A Corporate Welfare Economy

A Corporate Welfare Economy looks at the evolution, characteristics, and effects of America's economy since 1980. It demonstrates how corporate welfare and tax breaks have been influencing income and poverty trends, becoming one of the leading causes of decline in the American standard of living.

Although political rhetoric and public perception continue to assume that the United States is the very definition of a free market economy, in actuality an entirely different system has come to prominence over the past half century. This book demonstrates how government has come increasingly under the influence of corporate interests and lobbyists, skewing regulations in order to suit the interests of the privileged at the expense of well over 90% of Americans. The chapters in this volume expose the highly concentrated and powerful ruling nexus of the corporate welfare economy and the extensive trading of favors that exists behind closed doors. The final chapter focuses on an alternative community-oriented economy, with suggestions of how to establish it nationwide.

This book appeals to undergraduates studying the politics of economics as well as those interested in political activism.

James Angresano is a retired Professor of Economics. He has taught and done research at colleges and universities in the United States and throughout Europe, China, and Egypt.

Economics as Social Theory
Series edited by Tony Lawson
University of Cambridge, Cambridge, UK

For a complete list of titles in this series, please visit www.routledge.com

Social Theory is experiencing something of a revival within economics. Critical analyses of the particular nature of the subject matter of social studies and of the types of method, categories and modes of explanation that can legitimately be endorsed for the scientific study of social objects, are re-emerging. Economists are again addressing such issues as the relationship between agency and structure, between economy and the rest of society, and between the enquirer and the object of enquiry. There is a renewed interest in elaborating basic categories such as causation, competition, culture, discrimination, evolution, money, need, order, organization, power probability, process, rationality, technology, time, truth, uncertainty, value, etc.

The objective for this series is to facilitate this revival further. In contemporary economics the label "theory" has been appropriated by a group that confines itself to largely asocial, ahistorical, mathematical "modelling". Economics as Social Theory thus reclaims the "Theory" label, offering a platform for alternative rigorous, but broader and more critical conceptions of theorizing.

Other titles in this series include:

1. **Economics and Language**
   Edited by Willie Henderson

2. **Rationality, Institutions and Economic Methodology**
   Edited by Uskali Mäki,
   Bo Gustafsson and
   Christian Knudsen

3. **New Directions in Economic Methodology**
   Edited by Roger Backhouse

4. **Who Pays for the Kids?**
   Nancy Folbre

5. **Rules and Choice in Economics**
   Viktor Vanberg

6. **Beyond Rhetoric and Realism in Economics**
   Thomas A. Boylan and
   Paschal F. O'Gorman

7. **Feminism, Objectivity and Economics**
   Julie A. Nelson

8. **Economic Evolution**
   Jack J. Vromen

A Corporate
Welfare Economy

James Angresano

Routledge
Taylor & Francis Group

LONDON AND NEW YORK

First published 2016
by Routledge
2 Park Square, Milton Park, Abingdon, Oxon OX14 4RN

and by Routledge
711 Third Avenue, New York, NY 10017

Routledge is an imprint of the Taylor & Francis Group, an informa business

British Library Cataloguing in Publication Data
A catalogue record for this book is available from the British Library

Library of Congress Cataloging in Publication Data
A catalog record for this book has been requested

ISBN: 978-0-415-85838-0 (hbk)
ISBN: 978-0-415-85837-3 (pbk)
ISBN: 978-1-315-64063-1 (ebk)

Typeset in Palatino
by Saxon Graphics Ltd, Derby
Printed by Ashford Colour Press Ltd.

Contents

Acknowledgments

I have devoted my academic career to comparing and analyzing economies. In recent decades I have become increasingly irritated by the endless discourse that the US economy was a "free market economy" when the reality was something quite different. I therefore am grateful to Routledge for inviting me to write a book about a pressing contemporary economic problem, for which I had an ideal topic – corporate welfare as it has become pervasive throughout the US economy.

Many friends contributed encouragement, ideas, and feedback for various chapters which they kindly read. My son-in-law, Josh Mersky, was particularly helpful. His response to my observation that the US economy was headed in an undesirable direction was to encourage me to write something that explained how we could turn this direction around. Brian Schrag, Bill Scott, Ben Harris, and Chris Kober each read parts of the book and offered constructive suggestions for revision. Their friendship and support has been invaluable to me.

As always my wife Elizabeth, daughters Nicole and Michelle, and grandchildren – especially Lucas Mersky, provide both encouragement and incentives for engaging in the years of research and writing that the book has required. Lucas in particular inspired me to write this book in the hope that a new economy can be created that will make his life more enjoyable.

As always, any errors contained in the book are solely my own responsibility.

Introduction

We Americans are optimists – or at least we used to be. We had faith in the "American dream" that given the opportunities afforded to all citizens most of us could attain a satisfactory standard of living. That includes some television network news analysts who are proof that even intellectually challenged Americans can find a job that pays them an income well above the national average for people with below-average analytical skills. Since 1980, however, that faith has been challenged. Economic indicators reveal that a decline in the living standards of about 90% of Americans has been underway for at least three decades. The median family income has declined to below the 1998 level,[1] while health care costs have been rising at an average rate of over 6% for the past three decades. At the same time, there has been a dismaying trend towards consolidating income and wealth in the hands of a very small percentage of the population – with the upper 1% of American income earners receiving about 20% of household income and owning about 35% of our national wealth – the highest percentages since the 1920s. Both the decline in living standards and the concentration of wealth in the hands of the few are inconsistent with the traditional notion of America as the land of opportunity and upward social mobility.

Meanwhile, the US economy features many negative trends that began well before the 2007 recession. Since 1980 a combination of very low – or even negative – income growth, lower housing values, lost pensions and other benefits, and rising health care costs has reduced the living standards of about 90% of Americans. Some members of the lower 90% of income earners suffer from high rates of unemployment combined with a longer than usual period to find another job, if indeed they ever do so. It has also been estimated that as of 2015 at least one third of Americans lived either in poverty or very close to it. Not since the mid-1960s have poverty levels been this high. The official US government measure of the poverty rate is estimated to include almost 17% of Americans, or about 1 in 6. Almost 1.5 million Americans live in extreme poverty, which is to say that they exist on about $2 a day per person (prior to receiving food stamps), more than double the number compared to 15 years ago (Marisol, 2012). Meanwhile, there have been unforeseen profits for certain industries – particularly investment banks and pharmaceutical corporations, as well as for many defense contractors. Further, increases in income and wealth enjoyed by a small percentage of Americans have been unprecedented. According to a US Census report, inflation-adjusted average income growth for the top 5% of American families rose more than 60% to over $313,000 between 1979 and 2011 (Yen, 2011A) – and that trend continues. Overall, these trends have contributed to "the after-tax income of the most affluent fifth exceed[ing] the income of the other four-fifths of the population" (Pear, 2011A).

If such trends have not been due solely to the aftereffects of the 2007 recession, what other factors can explain the end of the American dream for most US citizens?[2] Why is the supposed "free market economy" (FME) of the United States a hallmark of the American dream and the rallying call of many contemporary politicians and economic policy makers, producing results that are so discordant with those we expect of an FME? This book will explore one important and as yet little-understood contributing factor to these negative trends, and in the process offer hope that we might be able to restore a sense of optimism in the American dream. That factor is the impact on the aforementioned economic and social indicators of the type of economy the United States has become – a corporate welfare economy (CWE).

It is no coincidence that lower standards of living for most Americans have occurred following the early 1980s shift away from the economic philosophy that guided the US economy throughout the 1932–80 period when there was general acceptance of redistributing income – including social security; banking was conservative and devoid of wild speculation, most profits were reinvested in the US economy, and tax evasion by the wealthiest Americans and corporations was the exception and not the rule it has become. During that time period poverty rates declined considerably and the distribution of household income became less unequal. The economic philosophy and corresponding policies that prevailed pre-1980 were replaced by a brand of free market philosophy and policies that were enthusiastically embraced by Ronald Reagan and many conservative economists. The essence of this philosophy is economic rationality that emphasizes the pursuit of efficiency and self-interest while glorifying a high retention of profits for oneself or one's corporation to the neglect of the impact of such retention on the greater community. Some post-1980 policies implemented based on this free market philosophy, including substantial income tax rate reductions, have contributed to the growing divergence in living standards between the wealthiest 1% and the rest of Americans; less sense of belonging to a community as Americans are becoming more divided and alienated; and the inability of many Americans to obtain a job that pays well above a living wage (roughly $18,000 a year for a single person and $35,000 for a family of four).

The book's central theme is that the rise of CWE post-1980 has been *one* cause of the lower and declining standard of living nearly all Americans are experiencing. The primary goal is to explain the CWE's evolution, characteristics, and effects as they manifest themselves in many industries and influence income and poverty trends. Reference will be made to economic philosophy, history, and industry examples to link the CWE's existence to the lower standard of living. A second goal is to recommend a different philosophy and reforms to recreate a type of economy far more likely to improve the standard of living of all Americans. The analysis and reform recommendations follow from the author's analytical perspective that differs considerably from that of orthodox economists, as explained in Appendix 1.

To summarize, this book will demonstrate: the CWE that now characterizes the US economy has been *one* of the main contributing factors to the sharp decline in the standard of living that has plagued an overwhelming majority of Americans. The CWE has been created partly through rules enacted by the government at federal and state levels that have "rigged" the competitive game, in the process benefiting a small percentage of Americans quite handsomely. As the following chapter will explain in detail, "rigged" refers to deviating from the rules of an FME while providing many forms of redistribution, tax reduction possibilities, public contracts awarded without any competitive bidding process, and bailing out reckless firms that suffer substantial losses – nearly all of which have benefited a small percentage of wealthy Americans. The effect of these rules has made a mockery of private enterprise philosophy – especially the relationship of the state to the private sector which emphasizes that the state should not establish public policies nor redistribute public funds primarily for the purpose of enriching a small percentage of Americans. It is noteworthy that, unlike in Canada and the European welfare states, a large portion of the US "welfare" spending is in the form of public funds redistributed to the wealthiest individuals and corporations who have very good political connections, but little need for public funds.

Analysis of the US CWE will be presented as follows. Chapter 1 will explain in greater detail the evolution of the CWE's principal characteristics: (1) a highly concentrated and powerful ruling nexus among wealthy private individuals and corporations, elected and appointed political leaders and their staff members, and major news media; (2) the ability of the nexus to influence public discourse and policy agendas; and (3) extensive trading of favors within the nexus that is highly beneficial to nexus members, albeit at the expense of a large majority of Americans. The second chapter will present a detailed account of changes in social and economic indicators for the United States since 1980, particularly indicators of declining living standards. Chapters 3, 4, and 5 illustrate examples of the CWE's characteristics in prominent sectors or industries that will include manufacturing; transportation and energy – especially oil and natural gas; agriculture; health care; college and university education; university and professional sports; national defense; real estate; and finance. Chapter 6 describes how the existence of the powerful nexus, shaping and limiting of policy discourse, and trading of favors among the CWE's nexus members contributes to the unfavorable (and to a privileged few, favorable) social and economic indicators plaguing the US economy. The concluding chapter summarizes the principal conclusions to be drawn from the analysis of the CWE. In addition, it focuses on some policy proposals that can transform the CWE with an economy based upon traditional American values that includes no welfare subsidies for wealthy individuals or large, highly profitable corporations. The subsidies given to these groups in their current form are both a gross misallocation of taxpayer funds and a means of corrupting our economic way of life that prevailed pre-1980 in the United States. A return to the values and policies prevalent pre-1980 will be much likelier to reverse the adverse trend of declining living standards being experienced by a large majority of Americans than adhering to a CWE economy that continues to foster upward redistribution policies as well as a close leading government officials–wealthy private sector individuals and corporations nexus that has emerged over the past few decades. An examination of that evolution and the CWE's characteristics is contained in Chapter 1.

Notes

1   Decline in the standard of living is based on a combination of negative trends in economic indicators affecting almost 80% of Americans. These indicators include (1) flat or declining real incomes, (2) declining housing values, (3) lost pension and other benefits, and (4) rising health care costs. Measures that refute this claim by pointing to Americans' rising consumption rates as the measure of standard of living do not account for the fact that much consumed was purchased on credit, that many of the credit obligations remain high or will not be repaid, and that the government has bailed out some of the financial institutions that have extended such credit.

2   Some analysts blame globalization effects, the relative loss of manufacturing superiority by the United States, or excessive government spending leading to unsustainable debt levels.

1 The Corporate Welfare Economy

> Today, wealthy individuals and well-organized business and financial groups exercise their power by means of costly public relations, advertising, and lobbying activities. By "investing" in the promotion of their interests … [they] have largely captured the major political parties in most democratic countries as well as the news media that communicate political events and debates to the public.
>
> (Van den Berg, 2014)

Introduction

The term "free market economy" (FME) is often used to describe the US economy by the typical news media, particularly if a corporate executive, consultant or orthodox economist is being interviewed. This constant repetition has led most Americans to believe that an FME exists and that the major threat to the continuation of such an economy is government intervention. This chapter begins by briefly explaining the main characteristics of an FME. Thereafter it will be argued that in reality the US economy has evolved into something quite different – a corporate welfare economy (CWE) – the characteristics of which then will be explained.

The Free Market Economy

The philosophy that became the basis for an FME was conceived in the United Kingdom during the late eighteenth century. Adam Smith and other political economy philosophers forcefully advocated an economy that would substantially increase personal economic freedoms, remove regulations of trade, markets, and prices, while maintaining social and economic order through the interaction of unregulated demand and supply forces within markets. This new philosophy was a reaction to the existing economy controlled by a small elite class who established that closely regulated commercial activity. These rules, and maintenance of traditional land tenure rights, contributed to the low standards of living and little opportunity for upward social mobility being experienced by an overwhelming majority of the eighteenth century British population. In the proposed FME the specific functions of the government would be reduced to three: protecting private property rights, maintaining a system of justice, and building and maintaining those public works and institutions private investors would not be interested in either building or maintaining. It was expected that government spending would be a small percentage of total spending.[1] Proponents of the FME believed that as they envisaged an FME it would promote economic growth and job creation sufficient to achieve full employment, and that subsequently rising wage rates eventually would greatly reduce poverty rates.

This economic philosophy, like that of all other social philosophies posited, is based upon certain assumptions and theories made up by its original proponents. The assumptions infuse the functions economic agents were expected to perform, those agents' behavioral traits, the interplay of morals and economic behavior, and contributions that the anticipated economic activity would make to economic growth and poverty reduction (Davidson, 2012). A basic assumption of Smith was his firm belief that "no society can be happy, of which the far greater number of the members are poor and miserable" (Jensen, 1976, p. 261). Smith's ultimate goal was to alleviate the prevailing poverty of his day. He believed entrepreneurs to be the primary economic actors whose profit making and reinvestment activities would boost economic growth, job creation, and wage rates which would result in the realization of that goal. Thus entrepreneurs were assumed to be the fundamental agents responsible for promoting growth and prosperity in the FME. These agents, it was assumed, would own private business firms, pursue the potentially profitable opportunities they recognized by organizing systems of production and distribution in the most efficient manner, and continually reinvest in new innovations from profits their firms earned as they sought more profits – creating employment opportunities and rising wages in the process.

A fundamental assumption was that a high percentage of those profits would be reinvested. One basis for this assumption was the further assumption that entrepreneurs, in their pursuit of riches, had a "natural" motive to save and invest, for the purpose of accumulating physical capital that would serve the purpose of generating more profits. It was further assumed that entrepreneurs believed that their pursuit of riches would bring them happiness. However, Smith argued that the "instinct" to pursue riches so as to satisfy the entrepreneurs' desire for satisfaction was deceptive, since the increasing appetite of the entrepreneur to achieve riches was, he believed, insatiable. Consequently, it was assumed entrepreneurs would continue to reinvest their profits in the pursuit of even greater riches. It was believed that entrepreneurs also were stimulated to reinvest their profits – and thereby initiate a process of economic growth, job creation, and higher wage rates for their laborers – because they would derive some pleasure from the improved well-being of the poor. All of the assumptions considered, Smith and most of the other nineteenth century Classical political economy philosophers believed that in an FME unregulated market mechanisms would cause the entrepreneurs' pursuit of self-interest to serve simultaneously as an "unconscious but effective servant of the economic welfare of the entire society" (Taylor, 1960, p. 2).

The philosophers also made assumptions about the moral underpinning of entrepreneurs' behavior. They assumed that as good Calvinists who adhered to the Protestant Ethic, entrepreneurs were morally bound to reinvest their profits to generate more means of production. This assumption followed from Smith's belief that people would make moral decisions in a free society that would have "favorable consequences for social order and harmony and thus for universal human welfare and happiness" (Taylor, 1960, p. 48). Therefore Classical economic philosophers assumed that entrepreneurs would use their faculties and power of reason to behave in "morally reasonable" ways in the pursuit of their "natural" desires, that is to always act "in the way that would fit in as appropriate parts of an orderly system of 'natural' social processes, on the whole conducive to the highest attainable collective welfare of all mankind" (Taylor, 1960, p. 48).

These assumptions were manifested in the actions of the quintessential American entrepreneur, Andrew Carnegie. He believed that the accumulation of wealth by the few can lead to a "reign of harmony and reconciliation of the rich and the poor as long as the wealthy use their riches as a matter of duty in the ways best calculated to produce the most beneficial results of the community" (Fusfeld, 2002, p. 81). In his own words, Carnegie argued that "[t]he laws of accumulation will be left free; the laws of distribution free. Individualism will continue, but the millionaire will be but a trustee for the poor; entrusted for a season with a great part of the increased wealth of the community, but administering it for the community far better than it could or would have done for itself" (Fusfeld, 2002, p. 81). Carnegie's point was that administering the wealth they had accumulated required successful entrepreneurs to engage in civic patrimony through reinvestment of that wealth back into local communities or the national economy. Carnegie himself lived by this principle.[2] When he sold the Carnegie Company (that later became U.S. Steel) in 1900 for $480 million, his personal share of the proceeds was $300 million. For the remaining 19 years of his life, however, "[h]e never saw them [these funds], and he never touched them; he gave them away. In giving them away he found peace" (Livesay, 1975, p. 188). The $300 million Carnegie chose to give society included the purchase or establishment of 3000 libraries and 4100 church organs. In addition, he established institutions such as the Carnegie Trust for the Universities of Scotland, Carnegie Hall in New York, Carnegie Institutes in Pittsburgh and

Washington DC, the Carnegie School of Technology, the Carnegie Foundation, and the Peace Palace at The Hague in the Netherlands (Livesay, 1975, p. 188).

Faith that entrepreneurs would spearhead progress in an FME has been reiterated throughout the twentieth century. Perhaps the best argument was put forth by economic historian and philosopher Joseph Schumpeter. He argued that the FME was superior to other types of economies because it would benefit the lower income members of the society more than wealthier members in terms of the relative shares of national income each group would receive. He defended this belief by noting that between 1870 and the late 1920s in the United States "measured in real terms, relative shares have substantially changed in favor of the lower income groups" (Schumpeter, 1962, p. 67). An essential assumption of Schumpeter's was that successful entrepreneurs would *choose to reinvest* a large portion of the profits they earned. Some of these investments would initiate a "process of creative destruction" "that incessantly revolutionizes the economic structure from within, incessantly destroying the old one, incessantly creating a new one" (Schumpeter, 1962, p. 83). This process featured the introduction of new goods, services, and systems of production or distribution. This process would contribute favorably to the greater social good because "by virtue of its mechanism [it] progressively raises the standard of life of the masses" (Schumpeter, 1962, p 68). This was due to there being more goods and services produced that sold for lower and lower prices. Many of these goods were purchased by members of lower income groups whose wages had been increasing, thereby raising their standard of living.

Both orthodox and heterodox analysts of the post-1980 US economy continue to agree that entrepreneurship is a vital ingredient for stimulating economic growth and employment opportunities. They emphasize that investment initiated by entrepreneurs operating within an environment unhindered by government regulations drives economic growth and job creation that will boost wage levels, and that poverty reduction should occur in the process. Further, they agree that high rates of job creation, wage level increases, and poverty reduction each will be dependent upon the extent that profits entrepreneurs earned are devoted primarily to reinvestment rather than to their own personal consumption or to giving up their American passports to avoid being taxed on income they have deposited in foreign banks to avoid having to pay their share of US income taxes (Badal, 2010). It is estimated that US companies have stashed over $2 trillion overseas to avoid taxes – a stockpiling of profits that would have served most Americans better had they been reinvested in the United States (Rubin, 2015). Further, it is noteworthy that the rate at which these wealthy Americans willingly have relinquished their US citizenship has increased dramatically, rising from about 500 in 1998 to over 3400 in 2014 (Griffiths, 2014). This is triple the number of Americans who renounced their citizenship in 2010 and represents a manifestation of a declining sense of civic duty.

Despite agreeing about the crucial place of entrepreneurship in an economy, there is not agreement as to what type of economy exists in the United States today. Some ideologues and conservative economists cling to the myth that a form of an FME still exists. However, there is considerable evidence that such claims are myopic and misguided at best, and blatantly hypocritical at worst. Although widely publicized deregulation reforms were introduced after 1980 ostensibly to reestablish the United States as an FME, less well known is that a wide range of redistribution measures favorable to upper income earners and large corporations continue to be introduced that have more than offset the effects of deregulations that began to be introduced during the Reagan administration. The net effect of this dual process on the average American's standard of living is not unlike the net effect ensuing from substantial increases in US beef production when concurrently pink slime was being added to chopped beef sold to American consumers.

The extent to which the US economy no longer resembles a free market economy has stimulated analysts to describe it in other terms. Nobel Prize winner Joseph Stiglitz, in reference to the 2008 bailout of the finance industry, used the term "ersatz capitalism." He argued that government policies were an inferior and artificial substitute for traditional government economic policies because they guaranteed losses to those investors whose decisions were reckless and quite damaging to the goods and services, labor, and money markets (Stiglitz, 2009B). Since this type of economy involves income transfers to specific wealthy individual and corporate interests, others have described it as "crony capitalism" epitomized by the close nexus between Wall Street investment banks and elected and appointed US government officials based in Washington DC (Chapter 3 explains the nexus in detail).

An insightful and powerful analysis of US government policies as they support the interests of a very small, wealthier percentage of Americans at the expense of poorer Americans and poorer citizens in other countries led author Naomi Klein to describe the US economy as an example of "corporatism." Such an economy

> erases the boundaries between Big Government and Big Business. ... Its main characteristics are huge transfers of public wealth to private hands, often accompanied by exploding debt, an ever-widening chasm between the dazzling rich and the disposable poor and an aggressive nationalism that justifies bottomless spending on security. For those inside the bubble of extreme wealth created by such an arrangement, there can be no more profitable way to organize a society.
>
> (Klein, 2007, p. 18)

A large portion of those outside the bubble have experienced declining living standards. This fact encouraged another observer to describe the US economy as an example of a "Banana Republic" (Johnson, 2009). Such a description formerly was reserved for Central American countries ruled by dictators that were permissive of American multinational corporations. One example concerns the United Fruit Corporation's activities in Guatemala. With the Guatemalan government's (and alleged CIA) complicity, the firm was instrumental in preventing land reform legislation from being introduced. Meanwhile, it was able to acquire ownership and control over large tracts of valuable land on which bananas were raised and "then operated plantations on its own terms, free of such annoyances as taxes or labor regulations" (Kinzer, 2006, p. 130). One outcome was more highly skewed distributions of income and wealth as well as an even higher incidence of poverty throughout that country – conditions not unlike those in the United States as of 2015.

Analysts Simon Johnson, James Kwak, and Edward Fulbrook have focused on how changes in the relative distribution of economic power in favor of a small percentage of Americans have affected the political structure, especially the election and appointment of agency officials throughout Washington DC.[3] Johnson and Kwak's emphasis is on the emergence of an economy dominated by an "oligarchy." This oligarchy is spearheaded by top officials at major Wall Street investment banks that successfully have translated their vast economic power into substantial political power. According to these analysts, "[t]he Wall Street banks are the new American oligarchy – a group that gains political power because of its economic power, and then uses that political power for its own benefit" (Johnson and Kwak, 2011, p. 6).

Fulbrook describes the new political structure as a "plutonomy" characterized by (1) a less democratic election process in terms of the influential power held by wealthiest Americans, and (2) a creative range of methods introduced by elected officials that serve to effectively redistribute income and wealth in an upward direction (Fulbrook, 2012, p. 147). Not coincidentally, during the rise of this new type of economy and plutonomy the incomes of the upper 1% of Americans have increased phenomenally. For example, this group's average real incomes (not including capital gains) increased from about $290,000 in 1950 to over $1,000,000 by 2008, while over the same period average incomes barely increased for the bottom 90% of Americans (Fulbrook, 2012, p. 141). The share of income (including capital gains) earned by the top 0.1% of Americans rose slowly from 4% to 6% between 1960 and 1995, then increased to over 10% by 2008 (Fulbrook, 2012, p. 141).[4]

The dramatic increase in the extent of income inequality is partly the result of an economy that has evolved in which there is an economic game whose rules have been rigged by public officials cooperating with wealthy private sector interests. Due to public redistribution benefits and favorable policies such as subsidies and bailouts to wealthier segments of the population the probability that substantial losses will be incurred by wealthy investors and major corporations has substantially decreased during the past half century. Further, when losses are incurred many of the privileged few receive redistribution benefits at taxpayers' expense. Such has been the case for many so-called private institutions, including private for-profit colleges and universities, which receive a majority of their income, and thus their profits, in the form of payments originating as federally guaranteed student loans.[5] Overall, the net effect of the new political structure and economy with rules designed to upwardly redistribute income has been the creation of a different institutional structure – the corporate welfare economy.

The Corporate Welfare Economy

The term "corporate welfare" was first coined by Ralph Nader. He describes it as

> the enormous and myriad subsidies, bailouts, giveaways, tax loopholes, debt revocations, loan guarantees, and other benefits conferred by government on business. It is a function of political corruption. Corporate welfare programs siphon funds from appropriate public investments, subsidize companies ripping minerals from federal lands, enable pharmaceutical companies to gouge consumers, perpetuate anti-competitive oligopolistic markets, injure national security, and weaken our democracy.
>
> (Nader, 2003)

In an article published by the conservative Cato Institute, corporate welfare is defined "as any federal spending program that provides payments or unique benefits and advantages to specific companies or industries" (Slivinski, 2007). This book embraces both definitions. What is most relevant is that over the past few decades the emergence of the CWE in the United States has coincided with the introduction of a wide range of creative, specific types of redistributions that primarily have enriched the upper 1% of American income earners across many industries – not only finance – to such an extent that corporate welfare in a broad sense has become systemic. The particular characteristics of this type of economy are presented below. While three characteristics are presented, it is important to bear in mind that these characteristics reinforce one another over time in a circular and cumulative causation pattern to exacerbate the privileged status of the wealthiest Americans as compared to most other citizens.

The Nexus

The CWE's first characteristic is a highly concentrated powerful ruling nexus between the wealthiest private individuals and chief executive officers (CEOs) of most major corporations, including financiers, many of whose wealth is measured in billions of dollars, and a class of wealthy politicians – with hazy and ever-shifting lines between these groups. Shifts have been occurring at more rapid rates. A study discovered that the ranks of Washington DC lobbyists comprised of former members of Congress and their staffers have nearly quadrupled since 1998. One infamous congressional representative, Democrat Joe Baca from California, introduced a bill that would reduce government regulation over payday lenders that are reputed to exploit low income Americans. Soon after Baca gave up his congressional seat he was hired by the payday lending industry as director of lobbying. An important lesson here is that this revolving door is dangerous for the public interest since wealthy corporations and industries can provide the "lure of corporate-lobbying money [that will be] … strong enough to orient both lawmakers and their staffs toward the values of their future employers" (*New York Times*, 2014F).

The powerful ruling nexus has contributed to the distribution of political and economic power becoming more skewed than at any time since the Great Depression. Fulbrook emphasizes that every step of the way the Wall Street–Washington DC nexus has been at the center of favorable rules that have benefited the richest Americans, and that one contributing factor to these rules has been the "revolving door" between Goldman Sachs and US presidential administrations. This is evident by the major appointments at high levels given to former executives of Goldman Sachs or their favored consultants (Fulbrook, 2012, pp. 147–8).[6]

A powerful close nexus has been created between those private individuals at the apex of the concentrated economic power and Washington DC elected and appointed officials. This nexus has taken the form of an oligarchical policy-making structure in which those representing the upper echelons of economic concentration have become part of the powerful nexus that solidifies the interests of the US oligarchy. The nexus enables private economic elites to translate their economic power into political power, and subsequently boosting their economic power through influencing policies and laws favorable to themselves regardless of the negative impact on nearly all other Americans. It is this nexus that "operates not by bribery or blackmail, but by the soft power of access and ideology, [but that] makes it no less powerful" (Johnson and Kwak, 2011, p. 7). The nexus enables the private sector members of the oligarchy to use their insider power to influence political appointments, including having their own cronies appointed to key regulatory positions in the federal government.[7]

An egregious example that illustrates the ability to enhance special interest influence within this nexus is the practice of "sending Wall Street veterans to Washington DC to work for the federal government – thus [these insiders are then] in place to shape power" (Johnson and Kwak, 2011, p. 7) in their own interest by controlling economic policy and appointments to powerful federal government positions. Such has been predominantly the case with appointments to the US Treasury, World Bank, and top presidential economic advisors. In return, Washington DC government officials and orthodox economists know that eventually they will benefit financially if they "serve the plutonomy's interests" (Fulbrook, 2012, p. 151). In exchange for private donations from large corporations and wealthy individuals to both Republican and Democratic governors this influential private group gains access to governors and other highly ranked officials and regulators who influence rules concerning public utilities regulations, environmental standards, and education policies (*New York Times*, 2014D).[8] Evidence indicates that among the corporations engaging in such practices are those representing power companies (e.g., the Edison Electric Institute), health insurers (e.g., Aetna and several Blue Cross affiliates), education sales (e.g., Amplify), and multiple lobbyists. They have been able to circumvent legal barriers while gaining substantial enormous influence and rules highly favorable to themselves.

Similar influence has been achieved by corporate interests that lobby state attorneys general for favors in return for campaign contributions. There is a pattern whereby corporate interests are served by lobbyists who meet with state attorneys general, provide them with large campaign contributions, in return for those attorneys general dropping investigations, changing regulatory policies, negotiating settlements favorable to the corporations, and using their attorneys general position to pressure federal regulators to act in the best interest of those corporations (*New York Times*, 2014C). This type of routine lobbying and deal-making occurs largely out of view. Given the examples illustrating the effectiveness of such lobbying the credibility of attorney general offices' decisions is being undermined. It is noteworthy that the nexus is also spreading to state judges in some states where outside groups representing large corporate interests are using their financial power to influence judicial elections.[9]

An example of privileged access to an attorney general is illustrated by the case of efforts by the distributors of 5-Hour Energy drinks. The firm was being investigated in more than 30 states for "deceptive advertising." In response they attended the Democratic Attorneys General Association meeting and lobbied aggressively for leniency. The lawyer for 5-Hour Energy was successful in having the investigation in Missouri ordered to be ended by the state attorney general after having been "courted [the attorney general] … at dinners and conferences with thousands of dollars in campaign contributions" (*New York Times*, 2014C).

The nexus is further strengthened by wealthy private sector interests hiring former members of Congress, former congressional staff members, or state governors to be "consultants" or lobbyists. This part of the nexus has become a particularly effective means for wealthy interests to influence government policy makers. One study discovered that between 1998 and 2012 the "number of active lobbyists with prior government experience had nearly quadrupled" (*New York Times*, 2014F). Undoubtedly it is lucrative for former members of the US Congress as well. Noteworthy is the hiring of former US senators or House representatives as "consultants" – although the reality is that they function exactly as paid lobbyists. For example, after their terms ended in 2012, 23 of these federal lawmakers participated in "Washington's well-oiled revolving door … spinning at breakneck speed … [as they began] new careers in the influence industry" (Salant, 2013B). These nexus members include Democrats: Representative Jason Altmire from Pennsylvania – health care (Blue Cross & Blue Shield of Florida); former Foreign Affairs Committee chair Representative Howard Berman from California – defense (for the law firm of Covington and Burling that lobbies on foreign relations for seven clients); and Representative Heath Shuler from North Carolina – energy (Duke Energy). Republicans were well represented by former House Foreign Affairs Committee representative Dan Burton who chairs the Azerbaijan American Alliance; and former US Senator and leading Republican on the Commerce Committee Kay Bailey Hutchison from Texas who joined Bracewell and Giuliani, a lobbyist for Yama Motor on consumer-product safety issues (Salant, 2013A).

The examples of two 2012 Republican presidential candidates, Newt Gingrich and Rick Santorum, are even more illustrative. Following their departure from Congress each earned millions in fees while engaging in what effectively were lobbying efforts on behalf of private and quasi private institutions seeking government funds or special rules to limit their tax liability or to secure benefits for themselves through some form of subsidy. Members of Mitt Romney's campaign staff uncovered that among Gingrich's activities was being paid at least $300,000 by Freddie Mac for being a "consultant." Some familiar with the lobbying culture that pervades Washington DC concluded Romney's supporters were correct – "Gingrich was a lobbyist even if he wasn't a lobbyist" (Negrin, 2012). He used his political contacts with influential public officials in a manner that benefited the private firm – despite being an outspoken advocate for an FME and opposed to the Washington DC political culture.

Santorum, who is on record as having stated that the Republican Party is unlikely to attract smart people in the future, was smart enough to benefit from his part in enhancing the ability of corporate interests to shape federal government economic policies. He reportedly earned over $3.6 million after he left the US Congress by effectively being a "stealth lobbyist," albeit while considering himself to be "consultant."[10] It was reported that Santorum "worked for at least seven different employers simultaneously, with several paying him a six-figure fee" (Mosk and Ross, 2012). One was the Ethics and Public Policy Center, a "think tank" funded by prominent donors with FME agendas such as the Koch brothers and the Coors family. The Editorial Director of the Sunlight Foundation, Bill Allison, argues that "[w]hat happens is canny operators like Newt Gingrich and Rick Santorum are able to avoid the lines drawn that would force you to register [as a lobbyist] … Obviously these folks are trying to influence the federal government" [to make rules upwardly redistributing taxpayer funds to private firms or protecting private firms from paying required taxes, fees, or penalties] (Mosk and Ross, 2012). Later Santorum was hired as a contributor to Fox News (Krugman, 2010A).[11]

One rule these stellar American citizens have been able to preserve is a tax loophole that provides a "multibillion-dollar tax windfall for an elite group of superwealthy hedge fund, venture capital and private equity managers" (*New York Times*, 2014A). The loophole defines profits received by hedge fund partners as "carried interest" which makes it subject to being taxed at the lower capital gains rate rather than at the rate applied to ordinary income (which is higher for upper income earners). Despite efforts by the Obama administration to close this loophole in every one of its budget proposals, both Republicans and Democrats have joined forces to preserve it. The estimated revenue that would be generated by closing this loophole is between $15 billion and $50 billion over the following 10 years.

Coinciding with the ruling alliance nexus becoming more highly concentrated has been the rising percentage of total income received by the upper 1% of Americans. Between 1979 and 2007 average household incomes rose less than 40%, increased about 65% for those in the 80th to 99th percentile, but grew a whopping 275% for the upper 1% (Leonhardt, 2012A). For all income earned in 2013, almost 20% went to the upper 1%. Comparative studies of the world's wealthiest countries indicate the extent to which income distribution has become more highly concentrated has been the greatest in the United States. The concentration of wealth has also increased considerably since 1980, as the share of wealth now owned by the upper 1% has risen from about one quarter to one third of all US wealth (Domhoff, 2015).

The concentration of media ownership has also increased as a higher proportion of major media is now owned and controlled by a few very conservative individuals or corporations. In the process the distinction between media and large corporate interests has become dangerously blurred. This high degree of income and media ownership concentration in the United States gives the upper 1% of income earners and wealthy corporations substantial influence over the contents of economic activity news media report and over what economic activity is not reported (Harkins, 2000).[12] Consider how rarely the significant increase in income inequality over the past few decades has been reported in major news media, or the absence of news stories concerning government policies that effectively would maintain or even further increase the inequality. The typical national and even local news media reports leave one with the impression that it is the corporate sector's interests that should be representative of US interests.

The disproportionate influence of wealthy special interests also is becoming pervasive throughout academia, among congressional and presidential economic advisors, as well as among appointed leaders in US government agencies (e.g., USAID), or international financial agencies (e.g., the International Monetary Fund (IMF), World Bank). Increasing the influence of wealthy interests are financial award decisions made by philanthropic foundations (e.g., Rockefeller Foundation, Ford Foundation, Aspen Institute, RAND Corporation), as well as by the World Bank, IMF, or USAID. The influence of these institutions occurs through their allocation of research grants, fellowships, payments for lectures, and consulting contracts. Orthodox economists hired by these institutions are used as "chessmen on the chessboard [world economy] through a system of elite clubs and think-tanks, whose members overlap and move in and out through the revolving doors" (Roy, 2012).

One orthodox economist who became a prominent architect of the 2008 Wall Street Bailout, then soon-to-be-appointed by the Obama administration US presidential economic advisor Larry Summers, reportedly was paid over $2.7 million during 2007–8 by "several troubled Wall Street firms and other organizations" for "speaking fees" – that included an April 16, 2008, talk at Goldman Sachs that paid him $135,000 (Greenwald, 2009). The justification for the bailout, as with many other orthodox economists' macroeconomic policy recommendations, was "not supported by their own theory and/or evidence, and thereby helped to impose certain policies on the larger public. [According to one prominent economic analyst] [i]t will be a huge step forward for democracy when economists no longer have this sort of power" (Baker, 2008).

Limiting and Shaping Discourse

The CWE's second characteristic is the growing ability of this ruling alliance to influence public discourse throughout academia, Washington DC, and among different media. This alliance has effectively steered policy discussions and decisions to a path highly favorable to their own special interest. One such factor is the narrow range of discourse concerning what for the United States should be a feasible type of economy, as well as the specific type of analysis done by those instrumental in proposing government economic policies, forecasting the impact of those policies on the economy, and analyzing the actual effect of the policies. There is little discourse concerning the low rate of creating high-paying employment opportunities are relatively few compared to the emphasis on tax reduction or financial and trade deregulation as being *the* means to create jobs and boost average incomes; that productivity has risen considerably over the past few decades while average incomes have stagnated or declined, along with norms of fairness regarding the existing distributions of income and wealth, also have been limited.

The combined effect of wealthy special interest influence has been that the dominant analytic and policy discourse reflects the ideology of a very small percentage of wealthy Americans. The US economy is described as if it were an FME, with no alternative considered. In the process orthodox economists have "turned ideology to faith" (Roy, 2012). One prominent heterodox economist concludes that "[t]he mainstream of the profession has taken positions that tend to support the existing economic and political power structure and effectively used its claim to expertise to deprive the public of the opportunity to freely debate policy options" (Baker, 2008). In the process an ideological position has become entrenched, namely that the FME exists, that it is *the only* feasible type of economy for the United States, and "that big, private, lightly regulated financial institutions are good for America" (Johnson and Kwak, 2011, p. 162).

The disproportionate influence stemming from concentration of power within the ruling alliance also has contributed to hypocritical rhetoric espoused by these same orthodox economists as well as some university researchers,[13] who extol the CWE "brand of conservatism" that is less a coherent ideology and more a movement funded by billionaires that rewards some pseudo-scholarly "mouthpieces" for producing claims and studies that will boost significantly the profits of those funding the research. It will be demonstrated later in this book that the finance industry has employed this tactic, much to their betterment. Some of these academic and "think tank" economists continue to shamelessly extol the virtues of tax cuts which, while purportedly advocated to promote economic growth and employment creation while being fiscally neutral, continue to enhance the income and wealth of the richest Americans while not delivering the promised job creation or fiscal neutrality – receiving substantial incomes and grants from organizations funded almost exclusively by a few billionaire families.

Then there are "conservative" politicians, executives of large corporations, and many citizens in self-proclaimed conservative states such as Alaska, Montana, and Wyoming spouting hypocritical rhetoric. The same voices that extol the virtues of an FME are among the first to argue in favor of receiving public funds for their special interest or some government protective measure from free market forces. A study of Alaska would indicate a long history of federal government expenditures to a state with a demonstrated voracious appetite for federal funds. The political culture has become one where elected officials "learn to manipulate federal budget levers at a tender age" (Powell, 2010). Alaska's political leaders are noteworthy for "identifying the federal government and pork-barrel spending as the enemy" (Powell, 2010). However, Alaska has benefited handsomely from wasteful pork-barrel spending to political supporters or constituents – particularly earmarks (directives by Congress as to specific funds that should be spent on a specific project) – compliments of the federal government. Comments made by Republican state lawmaker, Carl Gatto, of Alaska are illustrative. Despite being a critic of the "entire socialistic experiment in federal hegemony," he is reported as admitting "I'll give the federal government credit; they sure give us a ton of money. For every $1 we give them in taxes for highways, they give us back $5.76" (Powell, 2010).

One of the quintessential CWE players has been the American Legislative Exchange Council (ALEC), a front that has been influencing state lawmakers in particular. It is a consortium of state-level political leaders and corporations whose activities are secretive. It is financed by major corporations – particularly the Koch brothers. ALEC creates task forces consisting of corporate representatives and elected government officials to draft "model legislation" which it provides to other state and national government officials, seeking to have those officials use their influence to have approved and enacted the ALEC-authored legislation. Wisconsin governor and 2015 Republican presidential candidate Scott Walker has long held ties to ALEC, with some ALEC-sponsored bills being introduced in Wisconsin as one effect. ALEC also conducts "research" to promote its agenda: greater privatization, deregulation, and reduced taxes for both corporations and wealthy individuals. ALEC claimed that its "research" indicated that for the state of Kansas significant tax cuts for wealthy individuals and corporations would promote higher growth, more job creation, and lower budget deficits. Had they relied upon chimpanzees to predict the outcome of their policy package (see Appendix 2 for a discussion of how chimpanzee predictions are comparable to those of many economic experts) instead of a dubious economic theory concocted by ideologically driven economists with questionable research skills they would have arrived at different conclusions and saved many Kansas citizens from economic hardship.

Using ALEC's research as a justification, Kansas introduced an experimental fiscal policy in 2012 consisting of tax cuts to upper income earners that represented a higher percentage (25%) than cuts any other state had ever introduced. It also eliminated all taxes on business profits that are reported on individual income returns, while simultaneously reducing state-funded social services for lower income households. Proponents claimed it would boost the state's economic growth, job creation rate, and reduce the budget deficit. Unfortunately, as the chimpanzees may have concluded, the opposite occurred. Compared to its neighboring states Kansas' economy is growing more slowly, creating fewer jobs (Kansas was one of only five states that experienced lower employment levels during the first half of 2014), and experiencing a greater budget deficit – with its bond rating being downgraded in the process (Krugman, 2014C; and *New York Times*, 2014E).

Trading Favors

The CWE's third characteristic is extensive trading of favors among the powerful ruling alliance. These trades effectively result in an upward redistribution of income and wealth, and are not considered to be legally corrupt. The changes in the political structure and election process that facilitate the extensive transfers have been realized through organized, systematic, conceptualized, and financially motivated subversions of the trade which typically begins with wealthy private members of the ruling alliance channeling billions of dollars in political contributions to congressional candidates and presidential candidates. One of the most powerful political forces is the network funded to the tune of almost $870 million by the Koch brothers to shape the 2016 election – "an unparalleled effort by coordinated outside groups to shape a presidential election that is already on track to be the most expensive in history." The scale of such funding from any one group is unprecedented (Confessore, 2015). As of summer 2015, about half the nearly $400 million in donations for the 2016 presidential campaign came from fewer than 400 families, with most of these funds channeled to Super Pacs and the like eligible to receive unlimited funds with few restrictions on the giver (Confessore et al., 2015).

Many of the political authorities who receive such largesse are the same toadies who grant their private sector contributors special favors. All the while both sides extol the virtues of an FME. Those engaging in such trades avoid charges of corruption thanks to the US Supreme Court which in 2010 narrowed the definition of corruption primarily to acceptance of explicit bribes. This misguided decision has served to enhance the financial power of large corporations and wealthy individuals to obtain favors beneficial to themselves in return for favors that benefit elected and appointed officials rather than the public good.

There may be promises of employment for members of Congress, congressional staff members, or federal regulatory agencies after they leave the government. In return wealthy private members of this ruling class may be granted (1) public funds or specific legislation that provides private individuals and firms with direct or indirect payments, or confers to them unique benefits and advantages over domestic or international competitors; (2) additional indirect transfers such as perpetuating anti-competitive business practices such as trade rules that prohibit the importing of prescription drugs from other countries; (3) tax breaks that enrich primarily the upper 1%, as well as to multibillion dollar corporations;[14] (4) direct subsidies that "socialize" losses incurred by some wealthy private sector firms due to their having engaged in excessive, reckless behavior that leads to billion dollar losses; (5) excessive payments for services provided by private firms contracted by the government; and (6) lucrative defense contracts and other government contracts awarded without a strict, transparent competitive bidding process; public contracts awarded without requiring a competitive bidding process (Klein, 2007).

An egregious example of the trading process that would result in an upward redistribution that would benefit a few politically well-connected individuals is contained in a clause found in Wisconsin governor Scott Walker's proposed Bill 16.896. This bill has the objective of privatizing public utilities now owned by the state without taking competitive bids. The bill reads:

> Sale or contractual operation of state-owned heating, cooling, and power plants: (1) Notwithstanding ss. 13.48 (14) (am) and 16.705 (1), the department may sell any state-owned heating, cooling, and power plant or may contract with a private entity for the operation of any such plant, with or without solicitation of bids, for any amount that the department determines to be in the best interest of the state. Notwithstanding ss. 196.49 and 196.80, no approval or certification of the public service commission is necessary for a public utility to purchase, or contract for the operation of, such a plant, and any such purchase is considered to be in the public interest and to comply with the criteria for certification of a project under s. 196.49 (3) (b).
>
> (*Commons Magazine*, 2011)

Were this bill to pass, Wisconsin's ownership of the public utilities that provide heating, cooling, and electricity services could be, at the governor's discretion, privatized. According to the bill's provisions, the governor would be permitted to sell each state-run facility "without taking any bids, to anyone he chooses" (Krugman, 2011C).

Summary and Conclusions

Every economy is based upon some guiding philosophical principles concerning individual rights within an economy and the extent to which a government should be involved in the ownership and control over productive resources. Ideally, governing authorities use this philosophical basis to establish institutions and rules that are coherent and consistent with the values contained in the philosophy. The American public has been bombarded with hypocritical messages, namely that the US economy is an FME and that an FME is the only alternative. In reality a CWE has been created despite claims from apologists that it remains an FME. At present we have declining values and an incoherent philosophy of the CWE whose main feature is a close symbiotic relationship between the wealthiest Americans and federal government elected leaders and other high ranking government officials that has shaped the upward redistribution of income. The strength of the upper 1% is furthered by their extensive influence over news media and orthodox economists, as well as Washington DC policy makers.

The basic message of this chapter is similar to that contained in the book *Winner Takes All Politics* (Hacker and Pierson, 2010). The authors point out that over the past three decades the US distribution of income has come to more closely resemble that of a Third World oligarchy than the average income distribution for the rest of the world's 20 wealthiest nations. They attribute this distribution to the division between wealthy winners – nearly all of whom are in the upper 1% of income earners – and the losers who are the "rest of us." Members of the privileged group, particularly those in the richest financial and non-financial corporations, are able to protect themselves from economic loss or to profit handsomely from deals they create for one another, even during recessionary periods. An example occurred in 2012 when Al Gore not only was able to sell his cable network for an estimated $100 million, but was also able to sell his stock in Apple (for which he served on the Board of Directors) for $500 per share after having acquired it at $8 per share – a benefit enjoyed by members of Apple's Board of Directors.

As this income (and wealth) distribution has become more highly skewed Hacker and Pierson fear that the operation of our democratic institutions has been undermined as well, given the pattern and extent of contributions and favors provided to policy makers at the state and federal level. Partly due to favorable policies emanating from Washington DC there is less sharing of income broadly across our society as rules are established that overwhelmingly favor the upper 1% and wealthy corporations. Meanwhile, as the following chapter will demonstrate, the standard of living for most Americans has been declining along with the rate of upward social mobility. An increasingly higher percentage of the very rich, in turn, believe they have less responsibility to redistribute their income and wealth than many of their predecessors whose names can be found on some of America's largest foundations: Carnegie, Ford, Gates, Mellon, and Rockefeller.

The lesson seems to be that the rules by which our economy functions have become rigged, and that it reeks of "crony capitalism," with favorable laws riddled with loopholes exchanged for campaign contributions and the financial benefit of lawmakers. In regard to the Wall Street–Washington DC nexus one observer commented during a Bill Moyers interview that policy makers in Washington DC loaded the dice, then the Wall Street investment bankers rolled them – much to their favor. These insiders benefited, sometimes at the expense of the rest of us. This combination of wealthy interests' malfeasance and Washington complicity has dramatically changed the nature of our economy. The next chapter will explain in depth that coinciding with the CWE's emergence have been many negative economic and social indicator trends that have contributed to a more highly skewed distribution of income and wealth, some corporate losses paid for with public funds, much lower rates of high-paying job creation, a declining middle class which has realized little or no increase in the real incomes received by about 90% of Americans – while there has been substantial erosion in our democratic principles and practices.

Notes

1 For example, during the heyday of the free market economy in late nineteenth century England and early twentieth century US government expenditures were about 5% of gross domestic product (GDP).
2 Carnegie did, however, benefit from some government policies designed to enrich his corporation.
3 This theme runs throughout both Johnson and Kwak, 2011, and Fulbrook, 2012.
4 This data was taken from "The World Top Incomes Database," http://g-mond. paris.schoolofeconomics.eu/topincomes
5 Corporate welfare as it applies to education includes taxpayer-funded repayments of some unpaid student loan, with the for-profit academic institution receiving the payments issue.
6 Perhaps the most egregious example of this occurred in 2008 when the Obama administration appointed Lawrence Summers to be Chief Economic Advisor. Summers became one of the main proponents for the financial industry bailout that proved immensely profitable to Wall Street investment banks. Fulbrook notes that Summers had previously been on Goldman Sachs' payroll, and on one occasion was paid $135,000 to give a lecture (Fulbrook, 2012, p. 151).
7 Insider power that comes from being part of the Wall Street–Washington DC nexus was evident in the case of attempts to regulate investment banks. When Brooksley Born, a highly respected Chair of the Commodity Futures Trading Commission, sought to establish regulations on speculative investment bank activities in 2009 "thirteen bankers" convened in the White House to lobby a prominent member of the nexus, Lawrence Summers. They were able to use their power in this case to shape subsequent policies designed not to regulate derivative trading, a practice that inevitably led to financial collapse and the decision to bail out the finance industry with billions of taxpayer dollars. See Johnson and Kwak, 2011, p. 10.
8 Contributions are made through accounts – known in the Internal Revenue Service (IRS) tax code as 501(c)(4) associations – which are a form of secret political money.
9 The Koch brothers finance Americans for Prosperity whose state chapters purchase media spots to advertise their agenda against judges whose political and economic philosophy does not support the libertarian agenda.
10 For additional information see Eggen and Helderman, 2012, and Mosk and Ross, 2012.
11 Another example of a conservative choosing to be paid for influencing Washington DC lawmakers is Tim Pawlenty. As a presidential candidate he spoke out against some practices of Wall Street investment banks. However, in September 2012 he abruptly resigned his position as co-chair of Mitt Romney's presidential campaign staff to become the CEO of "one of Wall Street's most prominent lobbying groups in Washington" – The Financial Services Roundtable. According to one critic the finance industry, seeking to avoid regulations contained in the Dodd–Frank Act, has been very dependent "upon the Republican establishment to go to bat for them and try to slow down and water down all the reforms." Enter Pawlenty whose close relationship with elected Republican members of Congress is expected to achieve favorable results for the finance industry.

12 The Monsanto Corporation has been accused of exerting its extensive economic power over news media in its efforts to promote the benefits of genetically engineered or modified food. Monsanto allegedly was instrumental in creating a fallacious report that favorably evaluated its genetically engineered bovine growth hormone. Two TV producers who previously had refused to broadcast what they believed was a false report were fired by FOX News which owned the station where they worked – WTVT Channel 13 of Tampa, Florida. The reporters sued FOX, and ultimately were awarded $423,000 after they demonstrated that the reason they were fired was "for threatening to contact the FCC [Federal Communications Commission] and for refusing to distort the news (Harkins, 2000)."

13 It is noteworthy that many orthodox economists are university professors with tenure, and thus not subject to labor market competition from highly qualified younger professors who would accept that same position for a lower salary. Other orthodox economists are employed by the international financial agencies such as the World Bank or the US Federal Reserve System where their positions and salaries are protected even if it becomes evident that their economic analysis or policy recommendations were incorrect and led to highly unfavorable outcomes. An egregious example of this hypocrisy concerns the 1997 Asian financial crisis. Shortly after this crisis began "simplistic" free market solutions were foisted upon the Asian countries by the IMF and their Western orthodox economic analysts. Asian countries that encountered serious financial difficulty were told to raise interest rates, have a surplus budget, and allow distressed banks and businesses to go bankrupt. This was the formula proposed by the IMF's Western economists for all Asian countries with financial problems in 1997. Serious recessions ensued in the countries that accepted this advice. Yet when America and Europe faced their financial crisis in 2008, leading US policy makers proposed policies diametrically the opposite of what they urged South Korea and other East Asian countries to do.

14 It is true that the bulk of the income tax burden is borne by upper income earners (for example, the upper 20% pay about 75% of all federal income taxes) and that the upper 20% receive about 10% of entitlement funds – while the bottom 40% receives about 60% of entitlement funds while paying only about 1% of federal income taxes. However, a different perspective on taxes and public expenditures that includes either taxes not reported, or tax breaks or government expenditures not confined to "entitlement" programs such as Aid to Families with Dependent Children and unemployment compensation reveals a different picture. Data examined by the Center for Budget and Policy Priorities, Tax Policy Center indicated that in terms of distribution of actual federal benefits, in 2010 the lowest fifth of income earners received about 33%, the highest fifth only 10%; however, when they examined the distribution of tax breaks in 2010, it was evident that the highest fifth received 67%, and the second highest fifth 14%. Overall, the total dollar amount of tax breaks exceeds $1 trillion, of which about 70% goes to the top 20% of income earners, and the lion's share of this percentage goes to the upper 1%. For example, families earning over $1 million before taxes received almost $450,000 from tax breaks. See Porter, 2012.

2   Declining Economic and Social Indicators

Trends for most economic and social indicators that can be combined to provide a measure of the standard of living for a majority of Americans have been relatively poor. Some of these indicators have been declining for the past few decades. Poverty and near poverty rates have been rising, and a record number of Americans (over 45 million) rely on food stamps as a means of feeding themselves. Consumer spending remains relatively flat, while unfavorable labor market conditions persist (Smith, 2012), due in part to both business investment and job creation rates remaining below historical averages. The wealth of the median household has declined substantially since 2007, with one major source of wealth – housing – being in such a poor state that the percentage of Americans in 2012 who owned a home fell to the lowest level for the past 15 years (Lange, 2012). During the 2001–10 decade, the "mean net worth" of middle class families (value of a home *plus* retirement account, *minus* debt) fell 28%. In the private sector the trend is for businesses to reduce their workforce in the name of becoming "more efficient and more productive." Although worker productivity has been increasing and the revenue produced per employee of the 500 largest American firms "increased from over $375,000 in 2007 to $420,000 in 2011" (Brooks, 2012A), the typical worker has enjoyed a very small portion, if any, of this increased revenue.

A study by the Pew Foundation using these negative indicator trends finds that the "American Dream of upward social mobility [has] stalled for some people" (Lubin, 2011B). African-American males and women without a college degree are those most likely to have fallen out of the middle class, although all ethnic groups and both genders have been adversely affected. Those hardest hit include the unemployed. The officially reported rate has ranged between 5.5% and 9.5% since 2008. However, these rates understate the dire conditions in the labor market. There were about 5 million fewer jobs in 2014 than there were in 2007. If individuals who desire employment but have become too "discouraged" from seeking work as well as those "underemployed" (willing to work full-time or qualified for a much better job, but unable to find such a position) are included, then the "real" unemployment rate would be close to 15% during the middle of 2015. The "recovery" from the 2007–8 macroeconomic, finance, and real estate crises has been the slowest for the post-1945 period. Combining this dismal information indicates that many Americans are living in what one analyst calls a "modern day depression" (Rosenberg, 2012). Worse still, "judging by historical research of past debt deleveraging cycles, this 'modern day depression' is only halfway done" (Rosenberg, 2012).

The remainder of this chapter will describe in depth the economic and social indicators that affect Americans, both rich and poor. These indicators include declining incomes and rising economic insecurity; historically low housing values; rising health care costs; a grim labor market characterized by high unemployment with rising long-term unemployment, youth unemployment and underemployment – combined with low rates of job creation and a low percentage of Americans in the workforce; high rates of poverty and "near poverty"; and a range of unfavorable non-monetary indicators. The data for these indicators stands in sharp contrast to another indicator – rising inequality of income and wealth distribution. When all indicators are considered from a historical perspective that compares the United States to other countries that were formerly considered to be an empire based upon their relative economic and military power, it can be concluded that the United States has become a declining empire with a high proportion of its citizens experiencing a declining living standard.

Declining Incomes and Rising Economic Insecurity

Annual median incomes adjusted for inflation have been declining for decades, despite increases in labor productivity. However, many corporations have prospered in the face of layoffs and flat incomes,[1] while "the richest 1% of Americans – those making $380,000 or more – have seen their incomes grow 33% over the last 20 years, leaving average Americans in the dust" (Censky, 2011C). According to the IRS, the average income earned by an American after adjusting for inflation was about $33,400 in 1988, while 20 years later it was only $33,000 (Censky, 2011C). For the average American household in 2010 "income fell to $49,445 ... when adjusted for inflation, a level not seen since 1996. And over the 10-year period, their income was down 7%" (Censky, 2011C) as "[f]or the first time since the Great Depression, median family income ... [fell] substantially over an entire decade" (Leonhardt, 2012B). The median income adjusted for inflation in 2013 was lower by more than $2000 since 2009 when Barack Obama took office, and down by $3500 since George Bush became president in 2001 (Leonhardt, 2014A). Younger generations have not fared well. Median real wages for those aged between 25 and 34, except for those employed in the health care industry, have declined. Both globalization and information technology that has enabled more automation to replace workers are two key factors contributing to the downward earnings for youth. Not surprisingly, the share of national income earned by "labor" has "plummeted to a record low" for the 1950–2011 period, according to data from the S. Louis Federal Reserve Bank. Using 100 as the base for the index measuring share of national income, labor's share rose from 106 in 1950 to 111 in 1960 – but then declined to 95 by 2011 (Roth, 2011C). Meanwhile the wealth for the median American family fell from about $125,000 in 2007 to about $77,000 in 2010, and during that same period the percentage of families able to add to their savings declined from about 56% to 52% (Applebaum, 2012). This is not surprising, given that the rate of personal savings has declined since the early 1980s.

Declining incomes have increased the percentage of Americans suffering from economic insecurity since the middle of the 1980s. One measure of this indicator is the percentage of Americans falling below the level of income required to cover their basic expenses without their having to rely on public assistance. Over 20% of Americans realized a reduction in their household income of at least 25% during the 2008–10 period – with the median income falling to an inflation-adjusted level lower than any year since 1996. That percentage has improved only modestly since 2010. Meanwhile, the number experiencing economic insecurity increased to about 62 million (Luhby, 2011A). Between 1990 and 2012 the median household real income declined from about $55,000 to $51,000 (Blodget, 2012A). Another study of income insecurity, funded by the Rockefeller Foundation, defined someone as being economically insecure if they "experience[d] a decrease in their household income of 25 percent or more in one year without having the financial resources to offset that loss. Major medical expenses were counted as a decrease in available income" (Herbert, 2010D). The study "revealed that Americans are more economically insecure now than they have been in a quarter of a century, and the trend lines suggest that things will only get worse" due to rising unemployment rates and "skyrocketing medical costs," among other causes – all of which contribute to more and more families "facing utter economic devastation" (Herbert, 2010D). If this index were the basis for measuring economic insecurity, it would have measured about 12% in 1985, rising to over 20% by 2012. Given these unfavorable trends, it is not surprising that Americans have become less upwardly economically mobile than Canadians and many Western Europeans. For example, when the status of middle class teenagers in 1979 is compared to a similar group during the 2007–10 period, "28% fell out of middle class" (Lubin, 2011B) with dim prospects in the immediate future given rising health care costs and low job creation rates.

There are negative spillover effects from these adverse income and economic insecurity trends. The percentage of Americans filing for personal bankruptcy has risen dramatically since 2007 (*Business Insider*, 2010). Fewer people are able and willing to purchase a home, indicated by a rising percentage of young people ages 25 to 34 still living with their parents (from less than 12% in 2007 to over 14% by 2011) (Censky, 2011B). Many young cannot afford to live on their own as median wages for their generation have declined for workers in almost every industry except health. Another concern is the declining rate of retirement. During 2010, 25% of American workers indicated they had postponed their retirement. An international ranking of retirement security[2] ranked the United States 19th, partly a reflection of higher medical care costs and rising income inequality which has reduced the ability of most American families to save for retirement. Overall, over the past few decades major American corporations, particularly large financial institutions, have continued to prosper, but "average Americans are hurting with no end to the pain in sight" (Herbert, 2010D).

Historically Low Housing Values

The dramatic decline in home prices that began in 2007 has reduced the proportion of equity the typical family has in their home to its lowest point since the mid-1940s – particularly between 2001 and 2011 when the average equity in a home "plunged from more than 61 percent … to 38 percent" (Kravitz and Rugaber, 2011). Using the Standard and Poor's/Case–Shiller National U.S. Home Price Index home prices in 2007 were roughly equal to home prices in 1996, and this index has declined about 2% since then. Consequently, the average price of an American home in 2012 is below what it was in 1996, after adjusting for inflation. Even worse, about 25% of the roughly 75 million American homeowners have negative equity in their homes, with another 25% approaching that undesirable condition.[3] The extent of foreclosures has reduced the socioeconomic status of some neighborhoods to a below middle class status.

The likelihood that the declining housing price trend will soon be reversed "remains dim" despite fixed mortgage rates continuing to decline. There are too few people able to afford a down payment and the carrying costs associated with a home purchase. Exacerbating the problem is the huge glut of foreclosed homes banks still own, along with the glut of homes some Americans – particularly retirees   are attempting to sell. One analyst argues that by 2013 housing prices will have fallen 20% below the 2011 levels, and if that is correct the average price decline over the 2006–13 period will have been about 45% (Gold, 2011). Some analysts forecast that housing prices will not recover to the 2005–6 levels and begin to appreciate at a rate that covers inflation until after 2015.

Rising Health Care Costs

Total spending on health care in the United States has risen about 80 times the 1960 level, while the US GDP has increased only 20 times above the level of that same year. Meanwhile over the past three decades the typical family's income has hardly increased (kaiserEDU.org, 2012). As a percentage of GDP health care spending rose from about 5% in 1960 to over 18% by 2015. Compared to the rest of the world US health care expenditures on a per capita basis are about 70% higher, while our average life expectancy and infant mortality rate are both worse than in most other rich countries.[4]

For the typical American family health care out-of-pocket expenses between the late 1990s and 2012 increased from about 12% to 17%, while average health insurance premiums and typical out-of-pocket expenditures more than doubled (Social Security Advisory Board, 2009), as health care costs have continued rising much faster than family incomes. For those fortunate enough to have health care about 60% of their typical health care expenditures are paid by employer-funded insurance plans, but they must pay the remaining 40% (Milliman, 2009). This percentage is likely to increase because the cost of insurance premiums for employee-sponsored health care programs is predicted to continue rising (at about 7% a year), and it is expected that many firms either will be passing along some of these costs to their employees or (as studies of middle income families' spending patterns have revealed) suspending their purchases of health care benefits.

Rising health care cost burdens thus have "contributed mightily" to rising economic insecurity for many American families, as the "median household spent about 46% more for medical expenses than its counterpart in 1986" (Luhby, 2011A). The Social Security Advisory Board has argued that "the rising cost of health care represents perhaps the most significant threat to the long-term economic security of workers and retirees" (Social Security Advisory Board, 2009). Since the cost of health care is growing much more rapidly than the typical family income, standards of living are sure to decline as a result.

There is a long list of burdens created by rising health care costs. It has been estimated that a growing proportion of American families experience difficulty paying for their health care. For example, "[d]ata for the first six months of 2011 found that one in five families had difficulty paying medical bills, one in four pays bills over time and one in 10 can't pay medical bills at all" (Reinberg, 2012). Unfortunately, almost one American child out of four lives in such a family. Not being able to pay medical bills puts additional burdens, especially stress, on Americans. Many are contacted by collection agencies, use up all or much of their savings to pay their medical bills, and forgo paying for necessities – including food for an adequate diet – so that they can pay their medical bills. Of course there are many Americans without any health insurance – in 2011 it was about 18% on average, with 25% not having some coverage for part or all of the year (Morgan, 2012).

Forecasts are for all of these unfavorable health care cost indicators to worsen. It is estimated that health care costs will continue to rise about 7%

annually, which is more than three times the estimated growth rate for GDP, while real incomes are not forecast to increase more than 1% annually for the bottom 90% of Americans (Social Security Advisory Board, 2009). Consequently, family spending on health care is expected to double within the next 10 years. On a per capita basis, such spending is expected to grow almost 70% from $7800 per person in 2008 to $13,100 per person in 2018 (Social Security Advisory Board, 2009).

A Grim Labor Market

Exacerbating the degree of economic insecurity due to rising health care costs is a grim labor market that despite declining rates in the official measure of unemployment since 2012 has featured a historically low labor force participation rate; higher than normal rates of long-term unemployment, youth unemployment, underemployment, and discouraged workers; and low job creation rates for "good jobs" that pay at least $18.50 per hour.[5] When these indicators are taken together it is easy to conclude that "the overall job market and the experience of workers continues to decline or remains at highly depressed levels" (Gross, 2012B). This grim labor market exists within an economy that also features declining median wages – but continuously rising income received by a small group of wealthy Americans.

After averaging a little over 5% between 2002 and 2008, the officially reported unemployment rate averaged over 8.5% in 2009–12 before declining to 5.5% during mid-2015. However, despite this decline in the official unemployment rate the state of the labor market is "much bleaker" than the official rate leads one to believe. The following indicators are similar to those used by the Federal Reserve to assess the state of the labor market. What these indicators demonstrate is that a declining official rate of unemployment, while welcome, masks the grim state of the labor market.

Coinciding with a declining official unemployment rate has been a declining labor force participation rate (as well as a large number of baby boomers retiring). During mid-2015 the percentage of Americans considered as participants in the labor force (either they had a job or sought employment during the previous four weeks) fell to about 62%, the lowest rate since 1977. In 2014 the number of Americans in the labor force actually fell. For those classified as unemployed a higher percentage than normal has been suffering from long-term unemployment. In recent years the average unemployed worker had been unemployed for an estimated 35–40 weeks, double that of previous recessions (Krugman, 2010C), while at the start of 2015 over 30% of those classified as unemployed had been out of work for at least 27 weeks (Jamrisko, 2014) while during 2014 almost 3 million Americans were reported to be out of work for more than 6 months – which means they no longer qualified for federal–state unemployment benefits. As of late 2014 only about one fourth of those out of work continued to receive unemployment benefits (Krugman, 2014B).

There are a "staggering" number of Americans suffering from this problem as the "ranks of the long-term unemployed [have] swelled. ... [Many of these workers] have been disconnected [neither employed or in school] from the work force, and possibly even from society. If they are not reconnected, the costs to them and to society will be grim" (Riley, 2012). The degree of despair, marked by financial and emotional scars, for the long-term unemployed is even worse because for many families their housing values are declining, they may no longer qualify for unemployment insurance, and if they are between 50 and 61 they are too young to begin collecting social security.

Given they have little hope of finding employment, Americans between 50 and 65 years of age comprise a new class of Americans that has unfortunately been created, "the involuntarily retired" (Herbert, 2011D) many of whom fear "they may be discarded from the work force – forever" (Rich, 2010). This group is desperately in need of funds to support them after they reach 65. Another age group particularly hard hit by the grim labor market has been "youth" – those 18 to 34 years of age. Some believe this group has become "the most insecure" age group since 2007 as their unemployment rate has been estimated to be almost 25% (Luhby, 2011A). This group has fewer job openings to apply for than similar age groups in previous decades, partly due to low job creation rates and to lower retirement rates for Americans in their mid-sixties who cannot yet afford to retire. Consequently, a rising number of youth (age 16 to 24) feel disconnected from the economy. According to one study this problem affects almost 6 million American youths, putting them "adrift at society's margins" (Blow, 2013).

Among those officially considered "employed" almost 9 million of them are underemployed – those working part-time who wish to be employed full-time or those working in a job requiring far less than the education, skills, and work experience they possess. Some of this group are college graduates "scraping by in lower-wage jobs" (Wiseman and Leonard, 2011) – with their job prospects having declined "to the lowest level in more than a decade" (Yen, 2011A). For those college graduates under age 25 over half are either jobless or underemployed (Yen, 2011A). In addition, many people, especially those coming off long-term unemployment, get stuck in what is called "involuntary part-time limbo" – wanting to work full-time but unable to find a full-time job. The number of Americans with part-time jobs who have indicated they would prefer full-time work (known as "involuntary part-time workers") has been estimated to be about 7 million (Gillespie, 2014).

Many other Americans (estimated to be over 700,000) have become too discouraged to seek employment because they have been unsuccessful after an extensive job search and believe there are no jobs available for them for which they could qualify. There is a measure of unemployment known as U-6 which takes into account not only those actually unemployed, but also the millions of Americans who are either underemployed or "discouraged." In late 2014 this rate was about 12% (Jamrisko, 2014). One could conclude that among the reasons for the decline in the official unemployment rate has been the rising number of discouraged workers dropping out of the labor force as it is officially defined. Some analysts believe that discouraged workers represent only a fraction of the issue, and that there are others "missing" in the workforce that government data does not capture (Gillespie, 2014).

While much publicity has been given to the rising number of jobs created since 2012 less attention is being paid to the fact that the number of "good jobs" created has declined since the late 1970s as our economy is not creating the types of jobs and corresponding higher wages that we did throughout the 1940s to the late 1970s period. A "good job" has been defined by researchers at the Center for Economic and Policy Research as one that pays at least $18.50 per hour, and provides the worker with participation in both employer-sponsored health insurance plan and employer-sponsored retirement plan. Using these three criteria, in 1970 over 27% of all jobs could be considered "good," but in 2010 this percentage had declined to less than 25% (Scherzer, 2012). Over the 2010–14 period about 40% of jobs created by the private sector paid between $9.50 and $13 an hour, with another 25% paying between $13 and $20 per hour. Given that the average number of hours worked by the typical American worker is about 1700 annually, then 65% of these jobs created paid between $16,000 and $34,000. Indications are that most of these jobs were in food service, retail, and health fields – and with few, if any, benefits provided to many of the people who obtained these jobs (*New York Times*, 2014B).

While apologists for the poor labor market claim that the United States suffers from a shortage of skilled laborers, the fact that wages for employed skilled laborers have not increased substantially makes the apologists' claim questionable. What has contributed to fewer good jobs is a reduction in the percentage of unionized labor employed, deregulation of large industries, privatization of services previously provided by state and local governments, illegal immigration, and the effects of globalization. For example, in 1990 IBM employed 400,000 workers, with only 100,000 working outside the United States. In 2012 the total number employed had declined to 300,000 with only 100,000 being American workers residing in the United States (Scherzer, 2012).

How have government bodies on the local, state, and federal level responded to the suffering caused by this grim labor market and associated financial and psychological damage affecting many Americans? With governments at all levels facing tight budgets and revenue collections declining, spending cuts, layoffs, or salary reductions for those employed have occurred and more such cuts can be expected. The federal government has increased spending in one area – disability. As has occurred in Western Europe, elderly citizens unable to meet their expenses with unemployment benefits seek to become classified as disabled. In the United States the number receiving benefits from the Social Security disability program increased by 16% between 2007 and 2011 (Wiseman, 2011A). In contrast to increasing aid, Congress has delayed extending unemployment benefits over the past few years with one cause of the delay due to "senators in both parties [being] focused on preserving tax breaks for wealthy money managers and other affluent constituents" (*New York Times*, 2010A). One argument in support of either delaying or refusing to extend unemployment benefits is that this would "bust the budget." Some analysts refute that claim, arguing that such spending increases are only temporary, and that such benefits "support spending and jobs, they contribute powerfully to the economic growth that is vital for a healthy budget." The same analysts argue that ironically many members of Congress who opposed more generous unemployment benefits espoused this budget busting position – but did not believe that extending tax cuts for the upper 1% would bust the budget (*New York Times*, 2010A).

Overall, the labor market remains unfavorable for many Americans even while corporate profits and incomes of a small percentage of Americans have been rising. These facts prompted some analysts to describe the post-2008 economic recovery as more of a "profitability" recovery while the average family has yet to recover (Catts et al., 2013). Since the recovery began in mid-2009, inflation-adjusted figures show that the economy has grown by 12%; corporate profits by 46%; and the broad stock market by 92%. Median household income has contracted by 3% (Wiseman, 2011B). Corporate profits "accounted for an unprecedented 88 percent of economic growth during those first 18 months [post-start of 2008 recession]. That's compared with 53 percent after the 2001 recession, nothing after the 1991–92 recession and 28 percent after the 1981–82 recession" (Wiseman, 2011B). Evidence indicates that profitability of US manufacturers has increased substantially over the past five years, but wages remain flat. Owners are in a strong position to maintain this condition since they can threaten to move overseas to get wage concessions (or pension concessions), actually relocate their operations overseas, or relocate to parts of the Southern United States where there are not labor unions. Considering that the percentage of income earned by labor as a percentage of all income earned has declined while the gap between average worker pay and their productivity has been widening since the 1970s it can be concluded that much of the gains from increased labor productivity over the past decade or two "has all gone to corporate profits. This is unprecedented in the postwar years" (Herbert, 2010C).

Poverty and Near Poverty

Poverty and near poverty rates have risen to unprecedented levels. During 2009 the United States posted a "record gain" in numbers of people living below the poverty line that represented the "highest single-year increase since the government began calculating poverty figures in 1959" (Yen and Sidoti, 2010). By 2010 the absolute number of Americans "in need" (i.e., living in poverty) was the highest number measured since before the Great Society anti-poverty programs were introduced during the 1960s. "The number of people living in neighborhoods of extreme poverty (where at least 40% of the population lives below the officially defined poverty line) grew by a third over the past decade" (Tavernise, 2011). As of 2015 the poverty rate exceeds 15% while the percentage of children living in households below the poverty line is about 22% (versus under 10% in both Germany and France) (National Center for Children in Poverty, 2015).

If you find these figures depressing, consider that a new measure of poverty introduced by the US Census Bureau in 2009 that accounts for rising transportation, commuting, and child care costs would revise official poverty figures to be 15.7% instead of 14.3% for that year (Yen, 2010D). As of fall 2011 poverty rates, using the revised measure, had risen to the highest level in 17 years. During 2011 there was a record number of Americans, about 44 million, relying upon food stamps, up from 26 million in 2007 (*Business Pundit*, 2011). Among these unfortunate Americans, not only children but older people suffer disproportionately. These two groups comprise the largest share of the estimated 50 million Americans who go to bed hungry at night. Evidence indicates that since 2005 the number of older Americans who are retired but living below the poverty line has been "growing steadily" (Brandon, 2012). Meanwhile the poverty rate for those approaching retirement, the 55 to 64 age group, has been rising as well.

There are over 50 million more Americans living on incomes less than 50% above the poverty line – known as the "near poor." Therefore, for the United States about 1 in 3 Americans either is officially defined as "poor" or "near poor" (DeParle et al., 2011). Another report during mid-2012 found that "almost one in two Americans live in poverty or 'low-income' households" (Korn, 2012A). What is sad is the contrast in trends relationship over the past few years between corporate profits and poverty rates. A vivid, specific example occurred during the third quarter of 2010 during which "American companies have just experienced their most profitable quarter ever. Meanwhile the ranks of the poor swelled" (Herbert, 2010A).

Social Costs and an Erosion of American Confidence

Rising income and wealth inequality, among other undesirable trends affecting nearly all Americans, have come at the expense of rising social costs. Included among these costs is an increase in the divorce rate, that one study suggested was "presumably a byproduct of the strains of financial distress." The same study suggests that "inequality leads to more financial distress" partly because "inequality leaves people on the lower rungs feeling like hamsters on a wheel spinning even faster, without hope or escape" (Kristof, 2011). Stress due to high unemployment and less financial security – including the fear of bankruptcy – has contributed to changing family structures. Divorce rates among those over 50 are higher and a much higher percentage of adults are not marrying as compared to three decades ago. Meanwhile both birth and marriage rates have declined, partly due to lower actual or expected incomes (Steverman, 2014). Given these unfavorable social trends and growing levels of stress affecting many Americans it should not be surprising that while the United States still ranks first in international comparisons of mean household wealth, it ranked 12th in terms of "happiness" – while also featuring the largest gaps in income between rich and poor among the world's 36 wealthiest nations (Handley, 2012). Even worse, life expectancy is actually declining among Americans with low levels of education, reversing a trend that children born in each generation were expected to live longer than their parents (Tavernise, 2012).

Three indicators of a declining American confidence are the lack of confidence consumers have in the future of their material well-being, the disconnect between the rhetoric in favor of small government and an "(FME) market economy" and the reality of just who receives financial benefits from the federal government, and the loss in confidence that the US FME will be able to reverse the negative trends of the economic and social indicators described in this chapter. The Consumer Confidence Index, a widely respected measure of confidence, reached a historical high in 2001 and has declined since then (Conference Board Consumer Confidence Index, 2010). A similar trend has been identified by the University of Michigan's Consumer Sentiment Index.[6]

There has been a rising level of hypocrisy concerning the redistribution of federal funds, particularly to states in which a majority of voters profess to be "conservative" with disdain towards people relying upon government largesse. Evidence indicates that "the regions in which government programs account for the largest share of personal income are precisely the regions electing those severe conservatives … [for example] in 2010, residents of the 10 states Gallup ranks as 'most conservative' received 21.2 percent of their income in government transfers, while the number for the 10 most liberal states was only 17.1 percent" (Krugman, 2012D). One expert analyst argues that if the members of Congress they elected used their votes to eliminate many of the redistribution benefits they receive they would be quite angry and demand such benefits were continued. This likely would occur in states like Montana which receives about $1.50 in such benefits for every $1 paid in federal income taxes.

Throughout the United States, as well as in some other rich countries, there is a growing realization that "untrammeled, free-range capitalism is a myth" and that there exist many forms of government redistribution as the state has become present in all aspects of economic activity (Grant, 2011). One poll conducted by *The Economist* revealed that "faith in the free market is at a low in the world's biggest free-market economy. In 2010, 59% of Americans asked by GlobeScan, a polling firm, agreed 'strongly' or 'somewhat' that the free market was the best system for the world's future. This has fallen sharply from 80% when the question was first asked in 2002. And among poorer Americans under $20,000, faith in capitalism fell from 76% to 44% in just one year" (*The Economist*, 2011). One factor contributing to this loss of faith is the growing awareness that only a very small proportion of Americans have been experiencing improved standards of living over the past few decades, and that the extent of that improvement has been staggering.

Rising Income and Wealth Inequality

The degree of income inequality in the United States is greater than that in any other rich country. One indication that the degree of income inequality has increased dramatically in the United States is that the upper 10% of income earners account for about half of all consumer spending (Gorenstein, 2011A). The dramatic increase in the absolute amount, and relative shares of both income and wealth that have been received by the upper 1% of Americans over the past few decades is staggering when compared to the same levels and shares received by the rest of Americans. The upper 1% consists of about 3.2 million Americans living in a household with an annual income of at least $400,000 (Frank, 2012) – as opposed to the poorest 30% of Americans who earn an average of a little over $31,000 a year (Roth, 2011C). The percentage of all income received by this group is almost 25% – up from less than 10% in 1976 (Kristof, 2011). This percentage is now greater than at any time since the 1920s. Within the upper 1% are the 400 highest income earners whose average income for 2011 was over $270 million (Frank, 2012). One group at the apex of the income distribution are hedge fund managers, with the 25 highest paid receiving an estimated $21 billion in 2013 (Krugman, 2014D) – equivalent to the combined income earned by 500,000 Americans who received the median income.

Meanwhile the top 10% of American income earners receive almost half of all income and own 75% of the nation's wealth (Krugman, 2014A). The upper 1% also own about half of the stocks, bonds, and mutual funds owned by all Americans. One analyst calculated that the top 1% own 37% of our nation's wealth (Smialek, 2014). To put this in perspective, a family in the upper 1% has about 288 times more wealth than that of a family with median income (about $43,000) (*Bloomberg Businessweek*, 2013). The great bulk of the increased wealth over the past few decades has actually been received by the top 0.1%, the richest one-thousandth of Americans (Krugman, 2014A).

As a number of studies indicate, the rising income disparity has been occurring since the 1960s, and has accelerated since the 1980s, although there has been some reduction in income differentials since the 2008 recession. Between 1960 and 2004 the share of income received by the top 0.1% rose "dramatically" from about 3% in 1960 to over 7% by 2004 (Piketty and Saez, 2007). Between the early 1970s and 1998 "[t]he most comprehensive estimate of income distribution, by Lynn Karoly of the [very conservative] Rand Corporation, shows that the income of the bottom tenth of American families fell by 13 percent from 1973 to 1995" (Passell, 1998). It is noteworthy that this growth in inequality has been magnified by the decline of company-wide medical and pension benefits.

According to the Congressional Budget Office, during the 1979–2007 period "average household income for the nation's top 1% more than tripled, while middle-class incomes grew by less than 40%." Over the same period income earners in the 80th to 99th percentile experienced an income growth of about 65%, while for the upper 1% their "average inflation-adjusted household income grew by 275%." Further while the top 1% (1/100th) now receive about 20% of total income, up from less than 10% 40 years ago, the upper 1/10,000th of households – each earning at least $7.8 million a year, many of them working in finance – bring home almost 5% of income, up from 1% 40 years ago (Leonhardt, 2012B). However, income growth for the middle class was below 40%, and for the lower 20% of American income earners it was below 20% (Dickler, 2011). The share of income earned by the middle class declined from about 62% of all income in 1970 to about 46% in 2010 (Smith, 2012). Only in 2014 did the lower 99% experience an appreciable increase in real income (3.3%), although this increase pales in comparison to the 10.8% income increase realized by the upper 1% (who received over 21% of all income – and thereby the degree of income inequality increased) (Rugaber, 2015).

It has been demonstrated that in absolute dollars the richest Americans on average lost far more after 2007 than the average American family. There is a reported decline in average income for the upper 1/10,000th of earners from almost $40 million annually in 2007 to about $30 million in 2015 (Leonhardt, 2014B). However, it would be disingenuous to use this data to argue that income inequality is not a problem in the United States, or that the richest Americans have "suffered" more than the typical American family since 2008 – especially considering that between 1979 and 2013 the upper 1% enjoyed a 150% income increase versus under 5% for the typical American family (Kahn, 2013). Even though this data indicates a wildly divergent difference in income growth in the United States there are some who would argue that the data demonstrates that trickle down does occur.

During the 1920 to 1980 period, the share of increased income going to the top 10% and the bottom 90% was roughly the same. However, for the 1980–2005 period over 80% of all income growth was earned by the upper

1% of American income earners (Rosenberg, 2011). The share of gross personal income earned by the top 1% increased from about 8% in 1980 to over 17% by 2005 (Gross, 2007). Meanwhile, over the past three decades there has been a substantial relative decline in American middle-class family incomes, while simultaneously fewer of their jobs provide adequate health care and retirement benefits, the cost of health care and college tuition has risen considerably, while the average work week has increased (Carville, 2012). The extent of these income (and wealth) disparities is greater than at any time since the 1920s. It is true that the income for the upper 1% has risen over the past few decades in most rich countries, but in the United States "it is by far the largest and has grown the most" (Tyson, 2011). The income inequality has been worsening. According to Federal Reserve data, pre-tax income adjusted for inflation for each decile in the bottom 90% of Americans fell between 2010 and 2013, with those near the bottom dropping the most. Meanwhile, incomes in the top decile rose 3% (Rattner, 2014).

There has been a "dramatic" change over the past few decades between the ratio of CEO pay to that of the average worker (Domhoff, 2015). In 1950 this ratio was about 30 to 1, and increased to about 40 to 1 by 1980. However, it then rose to about 300 to 1 in 2000, and to about 400 to 1 by 2008 (*Business Insider*, 2010). It has been calculated that if the 1990–2004 percentage increase in CEO pay had been the same for minimum wage earners, their pay would have skyrocketed from $5.15 per hour in 1990 to over $23 per hour in 2004 (*International Herald Tribune*, 2006). What is noteworthy is that while CEO pay has been increasing rapidly there has not been convincing evidence that there exists a strong relationship between rising CEO pay and favorable performance of their corporation (Gorenstein, 2011B). As a former chair of the President's Council of Economic Advisors points out, "there is 'no definitive evidence' between the 'relative significance' of factors such as technical innovations creators or larger business size or growing premium for highly specialized skills or changes in CEO compensation and the dramatic income differentials changes" (Tyson, 2011).

Wealth disparities are even greater than income disparities. Between 1981 and 2007 the share of wealth owned by the upper 1% rose from about 25% to 35%, while declining for the bottom 99% from about 75% to 65% (Domhoff, 2015). Even though between 2007 and 2010 the absolute amount of wealth owned by the upper 1% has declined by about 11%, for the median American household it declined over 35% (Domhoff, 2015). Meanwhile the wealth gap between older and younger Americans "stretched to the widest on record by 2010 ... this wealth gap is now more than double what it was in 2005 and nearly five times [about 47 to 1] the 10-to-1 disparity a quarter century ago, after adjusting for inflation" (Yen, 2011B). In 2010 it was estimated that "the wealthiest plutocrats now actually control a greater share of the pie in the United States than in historically unstable countries like Nicaragua, Venezuela and Guyana ... [as] the top 10 percent controls more than 70 percent of Americans' total net worth" (Kristof, 2010). Meanwhile the wealth owned by America's 400 wealthiest individuals is equivalent to that owned by the bottom 50% of Americans (Moore, 2011). A microcosm of this disparity's effects can be identified within the housing market which, despite being in a depressed state in nearly all of the United States, is demonstrating "tremendous activity at the very high end of the market ... [where] the majority of these multi-million dollar transactions are paid for in cash" (Korn, 2012B).

This degree of income and wealth inequality has a number of consequences, especially the enhanced political power it gives to richest Americans as they have gained a greater ability to translate their economic power into political power through the nexus described in the previous chapter. Another effect of high income inequality is lower standards of living and declining social mobility. Currently social mobility in the United States is lower than that of wealthier European countries (with the exception of the UK) as well as Canada (Galbraith and Hale, 2014). These greater inequality and lower social mobility trends began in the early 1980s following the introduction of Reagan's economic philosophy and the rise of the corporate welfare economy.

Summary: United States – an Empire in Decline

For more than three decades the economies of Japan, most of Western Europe, and the United States have been declining in terms of every standard macroeconomic indicator – GDP, investment, real wages, among other indicators. Unfortunately for Americans, relative to these other rich nations the collective decline of US economic and social indicators has been among the worst (Blow, 2011). While public debt continues to increase "at an astonishing and unrelenting pace" (Brooks, 2010), wages for nearly all Americans remain stagnant, and high unemployment persists and is likely to remain high for the next few years. One analyst argues that there are at least 10 American industries unlikely to restore employment levels that existed in 2005, including automotive manufacturing, state and local governments, pharmaceuticals, big telecom, newspapers, and airlines (McIntyre, 2010). An overwhelming majority of Americans are experiencing declining living standards, particularly the poor and the families of typical workers. One observer fears that a permanent "white underclass" is being created. He argues that "[t]oday, I fear we're facing a crisis in which a chunk of working-class America risks being calcified into an underclass, marked by drugs, despair, family decline, high incarceration rates and a diminishing role of jobs and education as escalators of upward mobility" (Kristof, 2012).

Every major empire that eventually collapsed has experienced the same trends, some of which were discussed throughout this chapter while others will be explained in subsequent chapters: (1) financialization of the economy as it moves away from manufacturing to speculation; (2) high, unsustainable levels of debt; (3) extreme economic inequality with excessive conspicuous consumption by the wealthy class while the average family's standard of living declines; (4) costly military overreaching in search of cheap resources beyond the empire's border as the empire seeks to dominate the rest of the world – which comes at an increasingly higher domestic cost; (5) corruption and political ineptitude, with considerable favoritism, fraud, graft, collusion, and the diversion of public funds into private pockets. "Honesty is no longer valued. Lying and deception become the norm, even at the highest levels. ... The once critical press, now owned almost entirely by megacorporations, is shamelessly sycophantic to the regime" (Levisohn et al., 2009); (6) overconsumption that contributes to ecological degradation. Unfortunately, the United States is experiencing all of these trends while "gradually decaying within and becoming fragile and vulnerable" (Callenbach, 2008). The following chapters will give examples of corporate welfare throughout many industries that have been one cause of declining living standards.

Notes

1   One analyst notes that "the carnage that occurred in the workplace was out of proportion to the economic hit that corporations were taking ... the economic data show that workers to a great extent were shamefully exploited." This data indicates that from the fall of 2007 to fall 2009 GDP fell about 2.5%, but "employers cut their payrolls by 6 percent." See Herbert, 2010C.
2   The Natixis Global Retirement Index ranks 150 nations on 20 measures of health, wealth, quality of life, and material well-being that affect retirement security. The measures include per capita income, health care costs, and longevity figures published by organizations including the World Bank, World Health Organization, the United Nations, and Gallup, which polls citizens on their happiness and satisfaction. The study points out that the United States spends more per capita on medical care than any other country, but does not have higher indicators of heath (e.g., average life expectancy). See Tergesen, 2015.
3   Standard and Poor's/Case–Shiller National U.S. Home Price Index. The situation could be even worse. Many foreclosure sales have been delayed while federal regulators, state attorneys general, and banks review how those foreclosures were carried out over the past two years. Once those homes are foreclosed upon, they will cause prices to fall even further.
4   According to the Organization for Economic Cooperation and Development (OECD), health spending accounted for 16.9% of GDP in the United States in 2012 – the highest share among OECD countries and more than 7½ percentage points above the OECD average of 9.3%. OECD Health Statistics, 2014.
5   The issue of "good jobs" is discussed later in this section.
6   For additional information see www.advisorperspectives.com/commentaries/aci_050410.php

3 The Highly Concentrated Nexus of Power

> The farm bloc is an efficient, tightknit club of farmers, rural banks, insurance companies, real estate operators and tractor dealers. Many of its Washington lobbyists are former lawmakers or congressional aides. ... The benefits are heavily tilted to large commercial farmers growing a few row crops in a handful of states. ... The farm bloc, says former congressman Cal M. Dooley (D-Calif.), now an executive with a food industry trade group, is "committed and focused."
>
> (Morgan et al., 2006)

Every economy features institutions that combine elements of the state, private sector, and traditions to create the rules for production and distribution activities. Where economies differ is in the relative importance of each of these elements as well as the specific forms of governance, production and distribution mechanisms, and dominant traditions. Rules pertaining to economic activity are established by authorities to coordinate production and distribution activities. Therefore the authorities become *the* key participants in the rule-making process. What has become a unique feature, and one of the primary characteristics of the US corporate welfare economy (CWE), has been the growing importance in making key economic rules and policy decisions of a highly concentrated nexus between some key government authorities and some of the wealthiest private individuals and CEOs of many major corporations, including financiers – some of whose wealth is measured in the billions of dollars. Linking these two major groups within the nexus has been a dramatic increase in the number of lobbyists and private expenditures on lobbying efforts. Further, within the nexus there have been hazy and ever-shifting lines between these public and private sector nexus members. This shift over the past decade has accelerated via an increasingly faster and larger revolving door through which elected or appointed federal and state government officials (and members of their staff), some in the legislative branch, and others in either a regulatory or judicial position, leave public office either to become lobbyists or to work for industries which have benefited greatly from legislation and lax regulation promoted by those same public officials. Meanwhile some influential private sector nexus members have received appointments to prominent government positions responsible for economic legislation or regulation that subsequently becomes profitable to their former industry.

One factor propelling the revolving door is that becoming a lobbyist to represent very wealthy interests is far more lucrative than being a public official. Consequently, some public officials who have been friendly to specific corporate interests are able to leave government work and either find far more lucrative positions with lobbying firms promoting the same corporate interests they championed while in public office, or be hired by a corporation within the industry for which they provided profitable favors. Meanwhile, it pays off for a private sector executive to secure a position in public office (e.g., Treasury Secretary) since not only does that individual gain power and recognition, but as a high-ranking public official they are in position to help pass very favorable legislation that will both enrich their former industry and ingratiate themselves with that industry – and thus when they leave public office they may be welcomed back to their former industry on very lucrative terms.

For each industry described in this chapter a particular nexus has been formed that favors that industry (e.g., US Senators from California being friendly to cotton growers), but members of that nexus may not favor corporate welfare being given to other industries (such as defense or finance). The significance of these powerful nexuses, as subsequent chapters will demonstrate, is that emanating from the nexuses are two other CWE characteristics – the shaping of public discourse (Chapter 4) and extensive trading of favors among nexus members (so as to maintain and enhance their lofty political and economic status and wealth). Meanwhile, as the previous chapter demonstrated, important social and economic indicators have worsened for an overwhelming majority of Americans either unaffected or adversely affected by favors traded within one or more nexuses.

The remainder of this chapter will provide numerous specific examples of nexus members that have influenced tax laws as well as having promoted corporate welfare for the food, pharmaceutical, retail, defense, oil and gas, and finance industries, as well as cases of the revolving door within each nexus.[1] Rather than be exhaustive by providing examples for each major US industry, the examples provided are intended to show a different dimension of how industry nexuses generate corporate welfare by highlighting particularly relevant examples. The pattern by which industry nexuses are creating corporate welfare appears to be going on in all major industries.

Driving Nexus Economic Policy through Lobbying

Lobbying is the act of attempting to influence business and government or other public officials to create legislation or conduct an activity that will favor the lobbyists' particular organization – even if the economic outcome is detrimental to most citizens. When a highly concentrated nexus exists, lobbying becomes a powerful force shaping economic legislation and regulation by representing the political agenda of the private sector nexus members, as will be illustrated throughout the remainder of this chapter. The growing power of lobbyists is being fueled by the accelerating trend by which some members of Congress and their staff leave public office to often double or triple their income by becoming lobbyists. During calendar year 2012 the number of former Congress members who took a lucrative job with either a lobbying firm, trade association, or public relations for a private corporation or think tank increased 14% (compared to previous end-of-term years) after those members either retired or lost their most recent election. From 1998 to 2012 a total number of 338 former congressional members passed through the revolving door by going to work with a lobbying firm after leaving office – about 20% with firms representing the finance industry (Salant, 2013B). One study revealed that between 1998 and 2012 almost 800 registered lobbyists in Washington DC were receiving lobbying fees that exceeded $1 million annually. According to some observers former members of Congress, and some of their staff members, can earn incomes of up to $2 million per year "if he or she is 'willing to hustle'" (Edsall, 2015).

Among the more enterprising former members of Congress was House Minority Leader Richard Gephardt, a self-proclaimed populist who championed labor and public health care causes while in office. After leaving Congress he and a relative formed their own lobbying business which has become one of Washington DC's top lobbying firms dedicated to helping clients develop political and public policy strategies. One of his first clients was Goldman Sachs for whom Gephardt lobbied when the AIG bailout issue was being debated by Congress. He later lobbied to weaken financial regulations contained in the Dodd–Frank financial reform law (Jilani, 2012). Populism as a belief system typically focuses on the best interests of ordinary people rather than those of privileged elite. Apparently to "populist" Gephardt Goldman Sachs executives remind him of the good old folks in rural Missouri.

As the number of former congressional members, and their staffs, have become lobbyists the potential for conflicts of interest, unusual access to elected and regulatory officials, and temptation to vote while in office in favor of industries that would later become their source of lucrative employment opportunities has become clear. One non-profit organization, Public Citizen, identified 47 House and Senate members who would not be running for re-election and asked those retiring members of Congress to sign a pledge not to take a job with a lobbying firm. However given the principle of relative prices (or, in this case wages) the opportunity to boost their income from less than $200,000 while in Congress to at least $500,000 with a lobbying firm – the amount depending upon which powerful committees a former congressional member belonged – none of them would sign the pledge. Nearly all senators not retiring refused to sign a bill proposed by Colorado Democratic Senator Michael Bennett that would ban former senators for life from accepting a lobbying position.[2]

One of the most effective, and egregious, examples of lobbying power that effectively rewrites laws at the state level, some of which spew corporate welfare to its members, is the American Legislative Exchange Council (ALEC). This institutionalized nexus has become a highly influential political force, thanks in part to extensive corporate funding. It has created a national consortium of public officials at the state level and powerful corporate leaders. Its leading financial supporters include the Koch Industries and Exxon Mobil. ALEC seeks to establish big business control over legislators and legislation designed to enrich those same business interests. Over the past few decades it has been instrumental in extending corporate control over media and academia, while also weakening labor power and consumer protection, promoting industrial deregulation, and enhancing incentives for more outsourcing of jobs and tax avoidance. ALEC writes fully drafted pieces of bills which its loyal followers propose as state legislation. In the state of Virginia alone ALEC has written over 50 bills, many of which have become state law (Krugman, 2012B). The rhetoric from ALEC is free market with minimal government interference and an aggressive stance against corporate welfare, except when it sees an opportunity to have laws enacted that will provide corporate welfare for some members.

One example of such corporate welfare has been advocated by the ALEC education committee that contains members whose corporations provide computer software as a form of virtual education. ALEC bills that were written for state legislators (including some in Idaho, Louisiana, and Tennessee) to "encourage" or require public schools to sign contracts with these same software providers while making online education mandatory. Some of these bills were approved. Such a proposal that would have made online education mandatory was introduced by Jeb Bush in Florida. In Idaho the proposal made online education mandatory for Idaho public school students with the public funds also being required to purchase over 80,000 laptops – one for every student. Not surprisingly, the measure was promoted by former Idaho Superintendent of Schools, Tom Luna, whose election campaign contributors included an online computer company with ties to Idaho schools and the Apollo Group of Phoenix that owns the University of Phoenix. To their credit, Idaho voters rejected the proposal.

During late July 2015, ALEC hosted its annual meeting in San Diego. The featured speakers included representatives of ALEC, presidential aspirants Scott Walker (who has had past ties to ALEC) and Mike Huckabee. This festival gives the notion of a nexus its fullest expression. It has been described by Miles Rapoport, president of Common Cause, as a "closed-door deal-making by politicians, corporate executives and lobbyists" (Fulton, 2015). Protestors gathered in objection to what they perceive to be the abuse of power by billionaire individuals and corporations through writing legislation that willing members of Congress, some state legislatures, and city councils have proposed and had passed almost verbatim. Were Walker to win the 2016 presidential election the level at which ALEC could exert its influence would increase. Brendan Fischer, representative of the Center for Media and Democracy, pointed at the threat of corporations gaining too much power among city legislators. They blamed that power for funding a campaign that led to the rescinding of a bill already passed by San Diego City Council that would have increased the minimum wage to $11.50 an hour, prompting *Businessweek* to label the city as a "bulwark against minimum wage hikes" (Walsh, 2015). Some environmentalists in attendance spoke out against ALEC influence to defeat some local initiatives such as rooftop solar energy generating sources. Meanwhile, environmentalists warn that the draft conference agenda indicates that ALEC will pursue a familiar course in the coming year. According to Aliya Huq, climate change special projects director for Natural Resources Defense Council, ALEC is pushing measures to "defend polluters, hinder clean energy development, and obstruct climate solutions (Fulton, 2015)."

Tax Breaks: Having Friends in High Places

Unlike Garth Brooks' famous song about having "friends in low places," the nexus doling out tax benefits that reek of corporate welfare typically comes from private sector nexus members having friends in high (i.e., congressional) places. While countless members of Congress contribute to this practice, the most influential contributor until early 2014 (when he was appointed US Ambassador to China) was Senator Max Baucus, Chair of the Senate Finance Committee which wields considerable power over shaping tax legislation. He was the quintessential nexus player when taxes are concerned. The most prominent tax lobbying firms hired at least 28 of Baucus' former aides after he became Finance Committee Chair in 2001 (Lipton, 2013). No other member of Congress can boast of having as many of their former aides being hired as lobbyists. It has been estimated that efforts by Baucus protégés now serving as lobbyists have helped financial firms secure favorable legislation and tax benefits. One result of Baucus' influence was tax legislation he introduced in 2012 filled with corporate welfare that benefited numerous industries, including finance. Baucus' bill provided such companies with over $11 billion savings in tax deferments (Lipton, 2013). Among other beneficiaries was a liquor industry producer that continued to receive a tax break worth over $20 million a year. Of course, none of this welfare came without generous donations to Baucus' re-election campaign which were sufficient to rank Baucus' campaign funds among the Senate's top 10 fundraisers. It is little wonder that Baucus was referred to as the Senator from K Street "notorious for his numerous sellouts to special interests at the expense of his own constituents and the nation" (Korn, 2013).

Food: More Corporate Welfare for Well Healed (and Fed) Congressional Nexus Members and Agribusiness Firms – Less Welfare for (Not So Well Fed) Food Stamp Recipients

There are many current and former members of Congress who have benefited from the same federal programs that provide corporate welfare to wealthy agribusiness firms. One of the most notable over the past two decades was former Texas House Representative Republican Larry Combest who wielded power from his position on the House Agriculture Committee, with help from other committee members that included a cattle rancher, tobacco farmer, cotton farmer, corn and rice farmers as well as a hog farmer. The 2001 agricultural bill that Combest's committee proposed, which ultimately was passed, included "an eye-popping $50 billion, 10-year increase in price supports and income supports for farmers" (Morgan et al., 2006). The bill was so generous that some farmers were eligible for benefits even if they did not grow any crops. Conservation groups were among those strongly opposed to this bill. Combest and the rest of his committee were undeterred as they could count on the support of a multitude of agricultural organizations as well as their control over food stamp funding and the willingness to use their power to threaten a reduction in federal funding intended for those with nutrition needs if the proposed corporate welfare provisions they favored were not approved. Despite efforts by the Senate to cap the annual farm subsidy payment to any one farm or agribusiness at $275,000, Combest was able to eliminate that provision from the bill. According to US Department of Agriculture (USDA) records, large agribusinesses and farms owned by wealthy individuals have been the main beneficiaries of the generous subsidies. Between 1995 and 2012 the top 10% of agricultural subsidy recipients received about 75% of all payments. This group includes the major corporate sugar producers (discussed further below). Meanwhile owners of over 60% of all US farms received no subsidy payments (Tomaswell, 2014).

In 2014 a farm bill loaded with corporate welfare was passed by Congress even as the food stamp program was cut by more than $8.5 billion over a five-year period. The political haggling over how much food stamps would be cut and the size of crop subsidies ultimately was settled through a compromise along with "lots (and lots) of money from lobbyists" (Bjerga and Bykowicz, 2014). Included among the corporations that contributed an estimated $150 million in 2013 alone for lobbying efforts to protect their generous benefits were Monsanto, PepsiCo, and Dean Foods. There were some reductions in cotton grower subsidies that had been in effect, although a new provision in the bill would provide new subsidies to these growers should the market price drop too low. So much for the free market.

Agribusiness giant Monsanto, the Koch brothers, and the Grocery Manufacturers Association were able to identify and support former and current members of Congress when they sought to forestall legislation at the state level aimed at requiring genetically modified food (GMO) from being labeled as such. Monsanto have put their financial weight behind another prominent member of the agricultural nexus, former US Senator Blanche Lincoln. After leaving public office she formed her own lobbying firm, the Lincoln Policy Group, which was hired by Monsanto to fight food safety legislation. Lincoln, who received considerable campaign contributions from Monsanto while in the Senate, hired a former Washington DC civil servant who had served as her staff director for the Senate Agriculture Committee of which Lincoln was the chair. The currently elected side of the agricultural nexus features Kansas Republican House Representative Mike Pompeo, described by one Washington DC watchdog group as the "biggest fool in Congress" (Organic Consumers Association, 2014). Pompeo introduced a bill that would make it *voluntary* for producers to label food that included genetically modified organisms, and that would prohibit legislation making such labeling mandatory. Some cynically describe this bill as "The Monsanto Protection Act" (Matus, 2013). The Food and Drug Administration (FDA) supported this bill despite indications that an overwhelming percentage of Americans are concerned about adverse health effects from consuming GMOs. Despite Pompeo's claims that our food products are safe and do not need such information on labels, Colin O'Neil, director of government affairs for the Center for Food Safety, lamented that "[the] selection of Congressman Pompeo as their champion shows how extreme the proposal really is" (RT Question More, 2014). As of mid-2015 the proposal was still being debated.

A health-related issue that illustrates the contributions of the FDA to the agriculture nexus concerns the use of antibiotics. The health concern is that overuse of antibiotics leads to increasing bacterial resistance, with an estimated (by the Centers for Disease Control and Prevention) 23,000 annual deaths and an additional 2 million sicknesses in the United States attributable to illnesses due to antibiotic-resistant bacteria (Bittman, 2013A). What is significant is that about 80% of all antibiotics administered in the United States are given to animals. In this case the easiest and most effective way to reduce the number of deaths and cases of sickness is for the FDA, which has been given the power to establish mandatory guidelines, to restrict the use of antibiotics only to animals that are already sick. Unfortunately, the nexus between the FDA, pharmaceutical corporations, and agribusiness firms is quite healthy. The FDA has a number of industry-friendly administrators such as deputy commissioner for foods and veterinary medicine Michael Taylor who formerly worked for Monsanto as a vice president for public policy. Buttressed by support from this agribusiness giant as well as large pharmaceutical firms the FDA has continually avoided its responsibility for enacting mandatory limits on antibiotics given to the animals whose meat or produce (such as eggs) most Americans eat. Since 2007 legislation known as the Preservation of Antibiotics for Medical Treatment Act has been introduced, but it has been either defeated or watered down on four separate occasions. What the FDA has done is to create a "road map for animal pharmaceutical companies to voluntarily revise the F.D.A.-approved use conditions on the labels of these products to remove production indications" (Bittman, 2013A). Pharmaceutical firms would have up to three years to comply with what is essentially a toothless *voluntary* plan to modify their labeling. Consequently, thanks to their nexus' effectiveness these firms, and livestock producers and feedlot owners, will experience enhanced profits while producing food that potentially affects Americans' health adversely. It should be noted that some livestock producers have begun voluntarily to limit their use of antibiotics in livestock production, with some offering products (e.g., chicken) free of any antibiotics.

Prominent among wealthy agricultural producers receiving generous public support is the sugar industry. It has received corporate welfare for decades to such an extent that one observer argues that "[i]n a hall of fame for corporate-welfare queens, the sugar industry would occupy a place of special honor. For decades, powerful sugar growers have gotten politicians to enrich them with a protectionist scheme that inflates domestic sugar prices to the detriment of American consumers, American manufacturers, American farmers, and the American economy as a whole" (Steorts, 2005). Rules that generate about $1 billion annually in corporate welfare to sugar producing corporations include permitting sugar processors to receive USDA loans at rates (that pertain to the price per pound of cane or beet sugar) well above the world price of sugar. If processors choose not to repay the loan within a 9-month period the government will give them a price per pound that exceeds what their sugar could fetch in a free market. Consequently, multimillion-dollar sugar producers can only benefit from such a welfare scheme. The sugar industry pays well for this corporate welfare. Lobbying occurs to such an extent that although the value of sugar produced is about 1% of the value of all US agricultural production the amount of funds devoted to lobbying for corporate welfare that directly benefits sugar producers is over 15% of all estimated lobbying expenditures (Steorts, 2005). Meanwhile, the US price for sugar is kept artificially high by the USDA setting an import tariff rate quota (a high tariff is imposed on imported sugar once the quota is reached) as well as regulating the domestic supply by setting the amount of sugar domestic producers may sell. What is the effect on the US "market" price of sugar? In many years it has been well over 50% above the world price. In 2013 while the world price was $0.26 per pound, it was $0.43 in the United States. Not only do consumers pay more, but US producers of products (such as candy) that rely heavily on sugar as an ingredient must pay the higher price. In some cases jobs are lost as these firms either shut down due to higher costs or relocate to countries where corporate welfare for sugar producers does not exist.

Who are some of the main sugar industry nexus players? On the private sector side are corporate giants such as American Crystal Sugar Company and the Fanjul brothers – owners of the Domino Sugar and Florida Crystals firms. In return for being two of the prime recipients of sugar corporate welfare for decades the Fanjul brothers have been substantial campaign contributors to Washington DC elected officials. Perhaps the extent of their influence is exemplified by the following incident. While in office Bill Clinton allegedly interrupted a "meeting" with Monica Lewinsky to receive a telephone call from Alfonso Fanjul (Steorts, 2005). In Congress the sugar industry has counted on "powerful allies" that have included Michigan Republican House Ways and Means Chairman Dave Camp; the ubiquitous former Senate Finance chairman Max Baucus; some Minnesota House of Representative members (who benefit considerably from American Crystal Sugar's campaign funds) including Tim Walz, Erik Paulsen, and Chip Cravaak, along with Minnesota Senator Amy Kochubar; and House Agriculture Committee chair Republican Frank Lucas, from Oklahoma (Spencer et al., 2014). The House Agriculture Committee is of central importance in the establishment of food policy and the farm bills that specify the subsidies – many in the form of corporate welfare. Finally, sugar also has a sweetheart in Maryland Democratic Senator Barbara Mikulski who has been an "influential advocate" for the sugar subsidies, not surprising given that a sugar refinery owned by Domino Sugar is located in Baltimore (Hamburger and Wallsten, 2013).

Individuals belonging to ALEC enthusiastically endorse its free market agenda while being particularly outspoken in criticizing legislation that benefits labor, those unemployed, and the poor. Nevertheless these same individuals "check their principles at the door when it comes to accepting farm subsidy payments" (Tomaswell, 2014). For example, Louisiana former state House and Senate member, Noble Ellington, who had served for a time as ALEC's national president, willingly accepted over $300,000 in federal farm subsidies between 1998 and 2012. Among several other Louisiana ALEC members who received federal farm subsidies was Democrat State Senator Francis Thompson who raked in over $470,000 from 1995–2012 (Tomaswell, 2014).

Pharmaceuticals: Where the Nexus Protects Americans from the Free Market, while Major Pharmaceutical Firms Have the Healthiest Profits

Every country recognizes the necessity for some government regulation over the production, including testing, and sale of pharmaceuticals. However, conservative cries of "let the buyer beware" while consumer sovereignty rules seems to have been conveniently ignored in the case of pharmaceuticals. US consumers are hindered thanks to the health industry nexus from being able to easily purchase imported pharmaceuticals that have been tested and used for years in countries with health indicators more favorable than our own. In the case of Canada, their safety standards and methods for testing product quality are similar to what is done in the United States, as are their educational standards for becoming a pharmacist. The result of these import restrictions on consumers is much higher costs for medicine than the typical American needs to pay and a profitability rate for the pharmaceutical industry that is only rivaled among major US industries by finance.

As with other industries, there is not a lot of written information concerning the nexus players, specific lobbying efforts, and specific benefits reaped by major corporations within the health industry. The following cases have occurred over the past decade. What is clear is that a nexus exists, considerable lobbying funds have been devoted, and if profitability is the primary criterion the pharmaceutical industry has been rewarded for its lobbying and campaign contribution expenditures.

This was clear in 2005. Among congressional beneficiaries from corporate campaign donations that exceeded $100,000 were Speaker of the House Illinois Republican Dennis Hastert, and members of health committees including Senate Republicans Richard Burr and Arlen Specter, and Democrat Chris Dodd. The leading recipient of campaign contributions was House Representative Mike Ferguson whose powerful House Energy and Commerce Committee had jurisdiction over the pharmaceutical industry. Another key nexus member was Tennessee Bill Frist, a former surgeon who had the responsibility for overseeing which health-related bills would be debated within the Senate. Finally, former Republican member of the House Billy Tauzin reportedly was paid about $1 million annually after he left Congress to become head of the Pharmaceutical Research and Manufacturers of America – a powerful lobbying group.

The revolving door between Washington DC and major pharmaceutical firms has been quite active. According to the Center for Public Integrity, in 2003 over one third of the more than 1270 registered lobbyists for pharmaceutical firms in Washington DC were former federal officials, of whom 40 were retired members of Congress. One member of the National Women's Health Network noted that the pharmaceutical lobby was "one of the strongest, most well-connected and most effective lobbies in Washington. ... Going up against them is more often than not a losing battle" (Drinkard, 2005). It should be noted that this industry is heavily dependent upon government decisions and regulations as they provide the drugs for the Medicare, Medicaid, and Veterans Administration programs. As regulations and budgets for these programs increased so did pharmaceutical lobbying expenditures – almost doubling from nearly $80 million in 1998 to nearly $160 billion in 2004. Between 1998 and 2005 pharmaceutical firms' lobbying investment exceeded $750 million, greater than lobbying expenditures of any other industry during that time period. In addition to the lobbying expenditures and estimated $17 million in campaign contributions, drug companies also spent over $7 million on the Republican and Democrat national conventions in 2004 (Drinkard, 2005). One other expenditure has come in the form of flying key congressional nexus members on their corporate jets. One means for identifying some of the most powerful nexus members could be found by noting which powerful members of Congress were offered trips in corporate jets owned by pharmaceutical firms. While the political committee of each member was required to reimburse the firm for the equivalent cost of a first-class ticket, the chosen congressional representative did receive more luxury and convenience – in return for being escorted by the same firm's lobbyists on the trip. Pharmaceutical firms engaging in this practice as of 2005 included Pfizer, Schering, Novartis, and Abbott Laboratories (Drinkard, 2005). What did these firms receive for these investments? One benefit was legislation passed that prohibited cheaper imports from Canada and other countries from being readily available to Americans on the Medicare and Medicaid programs who could have chosen to purchase foreign-produced drugs on more favorable terms.

Four years later in 2009 the nexus had some different Washington DC figures, one of whom is noteworthy since he also has been part of the tax legislation (favorable to corporate and wealthy private interests) and the food industry. That would be former Montana Senator Max Baucus who from 2003 until he retired from office received over $3 million in campaign contributions from the health and insurance industries – an amount which ranks highest among all members of Congress. Of this total over $850,000 came from the pharmaceutical industry, ranking Baucus as the fourth among all former and current (as of 2009) congressional recipients of pharmaceutical campaign donations. Joining Baucus in writing major health care legislation that, of course, directly affected pharmaceutical firms were about 30 other members of Congress said to have financial assets in the health care industry (Ward, 2009).

As of 2014 the nexus was even stronger and larger. It was reported that the health care industry as a whole was spending more on lobbying in Washington DC (over $229 million) than any other industry (Center for Responsive Politics, 2014). Meanwhile the complexity of the Affordable Care Act contributed to the establishment of a new revolving door through which more public health care officials have become lobbyists for health industry firms. It was estimated by the Center for Responsive Politics that of all the "revolving door lobbyists" the highest percentage (12%) were specializing in health care lobbying issues. However, few of them are lobbying to change the drug importation laws, despite evidence that we Americans (both individuals and firms providing health care to employees) pay up to 50% more for prescription drugs than do Canadians for comparable drugs (Strauss, 2012). When some members of the Senate, including John McCain, have introduced amendments to the Prescription Drug User Fee Act that would legalize importing drugs through online pharmacies in Canada pharmaceutical industry lobbyists have acted swiftly and fiercely to kill such amendments. McCain lamented that "[i]n a normal world this would probably require a voice vote, but what we're about to see is the incredible influence of the special interests, particularly pharma, here in Washington, that keeps people who cannot – that have to make a choice between eating and medicine" (Strauss, 2012).

Killing attempts to offer American consumers a less expensive prescription drug option has not been the pharmaceuticals' only fierce lobbying effort over the past few years. A trade deal known as the Trans-Pacific Partnership initially was proposed in 2009. It would not be publicly debated until about 2013. During those four years the pharmaceutical industry included mention of this agreement in more than 250 separate lobbying reports as they, and other multinational corporations, engaged in what in effect were secret negotiations with congressional nexus members. The lobbying efforts were a good investment, for when the bill was written in proposal form for congressional debate it included terms "quite friendly to drug manufacturers, strengthening patent exclusivity and providing protections against bulk government purchasing" if industry profits would have suffered (Drutman, 2014). By 2015 critics of the proposed trade agreement were arguing that while the rhetoric for the bill was to promote freer trade worldwide, what it would most likely do would be to "strengthen multinationals at the expense of nearly everyone else" (Brodwin, 2015). Specific benefits for the pharmaceutical industry would be to gain some power preventing the production in poorer countries of generic drugs that would be sold at a much lower price than pharmaceutical giants now charge. Throughout the spring of 2015 congressional members of this industry nexus pushed to pass the bill (albeit unsuccessfully) that would have given fast track authority to President Obama for approval, and thereby they would not be on record as having approved of a trade pact so favorable to the pharmaceutical industry – among other industries.

Retail: Mr. Sam Benefits from Uncle Sam

Although the retail industry as a whole receives little in the way of corporate welfare compared to other US industries, both Wal-Mart, the world's largest retailer, and the Walton family, one of the richest families in the world, have benefited considerably. While this family is America's leading job creator (albeit mostly low-paying jobs) as well as a contributor to a range of charities, estate tax laws and local subsidies have enhanced their wealth. The family, thanks to a nexus that includes former Arkansas Senator Democrat Blanche Lincoln (who became a lobbyist for a firm that has Wal-Mart as a client after losing a re-election bid in 2010) and some

Republican congressional members introduced what even President Obama has referred to as the "Walton loophole" in the estate tax laws. Lobbyists, including Patton Boggs which was hired by Wal-Mart, worked with Washington DC legislators to write the rules for estate trusts that enable billions of dollars to be placed into trusts without there being tax obligations. One tax lawyer who reviewed the Walton family trust filings described the savings as "unbelievable" (Mider, 2013). Attempts by the Obama administration to close this loophole have been thwarted.

The Wal-Mart company has received over $1 billion in "economic development" subsidies from generous state and local governments in 35 states throughout the country (Sirota et al., 2004). These subsidies have come in the form of property tax relief, land at low cost or for free on which to build a new store, distribution center or warehouse, and even outright cash grants (*The Progress Report*, 2006). Of Wal-Mart's 91 distribution centers throughout the country, 84 received "economic development subsidies paid by taxpayers" (Mattera and Purinton, 2004). One analyst, referring to Wal-Mart as a "welfare queen," has found over 240 cases in which a new Wal-Mart facility was constructed with taxpayer assistance. A careful study of the economic impact on the local economy when a new Wal-Mart store opens would reveal that rather than create a large number of new jobs and significantly expand the income level of the local economy, much of Wal-Mart's sales cannibalize sales of existing retailers – causing some to go out of business with corresponding lost jobs. When urban sprawl and environmental effects of constructing a large retail store are taken into consideration the net positive economic impact Wal-Mart generates is smaller than government proponents of corporate welfare to Wal-Mart tend to argue. Another critic noted that the jobs Wal-Mart creates "tend to be poverty-wage, part-time and lacking in adequate healthcare benefits," while arguing "[t]hat a company with $9 billion in profits can wrest subsidies from state and local governments shows that the candy store game is out of control" (*The Progress Report*, 2006).

The Military–Industrial–Congressional Nexus

The defense industry has one of the oldest nexuses. It was first brought to the attention of Americans delivered in his farewell address by outgoing President Dwight Eisenhower in 1961. For well over half a century lucrative defense contracts have been facilitated by lobbyists and military advisors (who formerly were high-ranking military officers) funded by major defense contractors and aided by friendly members of Congress who, in return, have received generous campaign contributions. One distinguishing feature of this nexus is that unlike any other industry nexus it has been losing some of its political power as old, trusted congressional friends either retire or pass away.

Despite the passing of the guard reducing defense spending still faces formidable opposition. A case in point occurred in 2009 when the combination of President Barack Obama, his Defense Secretary, and Senator John McCain tried to limit "wasteful" projects such as a contract to build seven F-22 jets. However, the major defense contractor in the United States, Lockheed Martin, won this battle and was awarded the contract (Kiersh, 2009). Long-time congressional nexus member Representative John Murtha from Pennsylvania, who at the time was the congressional leader in total campaign contributions received from the defense industry, came to the rescue and used his influence to assist Lockheed Martin. It is noteworthy that Citizens for Responsibility and Ethics in Washington named Murtha "as one of the 20 most corrupt members of Congress" (Citizens for Responsibility and Ethics in Washington, 2009). He was known for being a champion of popular earmarks for special interest groups, who then were expected to donate to his campaign finance account once funding for their earmarks was approved.

One could argue that the popularity of defense contracts is the purported substantial economic impact contracts have throughout nearly every state that produces some type of military equipment. The primary recipients of this spending are the major defense contractors, especially Lockheed Martin, Boeing, General Dynamics, Northrop Grumman, and Raytheon, each of which lavishes campaign contributions on key congressional nexus members. In 2009 this group included Murtha, Georgia Senator Saxby Chambliss, a member of the Senate Armed Services Committee, Alaska Senator Ted Stevens, Missouri Representative Ike Skelton, and Washington Representative Norm Dicks. However, by 2013 Murtha had died while other key nexus members had either retired, been defeated for re-election, or put in jail. Ranked according to the amount of campaign contributions received from defense industry firms between 1990 and 2012, only 11 of the 30 House members receiving the most money and only 14 of the 30 most favored Senate members were still in office (Samuelsohn and Palmer, 2013). The defense industry is spending more than ever on campaign contributions, but the political power of those they are cultivating is less than that formerly wielded by Murtha and his fellow nexus congressional retirees. Some of the new foot soldiers who receive more campaign contributions than other congressional members include Senator Thad Cochran from Mississippi, Texas House member Mac Thornberry, and Illinois Senator Dick Durbin. The torch has now passed to these nexus members who, influenced by the more than $130 million lobbying expenditures from the defense industry in a typical year, serve as gatekeepers to secure defense contracts, earmarks, and maintenance of high levels of defense spending regardless of whether or not some particular projects enhance national security (Center for Responsive Politics, 2014).

One additional group that is prominent within the defense industry nexus are retired generals and admirals who serve as industry lobbyists, advisory staff members employed by a defense contractor, and advisors to the Pentagon – sometimes holding two of these positions simultaneously. One study discovered that between 1992 and 2012 the Pentagon feeder system provided about "750 of the highest ranking [retired] generals and admirals to be part of the 'rent-a-general' business" (Glaser, 2012). Some of these lobbyists retained an advisory role within the Pentagon. Between 2009 and 2011 the largest five defense contractors hired nine high ranking generals or admirals through what is a very lucrative revolving door (Greenwald and Sloan, 2012). Some of these high ranking officers also served on Mitt Romney's 2012 campaign advisory team – likely attracted by Romney's stating his desire to "massively increase US defense spending by \$2 trillion over ten years" (Glaser, 2012). This group of advisors who now benefit in part from the corporate welfare defense contractors receive included, among others, retired four-star general General James Conway (member of the Board of Directors of Textron, which manufactures helicopters and other aircraft and products for the military); retired former commander of United States Strategic Command James O. Ellis (member of the Institute of Nuclear Power Operations and board member at Lockheed Martin); and retired Air Force General Ronald Fogleman (member of the board of directors of four defense industry firms: Alliant Techsystems, AAR Corporation, Mesa Air Group, Inc., and World Air Holdings) (Glaser, 2012). Holding such a private sector position with any one of these defense industry giants has enabled the nexus' retired military officers to attend a few meetings a year and be remunerated an amount similar to their military salary. This is all legal, but the conflict of interest is glaring, especially when what at times can be considered corporate welfare is received by their defense industry employer – welfare for which former military leaders have been instrumental in securing congressional approval.

Oil and Gas Industry: High Profits and Generous Subsidies

What could explain \$4 billion annual corporate welfare in the form of tax breaks to an industry whose five largest firms – British Petroleum, Chevron, ConocoPhillips, ExxonMobil, and Royal Dutch Shell – realized combined profits for the 2000–10 period of almost \$1 trillion? Almost three fourths of Americans have indicated in surveys they believe this corporate welfare should be eliminated. During the Obama administration years both he and a few congressional members have advocated ending this generous subsidy. One analyst believes continuation of this corporate welfare is due to a "stranglehold on Congress that even when the Democrats controlled both houses, repeal of the subsidies didn't stand a chance" (Froomkin, 2011). An examination of the nexus reveals the key players and the economic and political power creating this stranglehold.

In addition to the major oil and natural gas producers (British Petroleum, Chevron, ConocoPhillips, ExxonMobil, Royal Dutch Shell, and Occidental Petroleum), other key members of the oil and gas industry nexus can be identified as indicated by the amounts of their political donations. Among them are the Koch Industries, Marathon Petroleum, and Western Refining. Each of these nexus members donated over $1 million to members of Congress – with 90% of these contributions going to Republicans (Center for Responsive Politics, 2015B). Koch Industries was by far the most generous contributor with almost $6.5 million. Another key nexus member is the industry's lobbying and trade association, the American Petroleum Institute. It wields enormous political and economic power to provide the industry's position and legislative preferences to key members of Congress when federal issues concerning the industry are either debated or proposals for debate are being made. It is such power that enables the oil industry to influence members of Congress to reject budget resolutions calling for the subsidies (i.e., corporate welfare) to be repealed. After a failed 2010 attempt to have a resolution passed by Democratic House member William Keating of Massachusetts, with no Republicans voting in favor of the measure, Keating lamented that this subsidy was retained in the face of congressional debate concerning cutting social programs such as Head Start, border security, and police protection (Froomkin, 2011).

The major congressional members of the nexus can be identified according to the amount of campaign contributions they receive. When those contributions made by the fracking industry are considered the leaders included Texas Representative Joe Barton and Senate Minority Leader Mitch McConnell. Barton is the chairman emeritus of the House Committee on Energy and Commerce. While he was chair of this committee Barton sponsored the Energy Policy Act of 2005 which provided an exemption to the fracking industry from provisions in the Safe Drinking Water Act – thereby reducing environmental cleanup costs for the industry (Center for Responsive Politics, 2015B). Using campaign contributions received from the oil industry as an indicator of key congressional pro-oil and gas nexus members the list also includes John Corny (R-Texas), Mary Landrieu (D-Louisiana), Speaker of the House John Boehner, and Senate Majority Leader Mitch McConnell (Center for Responsive Politics, 2015B).

The oil and gas industry ranks near the top of expenditures on lobbying and campaign contributions. During 2014 the most prolific lobbying spenders were Koch Industries ($13.8 million), followed by ExxonMobil ($12.6 million), Occidental Petroleum ($9.2 million), the American Petroleum Institute ($9 million), and Royal Dutch Shell ($8.4 million) (Center for Responsive Politics, 2015B). Total expenditures by the industry exceeded $141 million in 2014, which according to one estimate ranked it third among all US industries – behind pharmaceuticals/health products (over $229 million) and insurance (more than $151 million). Another estimate ranked it fourth behind pharma, electric utilities, and insurance

(Froomkin, 2011).[4] Further, there has been an upward trend in lobbying expenditures, rising from about $50 million in 2004 to over $170 million by 2009, although they declined to almost $145 million in 2014 (Center for Responsive Politics, 2015B). Lavish spending on congressional campaigns, either in direct donations or through political action committees, has also occurred. During the 2010 election cycle the industry donated about $25 million, while in 2014 the figure almost reached $35 million (Center for Responsive Politics, 2015B).

A controversial issue stimulating such campaign financing generosity has been the Keystone Pipeline. One analyst raised the question as to why this pipeline received so much attention from Congress (he referred to it as their "number one priority") when estimates are that construction of it would create a paltry 35 permanent jobs – fewer than are created by the typical new McDonald's restaurant. House Representatives who in early 2015 voted in favor of the bill received over $13 million in campaign contributions from the oil and gas industry as compared to the less than $2 million received collectively by those who voted against it (Kretzmann, 2015). Overall, a simple cost–benefit analysis of the industry's lavish spending on congressional campaigns indicates an exorbitant return on the industry's lobbying investment. Case in point was during 2011–12 when almost $330 million was spent by the oil and gas industry for campaign contributions and lobbying combined – while they received about $33 billion in corporate welfare over that same period. This translates to a nearly 10,000% rate of return – something that would make even Goldman Sachs envious (Kretzmann, 2015). Another contributing factor to a surge in campaign contributions between 2004 and 2012 was the boom in oil extracted by fracking. The boom (until 2015) has "yield[ed] gushers of campaign contributions for congressional candidates from districts containing hydraulically fractured wells" (Citizens for Responsibility and Ethics in Washington, 2015). The primary beneficiaries were congressional members from districts in which fracking activity was located. During the 2004–12 period the fracking industry's contributions to candidates from those districts rose over 230% as compared to (a still substantial) 130% to candidates from non-fracking districts (Citizens for Responsibility and Ethics in Washington, 2015).

The oil and gas industry employs almost 800 lobbyists, about 500 of whom went through the revolving door from federal government employment to persuade former colleagues to provide benefits, some in the form of corporate welfare, to their industrial employers (Froomkin, 2011). Perhaps some of these lobbyists formerly were US State Department employees. One investigative reporter uncovered evidence that a State Department official provided information to a lobbyist employed by the TransCanada pipeline company interested in constructing part of the Keystone Pipeline. The information concerned contents of a meeting that involved Hillary Clinton, and was allegedly provided to TransCanada's chief lobbyist in Washington DC who formerly was a prominent member of Clinton's presidential campaign team in 2008. The evidence includes email messages that "paint a picture of a sometimes warm and collaborative relationship between the lobbyist for the pipeline company, Trans-Canada, and officials in the State Department, the agency responsible for evaluating and approving the billion-dollar project" (Rosenthal, 2011). This is a significant part of the industry's nexus given that the State Department has the authority to grant permission for the construction of pipelines that cross from Mexico or Canada into the United States. It is supposed to act in the national interest – but the coziness of the relationships among nexus members with some State Department officials has all the appearances of conflicts of interest and that the "national interest" may ultimately be defined by these authorities as being synonymous with the oil and gas industry interests.

Finance: The Revolving Door Receives Its Fullest Expression

The strongest, tightest nexus among major American industries is exemplified by the deep-seated personal relationships that have developed between Wall Street investment banks, key Washington DC financial institutions, and ranking members of the executive and legislated branches of the federal government. Two effects of these relationships, both of which are detrimental to most Americans, is that they have "promoted the spread of the Wall Street world view in the corridors of political power. The prospect of landing prestigious or high-paying jobs in the financial sector may also have influenced the decisions of regulators and administration officials, who may have had an incentive not to make enemies among their potential future employers" (Johnson and Kwak, 2011, p. 96). Solidifying the nexus, at least prior to the 2008 financial industry crash, has been federal government officials permitting the top Wall Street investment bank officials to select their preferred primary regulator from among a number of Washington DC regulatory agencies – a practice "which created the incentives for a 'race to the bottom' in which agencies attract 'customers' by offering relatively lax regulatory enforcement" (Johnson and Kwak, 2011, p. 96).

For more than the previous decade leading up to the 2008 financial industry meltdown were actions by the nexus that contributed to deregulation legislation and the capture of rating agencies and federal regulators by Wall Street banks. Even after the meltdown when public sentiment for significant penalties against those investment bank officials who contributed mightily to the deep recession the financial services industry remains powerful. One US Senator observed that despite the United States being in a recession induced by the major investment banks "banks are still the most powerful lobby on Capitol Hill. And they frankly own the place" (Johnson and Kwak, 2011, p. 92).

In addition to the top officers at both the IMF and World Bank, the most prominent members of the finance industry nexus that has shaped regulatory policy and legislation highly favorable to the industry for the past three decades have included CEOs of the 13 largest financial institutions in the United States – who collectively comprise the "new American oligarchy – a group that gains political power because of its economic power, then uses that power for its own benefit";[5] former Federal Reserve Chairs Alan Greenspan and Ben Bernanke; Treasury Secretaries (particularly Robert Rubin, Lawrence Summers, Henry Paulson, and Timothy Geithner); and many members of Congress anxious to curry favor with this powerful industry. These have included former Senator Christopher Dodd, former House Financial Services Committee Chairs Spencer Bachus and Jeb Hensarling; and former New Hampshire Senator Judd Gregg (CEO of Wall Street's biggest lobbying group).

Greenspan's libertarian philosophy led to alleged laissez-faire policies highly profitable for the finance industry, but whose impact on the US finance industry was even more detrimental than policies introduced in states such as Kansas under the leadership of governors with a similar economic philosophy. Throughout his career as "financial maestro" of the US economy Greenspan was an outspoken advocate of deregulating the industry and preventing stronger regulation of what proved to be toxic financial assets such as credit default swaps. At times he blamed excessive government regulations for holding back the economy. Even after the 2008 crisis he refused to accept that the same deregulations and lax enforcement he championed as Federal Reserve Chair ultimately contributed significantly to the downfall. One critic of Greenspan's self-serving explanation of the slow post-2008 economic recovery argued that "Greenspan cites little positive evidence to support his claim that too much government activism is the reason why businesses haven't been investing" (Roth, 2011A). Perhaps the most accurate assessment of Greenspan's tenure as Federal Reserve Chair, taking account of his refusal to impose stricter regulations that likely would have prevented the disaster, was provided by the former head of the Commodity Futures Trading Commission, Brooksley Born. At an April 7, 2010, hearing conducted by the Financial Crisis Inquiry Commission she pointed out his "many failures" as Fed Chair, particularly his failure to heed her excellent advice to regulate derivatives (she offered such advice during the Clinton administration) that ultimately led to the financial and real estate crisis. She chided Greenspan for having "failed to prevent the housing bubble, failed to prevent the predatory lending scandal, failed to prevent the activities that would bring the financial system to the verge of collapse [and for having] failed to prevent many of our banks from consolidating and growing to a size that are now too big or too interconnected to fail" (Dayen, 2010). Greenspan's feeble attempts to defend himself included claiming that he lacked discretion as to what actions Congress would take. However, as he was considered somewhat of an "oracle" whose positions were followed carefully by all of those with financial industry interests his defense is far from convincing.

Bernanke followed in Greenspan's footsteps. Evaluations of his tenure as Fed Chair range from glowing to mixed. Criticism focused on his decision to let Lehman Brothers fail, his "conflicting role" as "puppeteer" (Sorkin, 2008) in the sale of Bear Stearns stock to other investment banks; his support for the AIG bailout; his unwillingness to press for stricter regulations of investment banks after he became Fed Chair in 2006 despite being well aware of the promiscuous lending practices; and for his failure to anticipate the real estate crash despite having access to evidence that would have raised many red flags that the rapid rise in housing prices pre-2008 was destined for a substantial fall. He did receive high praise for his part in preventing the 2008 crisis from escalating into a serious depression. Overall, his place within the industry nexus was prominent, and the remaining Wall Street firms profited handsomely from the monetary easing policies he promoted.

Rubin was a long-time nexus member who exemplifies the nature of, and ability to profit from, the revolving door between Wall Street and Washington DC. He was a top official at Goldman Sachs for over 25 years, Treasury Secretary in the Clinton administration, and temporary chair of Citigroup for two years. One of the quintessential Wall Street insiders, he was instrumental in placing a number of his protégés, such as fellow nexus members Tim Geithner and Jack Lew, both of whom served the Obama administration, in the position of Treasury Secretary as well. During his years with the Clinton administration he was influential, with fellow nexus members Greenspan and Summers, in reducing regulations on the finance industry – regulations that had served to prevent a serious financial crisis since the 1930s. In 1999, believing the US financial markets were over-regulated, Rubin used his influence to help sway Congress to repeal the Glass–Steagall Act. One cynical observer claimed that "repeal of this act" was "rewarding financial companies for more than 20 years and $300 million worth of lobbying efforts" (Snyder, 2009).

Rubin joined forces with Greenspan to oppose having credit derivatives regulated by the Commodity Futures Trading Commission. He also was a key player in the passage of the Gramm–Leach–Bliley Act of 1999. This act enabled investment banks to grow considerably – eventually becoming "too big to fail" that became the rallying cry for the post-2008 financial industry bailout. Rubin then held top positions with Citigroup at times between 1999 and 2009, serving as Director and Senior Counselor, and reportedly earning over $125 million. Critics point out that he joined Citigroup shortly after the Gramm–Leach–Bliley Act was passed, and that Citigroup benefited substantially from the new rules. Further, critics note that he played a prominent role in weakening financial regulations that would ultimately result in financial disaster. The federal government response to the disaster, thanks to the advice of finance industry nexus members, was to provide Citigroup with $45 billion in taxpayer dollars as well as to guarantee about $300 billion of Citigroup's illiquid assets. The harshest criticism of Rubin was that "[n]obody on this planet represents more vividly the scam of the banking industry," says Nassim Nicholas Taleb, author of *The Black Swan* (2007). "He made $120 million from Citibank, which was technically insolvent. And now we, the taxpayers, are paying for it" (Cohan, 2012).

The third most prominent member of the finance industry nexus over the past two decades has been Summers, former Treasury Secretary and economic advisor to President Obama. It was during his tenure with the Clinton administration that he joined forces with Greenspan and Rubin to "stave off the regulation of the very financial derivatives whose unlimited trading would eventually help bring down much of the financial system" (Goodman, 2009, p. 79). During that period Summers allegedly called Brooksley Born, head of the Commodity Futures Trading Commission – the agency responsible for financial contracts known as derivatives. In response to her advocating regulation of derivatives sales Summers is quoted as having told her, "I have thirteen bankers in my office, and they say if you go forward with this you will cause the worst financial crisis since World War II" (Johnson and Kwak, 2011, p. 9).[6] Overall, it was Greenspan, Rubin, and Summers whose arrogance and faith in financial markets contributed mightily to the 2008 meltdown – the worst financial crisis since World War II. However, as the remaining active nexus member among the most prominent three, Summers is still in good graces with other nexus members. It is noteworthy that he reportedly received over $2.5 million in speaker's fees from the same Wall Street firms that received federal government bailout funds – corporate welfare that he enthusiastically supported. It has been reported that he may rejoin the inner circle of the nexus should Hillary Clinton win the upcoming presidential election, despite his record for having argued forcefully for financial deregulation, including not regulating the derivatives market or failing to recognize the danger of a banks being too big to fail policy.

Two other non-congressional nexus members have been Hank Paulson, George W. Bush's last Treasury Secretary and former head of Goldman Sachs, and strong proponent of the Wall Street bailout, and Barack Obama's first Treasury Secretary Timothy Geithner. Paulson and Geithner worked together to prepare some of the bailout proposals the Bush administration began to draft during late 2008 (Goodman, 2009, p. 227). This is not surprising since as of 2008 Geithner had forged unusually close relationships with Wall Street CEOs during his five years as President of the New York Federal Reserve Bank. His mindset was theirs – equate prosperity on Wall Street with prosperity for the United States. Geithner would be instrumental in the creation and implementation of the $180 billion AIG bailout. As a loyal nexus member he undoubtedly was aware that after the bailout most of the AIG bailout money was funneled to the company's trading partners, banks, and other financial firms that would have lost big if AIG were allowed to fail. Calendar records from Geithner's first seven months as Treasury Secretary revealed that he was in contact with some of the Wall Street nexus members over 80 times, which far exceeded the number of his contacts with the chair of the Senate Banking Committee and House Financial Services Committee (Johnson and Kwak, 2011, p. 187).

Among the herd of congressional members who either were or wanted to be part of the finance industry nexus were former US Senator and Senate Banking Committee Chair Christopher Dodd, current Senate Budget Committee Chairman Kent Conrad, and House members Spencer Bachus and Jeb Hensarling. Both Dodd and Conrad demonstrated a brazen contempt for conflict of interest appearances as they accepted "sweetheart" mortgage loans with "special terms" from Countrywide Finance, a mortgage lender at the heart of the real estate crisis. Dodd and Conrad were not alone in this regard. An investigation determined that Countrywide "bought influence on Capitol Hill by issuing hundreds of sweetheart loans for members of Congress, their staffs and other government employees" (Christie and Stewart, 2012). However, in Dodd's case the conflict is especially glaring in light of his having accepted substantial campaign contribution dollars from the finance and real estate industry (Center for Responsive Politics, 2015A).

Dodd is not alone when it comes to appearance of corruption due to the interaction between the campaign contributions he received from the finance industry and his powerful position on the Senate Banking Committee. House member Spencer Bachus, former Chair of the House Committee on Financial Services who recently retired, was described as having "spent his career as a wholly owned subsidiary of the finance industry … in Washington, the view is that the banks are to be regulated," the Alabama congressman told the News. "My view is that Washington and the regulators are there to serve the banks" (Edsall, 2013A). Over half of the campaign contributions he received, according to OpenSecrets.org, came from the finance, insurance, and real estate industries, as well as receiving almost $500,000 from a political action committee (PAC) that was operated by companies from these industries. His tradition will live on in the person of House member Jeb Hensarling who succeeded Bachus as Chair of the Finance Services Committee. About half of his campaign contributions for the 2012 election came from the same three industries that avidly supported Bachus (Edsall, 2013A). Hensarling appears to be less of a cynic than a true believer in free enterprise for the finance industry – apparently having learned little from the 2008 financial disaster. He may have more faith in free markets than a saint does in God, as indicated by his assessment of what caused the crisis. He stated that "The great tragedy of the financial crisis … was not that Washington regulations failed to prevent it, but instead that Washington regulations helped lead us into it" (Finkle, 2014).

One final nexus member deserving mention is former Senator Judd Gregg who served on the Senate Banking Committee. He revolved from the Senate (where he argued against regulating derivatives and other strong provisions of the Dodd–Frank Wall Street Reform and Consumer Protection Act) to become an international advisor to Goldman Sachs, and later was appointed as CEO of Securities Industry and Financial Markets Association, Wall Street's largest lobbying group for which he has subsequently become a senior advisor (Hopkins and Schmidt, 2013). One wonders if Gregg's being one of the authors of the Trouble Asset Relief Program (TARP) to bail out the banks while a member of the Senate, and while he had substantial investments in Bank of America, had any influence on his subsequent appointments.

What the finance nexus has been successful at doing is writing rules that immensely profit the industry while offering post-Congress retirement positions to those instrumental in crafting legislation highly favorable to the industry. When the financial crisis occurred nexus members were needed the most, and those members who were key economic policy makers (Bernanke, Paulson, Geithner, and Summers) "devised an impressive range of schemes to shore up the banking system ... the common feature of these schemes was that they attempted to fill the gaping hole in the bank balance sheets with government subsidies, more or less crudely obscured" (Johnson and Kwak, 2011, p. 167). While the Supreme Court has ruled that Congress can regulate against "corruption and the appearance of corruption," behavior by members of the nexus seems to be widely accepted rather than subject to corruption consideration. One reporter questions the "relevance of the symbiotic relationship between the finance industry and the House Financial Services Committee and the current campaign finance case before the Supreme Court, *McCutcheon v Federal Election Commission*?" He concludes that "[c]orruption and the appearance of corruption are here to stay. The difference now is that the squalid character of the system has become institutionalized" (Edsall, 2013A).

Given the strength of its nexus and the multitudes of high level financial institution and Washington DC officials passing through a revolving door the finance industry spends less for lobbying and campaign contributions relative to other industries – but still receives a greater rate of return on the dollars spent thanks to generous corporate welfare and lax legislation approved by Congress and some favorable policies established by the Federal Reserve Bank. Therefore, in the case of the finance industry, more focus needs to be placed on the revolving door between Wall Street and Washington DC. Lobbyists are important, but when top officials from both Wall Street and the New York Federal Reserve Bank "move seamlessly" back and forth, they gain "power over political decisions affecting the financial industry" (Stiglitz, 2009A, pp. 84–5). Who needs lobbyists when your nexus can make the rules itself? One Nobel

Prize-winning economist concludes that the Wall Street nexus members were permitted "to write self-serving rules which put at risk the entire global economy – and then, when the day of reckoning came, [Washington DC officials] turned to Wall Street to manage the recovery" (Stiglitz, 2009A, pp. 84–5). When regulation enforcement began the revolving door between those who worked for the Wall Street banks as either consultants or attorneys and regulatory positions would resume with some receiving congressionally approved positions at the Securities and Exchange Commission (SEC). This pattern has strengthened the finance industry's ability to continue engaging in risky investment practices that remain highly profitable with a low probability of their receiving substantial fines for illegal practices. The pattern also continues the likelihood that should there be a repeat of the 2008 financial crisis similar bailouts would most likely be doled out to them.

An examination of the past presidential administrations would reveal a similar revolving door pattern, although the speed at which the door is spinning has increased. Both Paul Volcker and Greenspan had extensive Wall Street experience before being appointed Federal Reserve Chair. During the Clinton and Bush administrations many Wall Street bankers were given federal government positions that directly affected the finance industry, including Treasury Secretary, Treasury Undersecretary, Senate Banking Committee members, Director of the Office of Management and Budget, Chief of Staff, and Head of TARP, among other positions. Many positions at the Treasury department were staffed by former Wall Street investment bank managers. When Obama took office he chose to hire some of the same Wall Street nexus members that worked for Clinton or Bush, including Rubin, Michael Froman (Rubin's chief of staff who formerly worked for Citigroup), and Summers (Johnson and Kwak, 2011, p. 185). Obama brought on Geithner as Treasury Secretary. Geithner, in turn, recruited some managers from the same Wall Street firms (particularly Goldman Sachs) who were both a cause of the financial crisis and (at the time) candidates for billions of bailout dollars (Stiglitz, 2009A, pp. 84–5).

Summers has made almost as many revolutions through the revolving door as an ice skater. Perhaps these revolutions were part of the reason he was not nominated to be Chair of the Federal Reserve in 2014. Some critics cited conflict of interest issues that go as far back as the late 1990s when he played a prominent role in the repeal of the Glass–Steagall Act. After leaving Washington DC in 2010 where he was Obama's top economic policy advisor he worked with both Citigroup and the D.E. Shaw hedge fund, as well as either working or serving on the board of other financial institutions (Story and Lowrey, 2013).

What have been some outcomes from the deep-seated nexus and the revolving door between Wall Street and Washington DC? What are the consequences of regulators leaving government work to join the financial services industry, and vice versa? First, the revolving door has facilitated the ability of nexus members to translate their economic power into political power for economic gain, or to enhance their political power that later is translated into greater economic power (i.e., earnings). One critic pointed out that "the revolving door, which allows American financial leaders to move seamlessly from Wall Street to Washington and back to Wall Street, gave them even more credibility; these men seemed to combine the power of money and the power of politics" (Stiglitz, 2009A, pp. 84–5). In the process nexus members made financial decisions that contribute to deregulation and enhance their ability to capture both ratings agencies and federal regulators.

Second, the investment banks can continue their reckless lending practices buoyed by the conviction that they will be bailed out once again should another financial crisis occur – partly because they have convinced the public that they are "too big to fail." One analyst argues that Dodd–Frank legislation has done little to change the concentration of economic and political power exercised by Wall Street banks, arguing that due to the revolving door (that involves nexus members) "these banks are so big right now [and] they have access to so much of a percentage of the deposits of individuals ... [further] the leverage is so much higher on the back of those deposits, the bailouts that have happened for numerous reasons in the past 25 years have all been an indication that is okay to take more reckless bets" (Prins, 2015). These banks have been, and likely will receive favorable terms and assurances that their losses will be covered by the Federal Reserve, "which we know now has substantiated a lot of Wall Street losses" (Prins, 2015).

Third, there is evidence that some former investment bank employees who passed through the revolving door to become government financial industry regulators later became deferential to their former employers. That is not surprising given that the regulators are now dealing with lobbyists with whom they used to work. For example, in the year after the financial crisis almost 150 of the newly registered industry lobbyists used to be employed as lawyers for the SEC or as bank officials with the Federal Reserve (Lichtblau, 2010). Senate hearings have been called in response to claims of deferential treatment by regulators to "ensure that regulators aren't captured by the big banks in exchange for the hope of future jobs" (Prins, 2015).[7] Being deferential, to say the least, may explain why in the face of massive evidence of fraud and other illegal lending and ratings practices no high ranking Wall Street banker has been prosecuted for contributing to the 2008 financial crisis. One harsh critic offers an "insidious" explanation, namely that the existence of the nexus and revolving door has created "[a]n institutionalized double-standard, stemming from the fact that many prosecutors and regulators someday hope to work at Wall Street firms like Goldman Sachs" (Blodgett, 2011).

The impact of the financial industry nexus throughout the economy is more extensive than that of any other industry, both in economic power and in having the potential to create a serious recession. Unfortunately, the nexus remains as powerful as ever and seems committed to dramatically weaken the Dodd–Frank provisions that seem to be reducing the extent of abusive lending practices through greater regulation of financial derivatives. The response of the Wall Street banks to these regulations which are reducing their profits is to strengthen their political influence. They did this effectively in 2014 when "the vampires of finance bought themselves a Congress" (Krugman, 2015A) – most of whom are Republicans now determined on deleting or eliminating the Dodd–Frank reforms. What the banks want is a return to the days when they could engage in risky lending practices that were not subject to regulation. Their ability to influence the discourse related to bank regulation, as well as the ability of other industries to shape discourse in a manner that facilitates their receiving more corporate welfare, is the focus of the next chapter.

Notes

1   While a significant part of the nexus' influence throughout the economy comes from some major news media and think tanks, that influence will be examined in the following chapters – especially their influence over policy discourse.
2   Basically, this principle is that prices (or wages) are compared to one another by decision makers. As the price of good A (or wage from job A) increases more and more relative to the price or wage of B, more people will choose good A over good B.
3   Proponents have one more opportunity to have this proposal become law in a scheduled 2016 referendum.
4   According to estimates "business associations" also outspent the oil industry.
5   It has been documented that 13 of these bankers attended a meeting with Barack Obama in late March, 2009, to discuss federal government policy concerning bailout, among other regulations being considered for proposal. The bankers were the CEOs from the following institutions: American Express, Bank of America, Bank of New York Mellon, Citigroup, Freddie Mac, Goldman Sachs, JP Morgan Chase, Morgan Stanley, Northern Trust, PNC, State Street, US Bank, and Wells Fargo (Johnson and Kwak, 2011, pp. 3–4, 6).
6   Note that in 1998 during Bill Clinton's presidency the nexus recommended that custom derivatives be exempted from Federal regulation, and their recommendation was approved by Congress and Clinton to become law in 2000.
7   This quote is from Elizabeth Warren at a November 21, 2014, Senate hearing that was prompted by allegations by a former New York Federal Reserve examiner accusing some of her colleagues of being too deferential to Goldman Sachs.

4 Limiting and Shaping Discourse

The corporate welfare economy (CWE)'s *second characteristic* is the growing ability of the ruling alliance to limit and shape public discourse throughout academia and research institutes,[1] Washington DC, and the national media. The limiting and shaping of discourse by nexus members reinforces their growing ability to translate their economic power to "influence electoral, legislative, and regulatory processes through campaign contributions, lobbying, and revolving door employment of politicians and bureaucrats" (Edsall, 2013B). Private sector nexus members gain influence over the content of policy-related public discourse among cooperating academics, government officials, media owners, and media writers and reporters. This influence is achieved through financial awards (e.g., grants for research studies, professorships, fellowships, lectures, consulting contracts), campaign contributions or the promise of future employment at lucrative terms, the purchase of media advertising – or even the purchase of the media itself. Using this influence nexus members are able to exert influence over the content of policy-related discourse and decisions concerning those same policies, the rules pertaining to those policies, and enforcement of those rules that favor their own personal interests as well as those of their industry.

Academia and Research Institutes

In academia and research institutes some nexuses exert their influence by providing grants to these institutions, individual research grants to faculty and institute researchers, fellowships, as well as funds for lectures or consulting contracts. In return they may be rewarded with grateful recipients of corporate funding producing biased research highly favorable to their special interests, and having some of their cronies appointed to powerful positions such as college and university presidents, endowed professorships, research institute directors, or research institute researchers. This provides the industry with influence over courses taught, course content, or research results emanating from academia or research institutes.[2] That influence can be translated into public discourse limiting the policy alternatives to those destined to promote the nexuses' interests.

Within most academic institutions orthodox economic thinking is the dominant view. This way of thinking's influence on discourse begins with introductory economics textbooks written and adopted. Some critics have argued that one major cause of the 2008 financial crisis was that the pedagogy contained in these books has for decades misinformed students, the general public, and policy makers with its "fundamental misconceptions about the way economies, most especially their markets, function" (Fulbrook, 2009). The principles are presented in a formal, dogmatic manner with an emphasis on the free market economy being the only feasible type of economy for a country to adopt. There is an overriding theme that economies behave according to some natural laws, and that outcomes can be forecast with accuracy.[3] The fallacy of this latter belief is explained in Appendix 2.

The simplified messages contained in introductory economics textbooks and the claim that economics is scientific affect public discourse. Based upon those interviewed most often by the major news media there appears to be a bias within both the news media and among Washington DC policy makers in favor of the views held by orthodox economic thinkers – with a corresponding marginalization of (highly acclaimed) alternative policy advocates such as Dean Baker, Paul Krugman, and Joseph Stiglitz. Whether it be policies for financial markets or poor countries the discourse underlying the policy making originating with orthodox economics has suffered from its proponents practicing a "Cargo Cult Science" (Fulbrook, 2009) by appearing to follow scientific investigation without taking account of the non-economic factors that significantly affect the outcomes of economic activity. Orthodoxy received its fullest expression during the 1980s–2007 period when the pseudo-scientific "economic thinking undergirded the 'deregulation' mantra" (Patterson and Cowles, 2015) which contributed significantly to the 2008 financial and real estate crises. Deregulation discourse was accompanied by a plethora of statistical models as orthodox economic thinking dominated the policy-making process. What was consistently ignored was the expertise of other academics more suited to the topics at hand (Patterson and Cowles, 2015). Even worse outcomes have been experienced by poor countries where orthodox economic thinking has dominated discourse and policy making. The ahistorical mindset of orthodox thinkers, combined with a strong free market economy bias prevented them from admitting that the only countries that have experienced a significant development transformation have followed eclectic development policies heavily pragmatic and reliant to a degree on state intervention (Patterson and Cowles, 2015; Angresano, 2005).

How does this orthodoxy relate to the nexuses' influence over discourse? Some of the most prominent orthodox economic thinkers have profited handsomely from corporate payments for their research, consultation, or lectures. These payments have contributed to the nexuses' corporate values replacing academic values. An egregious example of research produced by economics professors at prestigious Ivy League institutions as well as MIT and Stanford that shaped discourse which ultimately led to policies disastrous for the US economy is presented in Charles Ferguson's *The Inside Job* (2010). The carefully researched documentary demonstrates that the 2008 financial crisis was partly due to some economics department professors being corrupted by financial institutions. Wall Street banks bought off these high-profile economists who prepared papers about financial markets while also being paid by some of the same banks who would profit from those papers shaping discourse and subsequently policies that were based upon the "research" indicating that (reckless) deregulation was a better policy than regulation of what would become toxic financial instruments. In doing so some of these highly remunerated economists whose work shaped the policy discourse behave more like sycophants than objective academic researchers. In the aftermath of the crisis some presidents of their respective academic institutions refused to comment on the corporate corruption of their own prestigious, and influential, academic institution. This example illustrates the danger of universities relying more and more on private corporation and wealthy individual donations. Rather than being the source of relatively unbiased research designed to promote the social good, cases where nexus funding influences research for private-sector profitability purposes compromises the important place academia should play in setting the boundaries for policy discourse.

The combination of orthodox economic thinking and the possibility of their currying favor with nexus members influences some economic researchers to reach conclusions not in the best interest of most Americans. Trade analysis and how economics affects the discourse and policies adopted is another example. One prominent heterodox economic analyst criticizes the prominent orthodox economists whose international trade research is most cited since they "use of their expertise to effectively act as priests ... [and are] accorded enormous respect by the major media outlets. [Consequently], any politician who challenges the prognostications from this group is likely to be ridiculed in the media. ... As a result of their ability to influence the media, economists can be incredibly important in steering public policy, often in directions that may not be supported by most of the country" (Baker, 2008, p. 23). What is ignored is that numerous previous forecasts made by orthodox economists about the outcomes from a free trade policy consistently overstated the positive economic benefits realized by a majority of Americans while understating the negative distributional effects – particularly as average workers were affected. Further, the cases of trade and finance are not the exception. One prominent critic observes that "[u]nfortunately, the role that economists have played in debates over trade policy [and which have influenced policies adopted] is typical of their role in public policy debates. The mainstream of the profession has taken positions that tend to support the existing economic and political power structure and effectively used its claim to expertise to deprive the public of the opportunity to freely debate policy options" (Baker, 2008, p. 32).

Among other issues where orthodox economists' research has had a substantial effect both limiting and shaping discourse are debt and tax havens. The Federal Reserve portion of the finance nexus appears to be influential concerning public debt policy. Its academic advisors typically are monetarist economists who believe the best policies are those that prevent inflation by avoiding full employment and rising wages for workers, but who are not averse to policies leading to deficit financing that creates more debt. The financial sector purchases most of this debt and repays it at low interest rates that continue to benefit the financial and real estate industries – but not many Americans who formerly held their assets in savings accounts that pre-2008 paid much higher interest. The discourse concerning debt continues to be shaped by some orthodox economists and political leaders "with an anti-government ax to grind and vested interests to defend and indeed, promote with regard to financial deregulation" (Hudson, 2011). Over time as the finance, insurance, and real estate industries have become relatively more profitable and powerful economically they have been able to donate more to academic institutions – particularly to graduate business programs and policy research institutes. Through this "academic lobbying" the nexus representing these industries shapes and limits discourse to their view of debt. In the process they have been successful in "steer[ing] students, corporate managers and policy makers to see the world from a financial vantage point" (Hudson, 2011) rather than the classical market economy viewpoint with entrepreneurs central to reinvesting in the production sector of the domestic free market economy to boost output of goods and services as explained in Chapter 1. A related issue is that given the plethora of tax havens worldwide it is a wonder why there is a paucity of economic research about the effects of these havens on reinvestment rates. The research that has been done typically argues tax havens are beneficial although not making it clear that it is almost exclusively the wealthiest Americans who reap the greatest benefit (Murphy, 2011).

Nexus financing of research institutes, for which "think tank" is a euphemism in some cases, has contributed to shaping discourse on a range of key policy issues. What is sad is that some of the economic ideas promoted by some of these institutes continue to be espoused by reigning and aspiring political leaders even after those ideas have been disproven by sound analysis and evidence. The term "zombie economics" has been coined to describe these ideas which, even after being disproven by highly respected economic analysts, continue to be proposed because the policies that correspond to the discredited ideas "serve a political purpose, appeals to prejudices, or both" (Krugman, 2013B). Good examples of (since proven erroneous) zombie economic ideas perpetrated by think tanks such as the Heritage Foundation have been that tax cuts for the wealthy would have a net positive effect on fiscal revenue – while also leading to substantial job creation, and the idea that financial deregulation would have net positive economic outcomes for a majority of Americans. Other discourse-shaping, and erroneous, claims have been that government deficit spending is a job destroyer and a driver to higher interest rates, although that argument was not used when the finance industry was bailed out in 2009 with hundreds of billions in taxpayer dollars. Evidence over the past few years indicates both claims are not correct, but such claims continue to be made.

Other false claims have been made by Heritage Foundation resident "scholars." One of these has placed a majority of the blame for the 2008 financial crisis on the congressionally created Fannie Mae and Freddie Mac that were charged with purchasing mortgages from lenders which were either held by them or sold in a package of loans as mortgage-backed securities. The claim made by the Heritage Foundation researchers was that the private sector of the finance industry was led "off the cliff" by Fannie Mae and Freddie Mac policies that made housing more affordable and supported extending subprime mortgages (Nocera, 2011).[4] Careful study reveals these claims to be false, and that it was the finance sector's private sector that led the way over the cliff. The source of this revelation was the Financial Crisis Inquiry Commission. One of its members was the same Heritage Foundation researcher who initially argued that his research indicated the blame should be placed on Fannie Mae and Freddie Mac. That position continues to be held by that researcher even as more evidence indicates that while guilty of padding profits and poor accounting practices the two government-approved agencies were not the main cause of the massive crisis.

Discourse Shaping and Limiting in Major Industries

When international comparisons of life expectancies and the influence of diets on life expectancy as well as debilitating illnesses are considered the diet of the typical American family is less healthy than that of nearly every other wealthy country. Dietary guidelines (that are taught in public schools), the public school lunch program, and agricultural policy are set by the USDA – which makes influencing this government agency a prime target for the agricultural industry nexus. Which products receive the most farm subsidies are contained in the congressionally approved "Farm Bill." A quick look at which *agricultural* products receive the most subsidies (corn, cotton, rice, soybeans, and wheat) indicates that vegetable and fruit producers are left out of what amounts to corporate welfare for the large agribusiness corporations that produce an overwhelming majority of the five heavily subsidized products. It should be no surprise that the agricultural industry nexus, particularly the multibillion dollar agribusiness firms, has been successful at influencing discourse pertaining to government-recommended dietary guidelines and regulations for labeling food products, particularly those containing genetically modified organisms (GMOs). Profitability objectives trump concern with encouraging the production of foods that would improve nutrition for Americans. The nexus has been able to have some members, or those beholden to them, placed as either USDA board members or advisory committee members. Some of these members have financial ties to the agricultural industry's meat producers associations, dairy associations and companies, sugar associations, and grain associations. The discourse concerning food policy continues to be strongly in favor of consuming heavily subsidized and somewhat unhealthy foods produced by these industries, despite growing evidence that if Americans were to eat a diet comprised heavily of vegetables and fruits health indicators would improve dramatically.[5]

Nexus influence over the discourse pertaining to the USDA recommended diet extends to the National Academy of Sciences where corporations exert influence over courses taught and research by academics friendly to the industry that provide some basis for government nutrition policy. The case of Cornell University Professor T. Colin Campbell, a world expert on dietary issues, is illustrative. Campbell's research led him to become an outspoken critic of the typical American diet. Allegedly bowing to pressure from the agricultural nexus the School of Nutrition prohibited Campbell from teaching some of the nutrition classes he formerly had taught. Campbell, now a Professor Emeritus of Nutrition, co-authored *Forks over Knives: How a Plant-Based Diet Can Save America* (Stone and Campbell, 2011). He and his co-author were featured in the documentary about their research and this revolutionary diet. Their research led them to conclude that their dietary recommendations, if followed nationally, would substantially improve the health of many Americans. In a 2011 interview with Bill Maher, Campbell stated that the USDA recommended food pyramid is "a joke" (TV. Natural News, 2011). He agreed that major agricultural producers have bought off government policy makers, citing his firsthand experience sitting on advisory boards and how the agricultural nexus successfully twists science to direct the discourse, and eventually agricultural policies, in a direction favorable to them.

The nexus is also powerful in shaping discourse concerning labeling of *foods*. A California case, which involved nexus member Monsanto, one of the nation's largest producers of genetically modified seeds, and the Academy of Nutrition and Dietetics, illustrates how conflicts of interests were ignored. This Academy has over 70,000 members, making its position on nutrition and diet matters significant for policy making. The issue is how the Academy responded to concerns raised by one member of a seven-person group appointed by the Academy to discuss and prepare a position paper about whether or not labeling of GMO food products should be required. That person, Carole Bartolotto, a registered dietitian in California, not avidly opposed to requiring labels for foods containing GMO labeling, was dismissed from the work group writing the position paper that would express the influential Academy of Nutrition and Dietetics' policy on foods made with genetically engineered ingredients.[6] She had raised conflict of interest concerns about two other appointed members who had ties to agribusiness corporations. One of them worked as a test farmer for Monsanto and had received a prize for being the "National Farm Mom of the Year" (Strom, 2013). The other member also served as the chair of the International Food Information Council that had ties to the major agribusiness firms – including Cargill. The Academy also hired an academic to write the position paper. Bartolotto objected when the Academy decided that this paper would be written "before the work group finished its review of the scientific materials" (Strom, 2015). Once she was dismissed any discourse emanating from this group seemingly was provided by those willing to ignore the conflict of interests and that the group's, and thus the Academy's, position would not be based upon all scientific evidence obtained. The Academy delayed taking a position on the issue once Bartolotto's concerns were made public.

How many calories are contained in processed foods and soft drinks is something that corporations producing those foods and their ingredients would like to downplay. This issue has become increasingly significant given the mounting evidence that excess consumption of soft drinks containing sugar or high-fructose corn syrup contributes to some of those consumers later becoming obese and likelier to suffer heart disease or diabetes. As sales of Coca-Cola have declined over the past few years the company has engaged in an effort to "sugarcoat the truth on calories" (*New York Times*, 2015C). They funded an organization called Global Energy Balance Network and hired scientists known to be friendly to the soft-drink industry to publish reports indicating that sugar-laden soft drinks should not be subject to any excise tax or other government regulations. The justification offered by the scientists whose income is dependent upon Coca-Cola donations argues that consumption of Coca-Cola and similar products will not have damaging effects on consumers' health. How objective are findings published by such scientists? An analysis published in the journal *PLOS Medicine* called the objectivity of studies written by scientists representing organizations financed by Coca-Cola or other industries producing either soft drink beverages or sugar into question. The analysis concluded that these studies "were five times more likely to find no link between sugary drinks and weight gain than studies reporting no industry sponsorship or financial conflicts of interest" (*New York Times*, 2015C).

The significance of the dichotomous discourse concerning climate change is exceeded only by the significance of the disastrous effects continued climate change will have worldwide. Among the more powerful nexus members shaping this discourse are *oil, gas, and coal* industry owners whose future profitability would be threatened by dramatic shifts in policies towards promoting the production and use of less harmful energy sources. Exemplifying this group's position and the means by which they shape discourse are the Koch brothers who control Koch Industries and its extensive oil and natural gas interests. While the Kochs are not alone among funders actively financing the propagation of climate change denial they appear to be spending the most to defend their industries that are "historically rooted in fossil fuel operations" (Greenpeace, 2015). They also have a longer, deeper record as industry nexus leaders seeking to sway discourse by using their vast economic power to build political influence. They have spent about $80 million since the late 1990s funding groups whose scientists do not have formal training in climatology, but who willingly deny what appears to be irrefutable scientific evidence concerning climate change – the same groups "that are working to delay policies and regulations aimed at stopping global warming" (Greenpeace, 2015).

ExxonMobil, another key nexus member, has also generously funded research institutes which are on record as having sought to shape discourse through offering prominent scientists a $10,000 honorarium if they would prepare an essay "that thoughtfully explores the limitations of climate model outputs as they pertain to the development of climate policy" (Allen, 2007). This offer was made by the American Enterprise Institute following an international conference of scientists in Paris that concluded that scientists "can now have a very high confidence" that human activities contribute to rising greenhouse gas concentrations, and thus to climate change. In doing so the Institute, which ExxonMobil has funded generously,[7] sought to shape environmental policy through undermining the conference's conclusion. In response the Union of Concerned Scientists accused ExxonMobil of funding many advocacy groups which, in turn, generated deceptive "disinformation" designed to influence discourse about the "reality of global warming" and the "science of climate change" (Union of Concerned Scientists, 2007).

This campaign seems to have influenced the discourse towards denying climate change used by public education officials in some of the major fossil fuel producing states – including Wyoming (natural gas), West Virginia (coal), and Texas (oil and natural gas) where climate deniers have attempted to pass legislation refuting the conclusions reached by virtually all climatologists about human-induced effects on climate change. Attempts to influence discourse were in response to the 2013 release of the National Research Council's report – the "Next Generation Science Standards" which recommended that students should study "the rise in global temperatures over the past century" and "the major role that human activities play" (Nussbaum, 2015). Wyoming legislators banned teaching this topic if it included that science had reached the conclusion that global warming was due to human activities. Attempts, albeit unsuccessful, were made to pass similar legislation in West Virginia and Texas.

Undoubtedly, these and other state legislators as well as congressional members who deny that human activity contributes adversely to climate change would not want the strong messages and evidence contained in Naomi Klein's *This Changes Everything: Capitalism Versus the Climate* (2014) to be part of any public discourse on the environment. Her book is a response to efforts by those such as the Koch brothers, ExxonMobil, the American Enterprise Institute, and other energy industry nexus members that are strong proponents of a discourse that contends either that climate change is not occurring or that such change is not due to human-driven economic activity. Klein argues that the root of the problem is the discourse endlessly favoring a free market economy, arguing that this "zombie ideology" promotes high levels of consuming goods and services that require production methods heavily dependent upon fossil fuels that are destroying our ecosystems. She fears that the political power of the major contributors to greenhouse gases will be able to sway both discourse and policy in a direction favorable to themselves. Klein concludes that for energy industry leaders to admit that their actions are causing climate change is for them to deny their core beliefs in the unfettered pursuit of profit through high rates of economic growth that relies heavily on extractive industries such as their own.

Part of the *health care* nexus determined to shape discourse and sway the public and members of Congress away from the Affordable Care Act includes the Club for Growth – the largest and self-proclaimed leading free-enterprise advocacy group in the nation, and Americans for Prosperity funded heavily by the Koch brothers. Both groups have more ideological than financial interests in health care policy. While neither is a research institute, they purport to have a basis for their positions that is more than simply ideological. They have spent millions of dollars opposing health care legislation (*New York Times*, 2013A). The Club for Growth uses a rating system to threaten Republicans who do not vote the way the Club wishes on key issues such as health care while rewarding those who adopt the discourse and take policy positions the Club favors. Those who voted in favor of the Affordable Care Act risked losing Club campaign contributions in favor of candidates who would oppose them in future primaries. "Defunding or repealing Obamacare" is the Club's mantra, and since that has not been successful they have opposed amendments to the Act such as one designed to aid people who prior to obtaining health insurance under the Act's provision had a serious pre-existing medical condition.

The Koch brothers fund Americans for Prosperity that has strongly opposed the Affordable Care Act on all fronts. They are not averse to using propaganda in the form of misleading advertisements to delay the introduction of health care benefits for the many Americans previously unable to afford to purchase private health insurance. One of their ads encouraged the viewers to visit a website called ObamacareRiskFactors.com which contained even more misleading information than the ad itself. For example, the website warned that if the Act were to go into effect employees in small firms should expect their wages and hours to be reduced – but this also is false since employers of small firms are not subject to the law (Robertson, 2013). The millions of dollars spent by groups such as Americans for Prosperity have had the effect on health care policy discourse that they intended, as some surveys indicate only about half of Americans correctly understand what the law is both trying to accomplish and what it has accomplished – such as more Americans now having health care insurance and health care costs rising more slowly than they have been for decades. Fortunately, nexus members were unable to sway the Supreme Court which upheld the constitutionality of the Affordable Care Act.

One of the more egregious examples of corporate welfare is that received by *for-profit colleges and universities* in the form of government-funded financial aid obtained by many of their students. Much of this aid is in the form of loans, a high proportion of which is not repaid. It has been estimated that over 100 for-profit colleges receive over 90% of their revenue from government funds – an estimated total each year of more than $30 billion. A Department of Education investigation revealed that there are "133 for-profit schools that are almost completely subsidized by taxpayers, receiving more than 90 percent of their revenue from a combination of Pell Grants, Stafford Loans, GI Bill funds for veterans and Department of Defense tuition assistance to active duty military" (Glantz, 2014). The estimated cost was about $9.5 billion as of 2012 when grants, loans, and other government financial programs are considered. Among the prominent nexus members is the Apollo Group which owns the University of Phoenix. This university has "collected the largest amount of federal money, with more than $5 billion coming from government student aid. DeVry University, Ashford University, Kaplan University and ITT Technical Institute each collected around $1 billion through federal aid dollars" (Kingkade, 2012). Overall, on average 86% of the revenue received by the 15 largest for-profit colleges is from the federal government (Farrell, 2014).

These colleges are exactly what they sound like: profit-seeking businesses. In fact, they are essentially the opposite of non-profits. Compared to non-profit public and private colleges and universities, for-profit colleges may be more expensive; the typical student incurs far more debt to attend; the quality of the education is suspect as the typical faculty member is less qualified; there are lower rates at which graduates are able to obtain jobs in the particular field of study they pursued; lower graduation rates; and most important for the purpose of exposing corporate welfare the loan default rate for students attending for-profit colleges is well above that of the non-profit academic institutions (Trull, 2015). The US Department of Education estimates that about 13% of all students in higher education attend for-profit colleges, but they account for about 31% of all student loans taken out and nearly half of all loan defaults (US Department of Education, 2014). This default rate is about double that of students with loans from non-profit institutions of higher education. This high default rate contributes to the unsettling fact that student loans received by students who attend for-profit colleges have a higher delinquency rate than any other type of consumer credit (Soederberg, 2015). The key point is that when these defaults occur corporate welfare is received by the colleges as the government forgives the loans, but the for-profit colleges retain all funds paid with these loans.[8] For-profit colleges typically get the vast majority of their revenue from federal student loans, while accounting for nearly half of the defaults on these loans (Lewin, 2015). The stocks of 15 for-profit college companies are publicly traded, and collectively the percentage of this group's total revenue that comes from government-sponsored sources (Department of Education student aid, GI Bill, Department of Defense Tuition Assistance) exceeds 85% (US Senate Committee on Health, Education, Labor and Pensions, 2012).

Another higher education industry nexus member benefiting from corporate welfare is Sallie Mae (the SLM Corporation), the most powerful private lending institution that extends student loan. It formerly was a government-sponsored enterprise, and later became privatized. However, even though it is now a private lending institution "the federal government continues to grant the company favorable loan contracts worth hundreds of millions dollars" (Ward, 2014). Sallie Mae is a master at receiving corporate welfare. It borrows billions of dollars at low interest rates from a federally backed bank and then extends loans to students at higher rates. According to Elizabeth Warren, Sallie Mae's profits are "boosted by special deals and breaks from the federal government" (Ward, 2014). It is noteworthy that Sallie Mae receives protection against financial losses if there are loan defaults, being insured by the Federal Family Education Loan Program. To their credit some members of Congress, and the Obama administration, have attempted to introduce reforms that would reduce the flow of corporate welfare to the for-profit colleges – only to be rebuked by Congress. The key education nexus member opposing such efforts has been House member John Kline who is the Chair of the Education and the Work Force Committee. His major campaign contributor is the University of Phoenix's parent company, the Apollo Education Group (Glantz, 2014).

A few years ago hearings were held by the Department of Education in response to concerns about for-profit college practices such as "recruiting students with little chance of academic success and leaving them with excessive debt," high loan default rates,[9] and low post-graduation "gainful employment" rates (Lauerman, 2013). A proposed regulation threatened to limit the debt levels incurred by for-profit college students. Nexus member Sally Stroup, former Assistant Secretary for the Department of Education who had become general counsel for the corporate Apollo Group that owns the University of Phoenix, among other for-profit institutions, argued that high debt levels were not a good "metric" for evaluating program quality. The for-profits claim that they offer "high-quality education" to students who otherwise would not be given the opportunity to enroll in college. Critics counter by pointing out that many of the low-income and military students with difficulty repaying debt were high-risk when they were admitted, and many had dropped out of their for-profit college program. One student says enrollment advisors at the University of Phoenix misled him about the length of time it would take to earn a degree and what the estimated total cost would be. The same student described the University of Phoenix as operating "kind of like a car dealership" (Hanford, 2012).

The for-profit institutions have sought to focus the discourse over financial aid policy towards giving disadvantaged minorities and military veterans whose academic credentials and likelihood of academic success are poor, the educational opportunity they offer, which they claim deserves to be supported with federally sponsored financial aid despite their being privately owned, for-profit institutions. They have used their influence in Washington DC to limit restrictions on the proportion of revenue they can receive from federal government sources, while settling some lawsuits without admitting any wrongdoing in cases where they were accused of misleading admissions practices. The lobbying effort launched by the for-profit colleges to forestall regulations that would reduce their corporate welfare flow reveals some of the major for-profit colleges' nexus players who are able to exert their influence in Congress. These include Goldman Sachs, partial owner of Education Management Corporation which operates some for-profit colleges; the chair of that corporation's board – former Maine Governor John McKernan whose wife is Senator Olympia Snow; Democratic House members Alcee Hastings and Robert Andrews; the Washington Post (which owns Kaplan University); and a major donor to the Democratic party, John Sperling, who founded the University of Phoenix, owned by the Apollo Group (Roth, 2011B).

In 2015 new rules were proposed by the Obama administration that would deny federal aid to either for-profit or non-profit colleges and universities that featured both unusually high levels of student debt and useless degrees with which the same students were unable to find "gainful employment." An estimated 99% of the cases of institutions affected by the rules were likely to be the for-profit colleges. In response Republican members of Congress in both the Senate and the House of Representatives, led by House Members John Kine (Education Committee Chair) and Virginia Foxx (Higher Education Subcommittee Chair) began to introduce bills to forestall enforcement of the new rules (*New York Times*, 2015A). This nexus support occurred even after findings that indicated the for-profit Corinthian Colleges, which filed for bankruptcy,[10] had practiced "the ethics of payday lending" (Lewin, 2015). This prompted the US Department of Education, in the first but not likely the last instance, to respond by forgiving the federal loans of tens of thousands of defrauded students who had attended the colleges, but either did not finish or had received worthless degrees. If that occurs then the cost to the federal government could be about $3.5 billion (Lewin, 2015). This amount of corporate welfare for economic disaster resulting from an industry's disreputable loan practices has only been exceeded in the past decade by that doled out to the real estate and finance industries.

In response to the claims of providing a quality education critics can cite comparisons of for-profit versus non-profit colleges and universities concerning the average spent by each per student on instruction. Department of Education analysts found that some of the largest for-profit colleges, including the University of Phoenix, spent less than $1000 per student on instruction while non-profit academic institutions in the greater Phoenix area spend between $3300 and $11,100 per student on instruction (Hanford, 2012). Meanwhile, the for-profit colleges' expenditures on marketing, advertising, recruitment, admissions, and CEO salaries were well above the less than $1000 per student expenditures and exceeded by far comparable expenditures by the non-profit academic institutions. The relatively higher priority placed upon non-instruction expenses, particularly among the 15 for-profit colleges that are publicly traded on Wall Street, should not be surprising given the profit motive driving these institutions at the expense of encouraging unsuspecting students to incur significant debt (with loans backed by the federal government) that provide them with corporate welfare for what a qualified group of academic analysts would deem to be academic programs with little merit.

Among the range of discourse perpetrated by the academic members of the *finance nexus*, which does not include Goldman Sachs CEO Lloyd Blankfein who reportedly said that as a banker he was "doing God's work," was the reductionist argument that self-regulating markets will correct imbalances and lead to positive outcomes. The main academic perpetrators of this belief were two of the three winners of the *Real-World Economics Review*'s "Dynamite Prize in Economics" for being the most responsible economists for causing the global financial crisis: Milton Friedman and Larry Summers.[11] Friedman provided a stream of simplistic free market economy views, including that markets are self-correcting, that influenced the creation of "fantasy-based theories" such as the Nobel Prize-winning economics professor and Friedman disciple Myron Scholes' efficient market hypothesis that provided the philosophical basis for justifying deregulation and lax regulation of derivatives. Summers can be credited for being instrumental in the repeal of the Glass–Steagall Act which unleashed a casino-type of behavior on Wall Street (*Real-World Economics Review*, 2010).

It was the discourse these prize winners provided that boosted the artificial profits earned by the finance industry in the run–up to 2008, while living standards for many Americans worsened as the top 1% received a lion's share of the rewards. This is a testimony to the problems created by the Corporate Welfare Economy's short-term profit focus. The convincing discourse they established was supported by economic models created by the investment bank researchers – particularly a formula for measuring risk that was hailed as an "unambiguously positive breakthrough, a piece of financial technology that allowed hugely complex risks to be modeled with more ease and accuracy than ever before" (Salmon, 2009). The method of analyzing using this formula was adopted throughout the financial industry despite some warnings that it oversimplified risk analysis. It became the basis for new (albeit toxic) financial instruments to be created and sold worldwide. It snowed ratings agencies into also adopting it. Nexus members of the Federal Reserve and US Treasury drank the cool aid as well. Only after the 2008 financial crisis did Federal Reserve researchers realize "how poorly traditional macroeconomic methods predict systemic bank failure and the domino effect it can unleash on the economy" (Greeley, 2012).

Finance industry nexus academic members were instrumental in shaping discourse in 2008 concerning how the government should respond to the financial crisis. Nexus members dismissed alternative (to the bailout) policies, as did many academic economists. Libertarian Harvard economist Jeffrey Miron advocated that the private owners who took the huge risks should bear full responsibility and be forced to declare bankruptcy, while the federal government should limit its expenditures to purchases of risky mortgages – then renegotiate the terms of these mortgages (e.g., 40 years at a lower interest rate) with owners. He also advocated that the federal government should phase out Fannie Mae and Freddie Mac and stop backing mortgages. His discourse was ignored, while nexus members and many academic economists dismissed the successful Swedish response to its 1991–92 financial and real estate crises which resembled to some degree the corresponding crises in the United States. Policies similar to Sweden's were advocated by Nobel Prize-winning economists Paul Krugman and Joseph Stiglitz. Sweden's policies to combat their financial crisis consisted of assuming the bank's bad debts, requiring banks to write down their losses, ensuring that bondholders and depositors suffered no losses, temporarily nationalizing the banks, and sharing any subsequent profits with taxpayers which brought the estimated cost to taxpayers to what has been estimated as between a very low percentage of Sweden's GDP to zero cost. The great irony is that in "welfare state" Sweden owners and managers of private banks were not bailed out. Rather they were required to bear the costs of their reckless investment decisions – unlike the generous corporate welfare received by the US "free market" economy's largest financial institutions (the extent of this corporate welfare will be discussed in the following chapter).

Washington DC

Limiting and shaping discourse is most significant when it occurs in Washington DC when policy matters are an issue. The revolving door between the private sector and federal government and the ties some nexus members have with prominent researchers at both academic and research institutions creates an overlapping of influences. This section will focus on the discourse that has been emanating from Washington DC that shapes policies for major industries. Emphasis will be placed upon what the particular discourse was limited to within the executive and legislative branches of the federal government rather than focusing on specific nexus members. Some of that discourse has been limited to only those alternatives the industry favors, thereby shaping policy discourse to a path highly favorable to the nexus members and their industry. The biases in favor of discourse that serves nexus interests by limiting the range of policy alternatives considered will be emphasized. The biases can be traced to Washington DC nexus members (presidents, members of Congress, Cabinet members, regulatory agencies) receiving campaign contributions and/or the promise of lucrative employment opportunities with the industry in question, and in return the sponsoring industry gets their like-minded cronies (or sycophants) elected president, to Congress, and/or have appointed some of their cronies to powerful policy or regulatory positions. In the process the private sector industry gains influence over the content of policy-related public discourse emanating from Washington DC, and subsequently some policies that guide corporate welfare in their direction. This section will provide some recent and past examples from a few industries to illustrate a pattern for how this process has not only favored some major industries, but also has been detrimental to a majority of Americans.

One reason policy-related discourse remains within limited boundaries even following a presidential administration change when a Democrat administration replaces a Republican administration, or vice versa, is that like-minded, trusted members of the nexus are appointed to similar Cabinet or regulatory positions, or retreads are brought back to Washington DC from past administrations of the same party. Note the 2016 presidential campaign.[12] In the case of 2016 presidential candidate Jeb Bush, his foreign policy advisors for campaign purposes are retreads from his brother's administration – "the very people who insisted that the Iraqis would welcome us as liberators" (Krugman, 2015B). As with previous administrations, particularly that of Lyndon Johnson, decisions that led the United States into the costly Vietnam war with defense contractors profiting handsomely are made based upon the discourse held by nexus members without input from government or academic experts with extensive knowledge of the country or region where war will be waged.

What the nexus hears is what conforms to their beliefs and agenda. Their policies are often based upon falsely contrived assumptions and scenarios (e.g., weapons of mass destruction). When the outcome of their policy is highly undesirable and counter to what they forecast, they find subordinates to facilitate lies that forestall discourse leading to alternative policies. When critics with the best interests of nearly all Americans challenge the policies and call for a wider discourse, nexus leaders turn on them and take measures to discredit those critics that suppress both democratic ideals and processes for future discourse. Lackeys for nexus leaders reap financial rewards and a sense of power at the expense of their own integrity and the country's best interests. While the Iraq and Vietnam wars are two highly egregious examples (Halberstam, 1992) this pattern of narrow discourse, poor forecasts, and lies to cover up the outcomes can be observed in non-defense industries as well – with corporate welfare flowing throughout the process.

A second reason that discourse tends to be limited is due to its being consistent with the economic ideology of major multimillionaire and billionaire donors. This financially elite group is anxious to see their political and economic agendas become reality, and seek willing aspirants to champion their message regardless of how poorly educated and intellectually limited these aspirants prove to be. One example is Scott Walker, current governor of Wisconsin and aspiring 2016 presidential candidate. Appealing to his major donor, the Koch brothers, Walker has "pledged allegiance" to the discredited supply-side economics proponents who have been forecasting since the Reagan administration that tax cuts would be job creating and deficit reducing – forecasts that repeatedly on the national and state levels have proven incorrect. Numerous research reports indicate that tax cuts for the wealthiest do not necessarily stimulate economic growth or reduce the federal budget deficit.[13] The same supply-side economists, referred to by some as "charlatans and cranks'" have steadfastly stuck to their false doctrines, including their incorrect prediction that the 2009 fiscal stimulus policies would drive up both inflation and interest rates (Krugman, 2015B). These mantras not only have been adopted by Walker, but by all other Republican Party presidential and congressional candidates. Other examples of limited (and biased) discourse to which presidential and congressional candidates continue to adhere include the false predictions that once the Affordable Care Act went into effect health care costs would soar, the deficit would explode, and more people would lose insurance than gain it. Perhaps the problem is the "intellectual bubble" within which seemingly willfully ignorant candidates (particularly 2016 Republicans) live, a bubble that provides the information that limits their policy discourse. One critic argues that these candidates, and their followers, "get their news from Fox and other captive media ... get their policy analysis from billionaire-financed right-wing think tanks, and they're often blissfully unaware both of contrary evidence and of how their positions sound to outsiders" (Krugman, 2013B).

Limiting and shaping discourse that inevitably leads to policies favorable to a small elite not only occurs throughout the major industries (discussed below), but also to discourse regarding issues such as the relationship of income inequality to international trade policies. While critics of free trade agreements argue that a majority of benefits tend to be reaped by owners of major industries to the detriment of average workers, the stale discourse of "greater efficiency" and "we all benefit" continue to dominate headlines and policy discussions. Lost in the discourse has been that globalization, while enabling us to purchase our tube socks and desk lamps much more cheaply than we ever could have imagined, has also contributed to lower incomes of average families throughout the richest economies in North America and Europe 30 years ago – many of which are now in a precarious economic state. In general, the post-1980s shift towards what the discourse calls "free market capitalism" has encouraged freer trade and contributed to lower rates of inflation. However, the detrimental effects of freer trade agreements and globalization on working-class Americans have all but been ignored. The same is true for immigration discourse that emphasizes upward mobility for immigrants and escape from political tyranny, as well as higher public education and health care costs, but does not focus on the relative distribution of benefits reaped by US employers as compared to either smaller wage increases, wage reductions, or lost jobs experienced by American workers attributable to immigration.

One of the industries that benefits most from immigration laws and enforcement, particularly lax enforcement of employing illegal immigrants, has been *agriculture*. This industry's nexus has spewed incorrect, hypocritical, and self-service discourse to support the flow of corporate welfare that has benefited overwhelmingly the wealthier agribusiness firms and multimillion dollar farm operations while limiting most subsidies to producers of corn, soybeans, and cotton as well as ethanol producers. It is widely recognized that agriculture is a unique industry that not only is vital to our national interest, but is also affected by adverse weather and lower revenue streams when due to agricultural productivity increases output rises faster than demand. Most Americans believe that preserving farming as a way of life merits government support. However, rather than focusing that support on family farms with net incomes below $100,000 per year the agricultural subsidies have become a glaring example of corporate welfare received by multibillion dollar agribusiness firms and family farms with, in some cases, multimillion dollar net incomes. A look at the discourse since the 1990s that has driven this stream of welfare payments illustrates that while agricultural policies regarding subsidies have changed substantially, the same discourse and flow of corporate welfare payments has survived quite well.

A 1995 Cato Institute study focused on the Archer Daniels Midland (ADM) agribusiness corporation as a flagrant example of corporate welfare (and higher food prices) whose CEO at the time, Dwayne Andreas, was quite adept at "fertilizing" key members of the nexus in Congress to limit and shape discourse concerning subsidies for sugar and ethanol producers to ADM's advantage. Andreas should be credited with dispelling the myth that a free market characterizes the US economy. He once cynically stated that "[t]here isn't one grain of anything in the world that is sold in a free market. Not one! The only place you see a free market is in the speeches of politicians. People who are not in the Midwest do not understand that this is a socialist country" (Bovard, 1995). The report's author concludes that the ability of ADM to use its influence in Washington DC has resulted in a perverse flow of taxpayer dollars to benefit this multibillion dollar "politically connected" corporation. This influence has steered discourse creatively to serve the best interest of ADM and other eligible wealthy farmers. Issues such as competitiveness, free market, profitability were not emphasized. Rather, claims made by Andreas that subsidizing ethanol production while serving corn producers also served to provide a good that is environmentally friendly while moving the United States towards energy independence and thus weaken geopolitical power held by Middle East oil producing nations.

This claim was repeated by congressional members friendly to agriculture and accepted by presidents from the mid-1970s until the past few years. However, research would demonstrate the claim to be false since burning gasoline mixed with ethanol increases hydrocarbon and nitrogen oxide emissions. Subsidizing ethanol production also served to shift corn use in that direction, thus driving up the price of feed for pork and beef producers – and ultimately consumers. To counter complaints from these groups the agricultural nexus claimed that corn farmers deserved to have their incomes supported, failing to add that it would be the multibillion dollar agribusiness corporations and wealthiest farmers that would benefit the most from the subsidies. The discourse continued to emphasize energy independence benefits from ethanol use throughout the 1990s. To further that interest trade restrictions that limited imported ethanol were imposed which further increased its price domestically. One critic argued that ethanol producers were able to justify their lucrative subsidies "only by spooking the public with bogey-men such as foreign oil sheiks, toxic air pollution, and the threatened disappearance of the American farmer can attention be deflected from the real costs of the ethanol house of cards that consumes over a billion dollars annually" (Bovard, 1995). When accusations were raised that the American corn (and other agricultural) producers were dumping some of their subsidized crops on world markets, aided by export credits the United States extended to purchasers of some agricultural exports, the agricultural industry defended the practice (which was hurting farmers in some of our poorest trading partner nations) by claiming that export revenue earned prevented a larger trade deficit.

Another agricultural product that has benefited handsomely from subsidies has been sugar for which import quotas and price supports have been imposed by the federal government. Again, the rhetoric was that taxpayers did not pay for import quotas and thus the policy was not costly. However, while there was no taxpayer cost American consumers of sugar and products containing sugar had to pay higher prices as the US price for sugar has been about five times what a free market world price for sugar would be. Taxpayer-funded price supports guarantee producers against losses, which advocates claim is to prevent producers in the event prices fluctuate substantially. The outcome is more guaranteed profits for sugar producers, with incentives to produce more unhealthy products such as high fructose corn syrup. Left out of any discourse concerning agricultural policy has been the considerable rise in health care costs that are attributable to diabetes and other obesity-related illnesses partly due to consumption of large amounts of this syrup produced with highly subsidized corn.

During the last years of George W. Bush's administration he, along with some congressional leaders, sought to change agricultural policy due to mounting criticisms that such policies were "enriching big farm interests, violating trade agreements and neglecting small family farms" (Herszenhorn, 2007). However, substantive reform was forestalled, aided by discourse used by congressional friends of agribusiness and some wealthy farmers who maintained that the existing subsidies and favorable trade restrictions were justified since the policies were "keeping the dollars at home" (due to less imported petroleum), and the policies enabled them to use a renewable product fueled by sun, water, and (unfortunately) chemicals to produce needed fuel (Morgan, 2007). There was also the claim that these subsidies would help maintain family farms rather than seeing these farms sold – which did not occur for the smaller family farms. Biofuel production, aided by generous federal subsidies, was making many wealthy corn farmers even wealthier. Nevertheless, the House of Representatives passed a bill authorizing over $10 billion in subsidies for corn growers for 2007–12 even if the price of corn remained high. The likelihood of this price remaining high was enhanced when the Senate passed a bill that would double the required use of ethanol from corn.

By 2013 the corporate welfare flow to the agricultural industry's wealthiest was so prominent, despite this largesse driving up prices for consumers and feed purchasers as well as increasing greenhouse gas emissions, that one member of Congress remarked, "I can't think of another product in the American economy that really had the trifecta – a tariff barrier, a subsidy, and a mandate" (Taxpayers for Common Sense,

2013). Undeterred, Iowa Senator Tom Harkin and other members of Congress proposed even billions more taxpayer dollars be directed for new ethanol subsidies while simultaneously arguing that food stamp funding should be reduced, or even eliminated. Their discourse included that the government did not have the right to reallocate money from the rich to the poor – ignoring that farm subsidies to agribusinesses force people to pay taxes and give to agribusinesses and the wealthy. Stephen Fincher is an egregious example of a member of Congress justifying food stamp cuts but who receives USDA farm subsidies (almost $3.5 million from 1999 to 2012). He defended his vote to cut food stamp funding by quoting the Bible "[f]or even when we were with you, we gave you this command: Anyone unwilling to work should not eat" (Bittman, 2013B). He conveniently or willfully ignores the fact that most food stamp beneficiaries are children or the elderly who are not part of the workforce. Critics responded to this blatant self-serving discourse with the same criticism leveled at corporate welfare given to agriculture in the 1995 Cato Institute analysis, namely that "[o]ver the years … farm subsidies became a fraud-ridden program that mainly benefits corporations and wealthy individuals" (Krugman, 2013A).

Producers of unhealthy food such as corn and corn products continue to be highly subsidized, unlike producers of much healthier food products such as fruits and vegetables. A lion's share of the subsidies is going to industrial producers of food that is less healthy via a process that is neither sustainable nor environmentally friendly as opposed to small-scale farms and non-industrial organic farms. As demand for organically produced agricultural products has increased so have attempts by industrial food producers to influence what can receive the National Organic Standards Board's approval of what can be labeled organic. Using their considerable economic and political muscle agribusiness corporations have been able to have some individuals who will champion their interests appointed to this board. By law the Board is to be comprised of farmers, conservationists, consumer representatives, a scientist, a retailer, a certification agent, and representatives of companies that process organic food. This did not deter the Secretary of Agriculture from appointing someone to one of the Board's designated "farmer" positions who neither owned nor operated a farm. Overall, the Board increasingly has become dominated by appointed members sympathetic to agribusiness interest in expanding their product line to include higher value-added organic food products, but with products that increasingly contain more non-organic ingredients. One organic purist from Eden Foods familiar with the National Organic Standards Board stated that "[t]he board is stacked. Either they don't have a clue, or their interest in making money is more important than their interest in maintaining the integrity of organics" (Strom, 2012). This critic was so disgusted that he refused to put the Board's certified-organic label on Eden Foods because these labels, he believes, are a fraud.

Discourse has changed in recent years in response to recognition that false, self-serving claims were not justifiable to continue the flow of corporate welfare. Some new farm programs were introduced. In early 2015 Senators Pat Toomey and Diane Feinstein proposed a bill that would eliminate one source of agribusiness corporate welfare: namely that oil refineries would not be required by the federal government to purchase ethanol and blend it into gasoline. Fearing that the gravy train for ethanol producers may be reduced Bruce Rastette – ethanol mogul and founder of Heartland Park, one of the largest pork processing corporations in the United States, who is a major donor to Republican presidential candidates – organized a March 2014 "agriculture summit" that was held at the Iowa State Fairgrounds in Des Moines. The purpose of this summit, to which all major Republican presidential candidates were invited, was to have them state publicly their position on agricultural issues, particularly corn and ethanol subsidies. The intent, of course, is to focus discourse on a continuation of the existing policies that profit corn and ethanol producers. These policies, which provide subsidies and federal requirements favorable to ethanol producers, represent according to Senator Toomey, "the government using corporate welfare to shower money on a favored industry" (*Bloomberg Politics*, 2015).

The prices for prescription drugs charged by the *pharmaceutical* industry is a complicated issue, and this is reflected in the discourse concerning federal government drug policies. Critics of high prices point out that American consumers pay much more (for some drugs at least double) than people in other countries for the exact same drug even if that drug is only produced in the United States. Although Canadian drugs are available, on average, at half the price of their American equivalent,[14] US consumers are currently prevented from purchasing them because of a prohibition on the importation of prescription drugs. American consumers have access to the highest quality drugs available worldwide, and we rely heavily on the quality of prescription medicines to improve the quality of our health. The issue, however, is what these drugs should cost – especially considering that the health of many Americans is below what it could be if these drugs were more affordable.

One factor contributing to drugs being unaffordable for some is the size of profit margins pharmaceutical firms receive. According to Forbes, in 2013 the average profit margin earned by pharmaceutical firms was the highest among major industries, slightly above that earned by banks. Pfizer, the largest pharmaceutical firm in the world, realized a 42% profit margin (Anderson, 2014). Pharmaceutical firms claim that the high prices and profit margins they receive are justified because of the high fixed costs they incur, especially for research and development, to introduce a new drug. This discourse is true, but they fail to add that they spend far more on marketing than on research and development. Pfizer spent almost twice as much on marketing than they did on research and development in 2013. What has not been prominent in the policy discourse is why, unlike in other wealthy countries, there should be some of our citizens unable to afford needed prescription drugs while the firms producing those drugs are on average more profitable than firms in any other industry.

Pharmaceutical drug defenders point to the need for laws, including import restrictions, to allegedly protect the health of American consumers. What is not included is freedom of choice that consumers should be given. If someone is free to consume the revolting range of unhealthy junk food found in every roadside service area along our highways why should the consumers not be free to choose their source of prescription drugs – especially from Canada where standards for drug development are as high as they are in the United States? Pharmaceutical industries and the FDA claim there is no supervision over these drugs. However, there is a mass of evidence that Canadians who consume these drugs suffer no more ill effects than do Americans consuming the same drug.

In 2015 two Senators, John McCain and Amy Klobuchar, introduced the Safe and Affordable Drugs from Canada Act that would permit Americans with a valid prescription from their licensed physician to purchase from a licensed Canadian pharmacy a 90-day supply of the drug they need. The Senators emphasize that these drugs are cheaper and that Canadian safety standards are similar to ours (Silverman, 2015). Undoubtedly there will be fierce efforts launched by the pharmaceutical lobby that will shape the discourse debate, emphasizing that by prohibiting imports American consumers will continue to be protected from "unsafe" medications produced abroad. If past experience is any indicator the industry likely will be successful in having their views prevail. Overall, the "health industry" outspends all other industries for lobbying purposes, and the number one category for lobbying expenditures by this industry is "pharmaceuticals/health products" (OpenSecrets.Org, 2015). What this intensive lobbying effort has bought the industry includes lawmakers not discussing the "predatory pricing practices while enjoying exclusive rights to manufacture drugs for 20 years or more" resulting in a widening difference between what Americans pay for drugs and the price of those same drugs abroad; preventing Medicare administrators from negotiating for lower prices with the same pharmaceutical firms – something the insurers and Department of Veterans Affairs are permitted to do. Estimates are that over $100 billion could be saved over the next decade if Medicare were permitted to negotiate prices (Potter, 2013). The revolving door from Washington DC to firms lobbying for the pharmaceutical industry is wide, making it "one of the strongest, most well-connected and most effective lobbies in Washington" (Drinkard, 2005). In hearings concerning drug safety issues held by the FDA it is not uncommon for witnesses (including from the American Enterprise Institute which receives pharmaceutical industry funds) to include those receiving payments for various services from the pharmaceutical industry – clearly an effective way to shape discourse. An additional, highly effective way the industry shapes discourse that occurs between doctors and their patients is revealed by a report indicating that American doctors who received payments for various services from pharmaceutical companies were twice as likely to prescribe the drugs these same companies produced (Anderson, 2014).

Owners of *professional sports teams* are masters at reaping profits in the hundreds of millions from first receiving corporate welfare to fund their team's new stadium or renovation, then reaping huge profits when they sell the team. In the process they are bolstered by friendly treatment from Washington DC defenders of corporate welfare. As with agriculture, pharmaceuticals, and finance (see below) professional sports teams have successfully limited discourse in a direction that ultimately favors them quite lucratively. This can be demonstrated by comparing a detailed late 1990s analysis of the discourse, and overall strategy, utilized by professional sports owners to secure corporate welfare for construction of new stadiums with similar strategies being utilized by owners such as the National Football League's (NFL) San Diego Chargers and the National Basketball Association's (NBA) Milwaukee Bucks, as well as the owners of a lower tier minor league baseball team – the Boise Hawks. The analysis is powerful, concluding that many new professional sports facilities were constructed at taxpayer cost that occurs within a climate of "deceptive politicians, taxpayer swindles, media slants, the power of big money, and most of all, a political system that serves the rich and powerful at the expense of the average fan, the average taxpayer, the average citizen" (Anderson, 1998). In that analysis, contained in Joanna Cagan and Neil deMause's *Field of Schemes: How the Great Stadium Swindle Turns Public Money into Private Profit* (1998), the authors identify a seven-step process utilized by owners to bully unsuspecting taxpayers to approve the use of public funds to partially finance construction of their new stadium or arena. These steps are: (1) a claim by team owners that the existing facility is obsolete and insufficient for catering to the desires of the teams fans; (2) a threat (often backed by the commissioner of the league) to move the team to another city if a new facility is not built on the team's terms; (3) a claim by owners that a new facility is necessary for the team to be "competitive" (which seems to mean even more highly profitable for the owners); (4) friendly consultants with a track record of producing a cost–benefit analysis demonstrating how profitable it will be to the city if a new stadium and "development" of the greater stadium are both constructed; (5) the municipality is put under time pressure that makes it difficult, if not impossible, for a public referendum to vote on the matter to be held, with the owners claiming that "the window of opportunity on a new stadium will only remain open for so long, leaving unstated what disaster will befall the city if the window should be allowed to slam shut" (Anderson, 1998); (6) teams ensure that cost overruns will be paid for by taxpayers; and (7) without gaining approval owners start the process again with renewed threats from themselves and the league commissioner that unless the stadium or arena is built on terms favorable to the owners they will move the team elsewhere.

During 2012 I participated in a panel concerning a request by the previous owners of the Hawks for a new stadium. The local newspaper, *Idaho Business Review*, covered the session. The story that ran in the paper only included positive aspects of new stadium construction, while critical remarks made by one Boise merchant and myself were omitted. Including as part of the reported discourse only those in favor of corporate welfare for professional teams is not uncommon. This discourse shaping is not unprecedented. The Milwaukee Bucks (see below) successfully presented their case to the Wisconsin State Legislature with only those in favor of their receiving public funds invited to attend the session. Fast-forward to 2014 when the new owners of the Boise Hawks flew into town and started the discourse in a familiar fashion. They pointed out that the existing stadium (which for the record was constructed with private funds) was almost 25 years old, and had problems such as a "cramped clubhouse" and a scoreboard that lacked video capability (Berg and Southorn, 2014). (Imagine what a hardship it must have been to play baseball for well over a century without such an electronic marvel.) There was no immediate threat to move the team, but there was emphasis on having a competitive team so as to resolve the "baseball problem" in Boise. The usual study was produced claiming that a stadium would be part of a "mixed-development" project that would serve as an entertainment district by featuring retail shops, office space, and residential units. Conveniently, the new owners pointed to a similar project which they owned located in North Augusta, South Carolina. Projections included rising attendance and more fan spending. While cost overruns were not part of the discourse, the new owners did seek to soothe concerns about taxpayer funds by stating that they wished to explore alternatives that would not include the "risk" of taxpayer funds having to be used. Perhaps the new construction would strike oil or a gold vein and save taxpayers from having to pay. The window of opportunity card was also played, with the year 2017 for completion of the fiasco designated as the goal. One owner stated that the process would be difficult "but I think we're still in a window where that's still possible" (Berg and Southorn, 2014). The seventh step has yet to be reached, but give the owners time.

By July 2015, the Boise Hawks ownership group came up with a new tactic that it had used successfully in Fort Wayne, Indiana, and Augusta, Georgia, a tactic other professional sports team owners have adopted (see Milwaukee Bucks below). Instead of just proposing a new baseball park by itself the proposal is to make the park the "central part of a mixed-use development that includes hotels, restaurants, conference centers, office space and residential housing" – a carrot to entice the Boise governing officials to agree to "chip in" with the costs. The owners billed this proposal, of course, as one that would generate substantial revenue for Boise rather than become a "burden on the backs of taxpayer" (Lycklama, 2015). That claim seems ludicrous given the record of previous such projects across the country and that in the case of both the Indiana and Georgia projects taxes were increased on those districts dedicated to developing their central city area. Boise already has a vibrant downtown area currently experiencing a building boom with considerable development funded by the Simplot Foundation and Zion's Bank, among other investors.

In San Diego the same story is playing itself out as the owners are ramping up their criticism of the city's effort to build them a new stadium. Here the threat of leaving is real. The discourse used by Chargers' management includes that it would be justified for them to move to nearby Los Angeles because then the Chargers' "local revenue stream" would be reduced (Williams, 2015). Management was playing hardball, threatening to identify elected city officials who sought "political cover" (read would not approve public funding, but would not want their own name tied to that proposal). Management arranged for NFL executives to join the process. One has to give Charger management credit for not being bashful. They have argued for a "real world solution" including that there should be a tax increase to provide funding for the stadium – or else. To entice the city to meet their demands Charger management, as did that of the Hawks and the soon-to-be discussed Milwaukee Bucks, offered a proposal that would be for a "multi-use stadium" to serve as an expansion of the convention center. As with the Boise and Milwaukee cases, this would give the team possibilities for tapping into city funds targeted for hotel and infrastructure purposes. By mid-2015 the Chargers were asking the NFL to let them move to Los Angeles because, having "done everything possible," their nine proposals had been rejected by the city officials of San Diego who for some unknown reason decided that dealing with the city's pension liabilities should take priority over providing corporate welfare for the Chargers' owners (Garrick, 2015). The window of opportunity threat was used when the city decided a public vote on the funding issue should be scheduled.

Owners of the Milwaukee Bucks successfully received taxpayer funding for a new arena (see Chapter 5) by employing the same seven-step pattern that has become a tradition among professional sports team owners interested in having a new stadium or arena built with corporate welfare in the form of taxpayer money. The existing arena, the Bradley Center, has been deemed obsolete. The weight of the NBA is behind the threat to move the Bucks to another city if the 2017 imposed deadline for a new arena is not met. Essentially the league is letting Milwaukee know that if they do not agree to provide funding – corporate welfare to the billionaires who own the team – so that a new arena can be completed, or nearly completed, by the start of the 2017 NBA season it will approve a proposal from the current owners to take the franchise to Las Vegas or Seattle.

The usual claim about the need for the arena to make the Bucks competitive has been trumpeted. The friendly consultants produced a grand scheme for a $1 billion project that would include a new arena and all sorts of entertainment, eating, and office establishments that would be part of the promise that the grand project will revitalize the downtown area. Some of the discourse claims that taxpayers would be protected from cost overruns, but they would not be protected from the principal plus interest to the tune of $400 million (which would amount to over half the cost of the new arena) – and perhaps more depending upon the cost overrun situation. One cynic called Governor and presidential aspirant Scott Walker's proposed plan for the new arena "an outrageous example of corporate welfare" (Rmuse, 2015). This proposal is highly contradictory to Walker's self-proclaimed fiscal conservativism, demonstrated by his not bashful proposal for excessive cuts to education and transportation. Walker is not alone in being subject to criticism in this case. Milwaukee County Executive Chris Abele, an ardent supporter of the corporate welfare that would accrue to the Bucks' new owners, would realize a considerable increase in the value of his recently purchased $2 million condominium that is conveniently located next to the proposed site for the new arena (Rmuse, 2015).

The discourse surrounding the proposal does not include that the average Milwaukee County citizen who will contribute to the new arena will be unable to afford the expensive tickets, the price of which is sure to increase if the new arena is completed. Some of the economic benefits cited for this arena, and other similar arenas and stadiums, have been discredited in numerous studies by economists. The claim that dollars spent on basketball tickets would boost the city economy ignores evidence that local fans, either companies or individuals, have a fixed amount of funds they plan to allocate for entertainment purposes. Therefore, more spent on tickets will take away from entertainment expenditures elsewhere. The consulting reports prepared for the Bucks' owners, like proposals in other cities, assume an influx of fans from outside the area that would boost revenue spent in Milwaukee. If the example of other arenas and stadiums is examined, this forecast would be incorrect.

Numerous economic analysts agree that there is a considerable difference between purported claims that new arenas will generate net positive revenues for the city and what has occurred. The Cato Institute published a study in 2004 that concluded the projected net revenues for new stadium and arena construction tend to be greatly overstated – except for the owners and those who construct the new monument (Coates and Humphreys, 2004). A 1997 study by two acclaimed economists reached similar conclusions (Zimbalist and Noll, 1997). Among the findings were that most funding for new stadium construction came from public sources, with federal, state, and city funds provided; the typical sports facility was a net cost to the respective city; that the claim that job creation will ensue from construction is short-sighted, since once the construction is complete most jobs are low-paid service jobs and are seasonal; further, consultants' reports overstate the increased number of tourists attracted to see the team play in the new facility. Overall, the economists concluded that "bad economic analysis" was at the heart of the discourse justifying the benefits created by the proposed new stadiums or arenas (Zimbalist and Noll, 1997). One would think that with all this evidence Congress would reconsider the protection from antitrust enjoyed by professional teams. Not so. The influence of the billionaire team owners combined with local political leaders wanting to appease some rabid fans has kept Congress from reconsidering protection of professional sports teams that can limit entry into their industry and set salary limits not permitted by any other industry.

The *oil and gas industry* has successfully focused on the need to maintain its multibillion dollar subsidies (i.e., corporate welfare) it receives by using its economic power to sway friendly Washington DC officials despite polls indicating that an overwhelming majority of Americans would vote to have the subsidies eliminated (Froomkin, 2011). The welfare they receive directly includes exploration and drilling subsidies, generous depletion allowances (for tax purposes), and some federal financing for fossil fuel projects outside the United States. Indirectly the industry is subsidized by not having to bear the enormous costs they impose on the environment, the portion of military spending directly related to protecting US oil interests abroad, and health care costs due to spillover costs ensuing from the production and distribution of oil and natural gas. These costs are rarely, if ever, part of government policy discourse when this industry is concerned.

Discourse promoted by the industry focuses on the need for continued subsidies to promote economic growth, preventing existing jobs from being lost – what analysts argue is an exaggerated claim, and the need to achieve energy independence for the United States. The industry also claims these subsidies are needed to keep gasoline prices low. However, some industry analysts argue that the retail price of fuel is determined more by international market factors than by the production cost of extracting and refining petroleum and natural gas. The industry also makes considerable efforts to promote discourse that denies climate change is due to industrial activities as well as to limit federal actions taken against industry giants whose drilling operations result in damaging oil spills that would require these firms to pay the full cost of their oil extraction activities. It is not surprising that the industry also is influential supporting those who would reduce funding for the Environmental Protection Agency (EPA) while also making existing environmental regulations much more lax. The industry is so powerful in shaping this discourse that there are Republican members of Congress who allege to be cognizant and concerned about climate change, but who recognize the wrath of the industry in the form of campaign dollars to opponents who would challenge them in their next election should they support policies designed to reduce the impact of the oil and gas industries on climate change or to limit output of greenhouse gas emissions (Froomkin, 2011).

The industry also wields its influence over discourse on the state level, focusing on state attorneys general. There are cases that reveal discourse in the form of letters written by oil and gas industry representatives for attorneys general, who then send the letters to Washington DC regulators. Of course, the content is highly biased and favorable to the industry. One example occurred in Oklahoma where the attorneys general passed along a letter he had received from one of the biggest oil and gas companies in the state to the EPA. The letter argued that "[f]ederal regulators were grossly overestimating the amount of air pollution caused by energy companies drilling new natural gas wells in his state" (Lipton, 2014A). One study by a *New York Times* analyst discovered that oil and gas industry campaign contributions to attorneys general in at least 12 states were shaping both discourse as well as being influential in some decisions to end investigations of abusive industry practices or to reach favorable terms in settlements involving the industry. The same analyst uncovered cases of the industry preparing legislation highly favorable to industry interests, then giving it to state attorneys general to pass along to their respective state legislators for enactment (Lipton, 2014A).

The *finance* industry had no such need to prepare written legislation to pass along to friendly members of Congress for enacting policies that would generate corporate welfare in the form of deregulation that permitted toxic financial instruments from being sold worldwide – culminating in bailout billions given to those who created the financial crisis. They already had some of their own in high positions throughout Washington DC – as discussed previously. These friends of Wall Street spread discourse, dreamed up stories that deregulation that permitted the sale of derivatives and subprime mortgages packaged and rated as low risk would generate "economic progress" – discourse one critic describes as "financial make-believe" (Goodman, 2009, p. 15). This world of make-believe was carried out in a casino-like atmosphere which, unlike a Las Vegas casino, did not require those dealing the cards to have on hand sufficient funds to pay off all bets. Discourse was concocted on Wall Street, and repeated by congressional lackeys, that the financial system operated within self-regulating markets in which risks would be regulated by private individuals. Whether it was the 1990s with Greenspan as Federal Reserve Chair and SEC chairs such as Arthur Levitt, or Bernanke after he became Fed Chair, Congress, when it bothered to inquire, was continually offered assurances that financial markets were stable. Even worse, Summers and other like-minded nexus members vehemently argued that any attempts to regulate investment banks would be disastrous.

Over time "Wall Street's positions became the conventional wisdom in Washington; those who disagreed with them, such as Brooksley Born, were marginalized as people who simply did not understand the bright new world of modern finance. This group think was a major reason why the federal government deferred to the interests of Wall Street repeatedly in the 1990s and 2000s" (Johnson and Kwak, 2011, p. 97). With the aid of friendly congressional members, especially Republicans, the discourse originating on Wall Street was twisted to the distorted position that deregulated financial markets will promote economic progress, a view that served to maintain an ideological vision of the market which continues to serve the finance industry quite well.

Of course, once these fantasies were proven disastrously false cries from avowed free market libertarians immediately arose that justified bailing out the private investment banks. This message was sold to the public and throughout the halls of Congress, and to Barack Obama. First, there were (false) cries that the bailout was needed because credit was not available. For example, former Idaho Senator Larry Craig fomented fear among Idahoans by telling them that there was not credit available, which contrasted sharply with what managers of Boise area banks were telling me at the time. Obama, his Treasury Secretary, and his Federal Reserve Chair fostered fear by using the term "depression" that presidential administrations, in the interest of not creating panic in markets, have avoided for decades. During the few years following the 2008 crisis slick finance industry marketing combined with proclamations by friendly members of Congress served to cover up the massive fraud that had occurred throughout the finance industry. On top of this the "too big to fail" argument was used to justify the massive corporate welfare given the investment banks after the crisis in lieu of replacing the management, temporarily having government assuming ownership and control of these banks until stability was restored and new buyers found. In the process Washington DC finance industry supporters convinced the public to sanction the reckless pursuit of private profit which resulted in trillion dollar losses by socializing risk and responsibility assumption. Americans were still being told that "big, private, lightly regulated financial institutions are good for America" (Johnson and Kwak, 2011, p. 162). The massive bailouts rewarded the finance industry for being able to have the biased discourse they perpetuated translated into reckless deregulation followed by bailout billions – a demonstration of their "near-total control of the policy levers, rolling back the regulatory encroachment of government in many commercial realms" (Goodman, 2009, p. 35).

After reforms were demanded by the public as well as responsible members of the economics and finance profession, discourse from finance industry supporters shifted to lies about who was responsible for the crisis – with blame placed heavily on Freddie Mac and Fannie Mae. The "Big Lie" began with the plausible hypothesis that these institutions were responsible, then finding someone in Washington DC to perpetrate the myth. In this case it was two "scholars" at the American Enterprise Institute whose faulty, intellectually dishonest analysis was fodder for shaping discourse in a direction favorable to the finance industry. Critics countered by pointing out the very mortgages linked to Fannie Mae and Freddie Mac were actually created by the "unholy alliance between subprime lenders and Wall Street" (Nocera, 2011). The big lie, however, then is printed by "sympathetic publications" (e.g., *Wall Street Journal*) and becomes part of the discourse used wholeheartedly by many Republican members of Congress anxious to appease Wall Street by not having substantive financial industry reforms introduced (Nocera, 2011).

A bipartisan congressional commission was established to analyze the causes of the 2008 financial crisis. The bipartisan Financial Crisis Inquiry Commission quickly divided along party lines, with the Republican members shaping the discourse by voting to exclude terms that would influence substantially the final report's message. Among the terms excluded were "deregulation" and "Wall Street" (Krugman, 2010A). Democratic members' protests failed to deter the four finance industry sycophants who then chose to write their own report. Also in the aftermath was little in the way of Washington DC discourse concerning punishments that should have been meted out against the finance industry ratings agencies (e.g., Moody's, Standard & Poor's and Fitch) for their fraudulent ratings of what ultimately were deemed junk bonds – despite it being widely known that substantial conflict of interests existed between the agencies and Wall Street banks who not only could choose which agency would rate them (and be paid to do so), but who could also hire ratings agency members to consult for these same banks. By 2015 little had changed, at least on one side of the aisle in the Senate or House of Representatives. The Wall Street "vampires," according to one harsh critic, had pushed to have their discourse translated into friendly policies by purchasing for themselves many members of Congress – nearly all Republicans – "who came to power this year [and] are returning the favor by trying to kill Dodd–Frank" (Krugman, 2015A), likely because it is reducing investment banks' profitability by eliminating many abusive lending practices while regulating financial derivatives.

News Media

Through purchasing advertising, or the media itself, major industries are in the driver's seat for limiting and shaping discourse in a favored direction – at the expense of subverting the role independent media should play in a democracy. Not only can the industry influence who does and does not work for the media, but it can exert control over the content and veracity of information that media provides to the public. The industry nexus has effectively used the media to influence Washington DC officials who introduce or rewrite laws promoting the distribution of corporate welfare to multibillion dollar corporations and the wealthiest Americans who year by year pay a smaller share of their income in taxes for this largesse. Critics argue that many industries have been able to receive a redistribution of income upwards in their direction, some in the form of corporate welfare "through organized, systematic, conceptualized and financially motivated subversions of the democratic process" – and in the process succeeded in pumping through the media what at times is propaganda in the form of distorted discourse that dupes unsophisticated, unsuspecting voters into voting against their own interests (Fulbrook, 2012).

At its worst, as exemplified by Fox News, the media engage in blatant fearmongering without concern for decency or the truth. This media behemoth provides vivid evidence of the close link between major news media and Washington DC and the number of Republican presidential contenders over the past two election cycles who have been paid to contribute to various programs. Many of these programs feature climate change deniers, economists whose forecasts for the benefits of tax cuts have continually been proven false, people holding a doctorate who swear there is no institutional racism in the United States, among other paid contributors who willingly spout nonsensical discourse. This shaping of discourse on what is the most viewed news program in the country is part of "a movement shaped by billionaires and their bank accounts, and assured paychecks for the ideologically loyal are an important part of the system" (Krugman, 2010B). The discourse is heavily laden with the brand of conservatism that is about enriching the richest, often with corporate welfare being the means.

When some of these news broadcasts contain factually incorrect points (a euphemism for lies in this case), only a few other news programs (e.g., the *Daily Show*) are willing to point these out. One NBC News director "abdicated his responsibility as a journalist while demonstrating his station's complicity in supporting the spewing of false discourse that serves wealthy business interests, by claiming that it was not his job to correct 'Republican lies' about issues such as the Affordable Care Act" (Easley, 2013). NBC further demonstrated their ability to shape discourse in a direction favorable to multibillion dollar business interests when, unlike virtually every other major news media on the same day, they failed to report in 2011 that General Electric had paid $0 taxes to the United States despite receiving profits that exceeded $14 billion worldwide – courtesy of congressionally sanctioned "creative series of tax referrals and revenue shifts" (Lehmann, 2011). One should not be surprised to learn that General Electric owns the media giant that owns NBC News. This combination of discourse limiting and shaping by congressionally approved tax laws is one clear demonstration of this chapter's theme, namely the ability of the ruling alliance to limit and shape public discourse throughout academia and research institutes, Washington DC, and the national media.

Notes

1   These include the American Enterprise Institute, Cato Institute, Heritage Foundation, Hoover Institution, and the Rand Corporation.

2   Nearly all academics and many institute researchers teach their courses or do their research in an honest, objective manner. There remains, however, a small minority of individuals who wittingly or not contribute work that shapes the discourse and subsequent justification for policies to be established that are profitable for industries supporting those faculty or researchers, but that are not in the best interest of most Americans.

3   An alternative would be economics textbooks written from a heterodox perspective, pluralist textbooks that look at real-world economic problems from different points of view.

4   Among the financial contributors to the Heritage Foundation have been the Scaife Foundations (named for the heir to the Mellon industrial and banking empire fortune), Koch brothers, and even the South Korean government.

5   For an excellent analysis of the benefits of a plant-based diet see Stone and Campbell, 2011.

6   This incident arose at a time of growing consumer awareness and debate over genetically modified foods – with more than 30 states considering labeling laws – and rising pressure on companies to reduce their use of genetically engineered ingredients.

7   One source disclosed that the American Enterprise Institute received over $1.5 million from ExxonMobil, and that many of its staff members had been paid consultants for the George W. Bush administration (Allen, 2007).

8   It is not agreed upon as to what the federal government cost will be from all student loan defaults. Differences in estimate depend upon accounting methods used and forecasts of future repayment rates. Estimates range from no cost (with the government earning a profit) to almost $90 billion loss for all student loans. When administrative costs are taken into account there will be losses to the federal government (Barshay, 2014).

9   "More than half of the students who enrolled in [for-profit] colleges in 2008–9 left without a degree or diploma within a median of 4 months" (see www.help. senate.gov/imo/media/for_profit_report/ExecutiveSummary.pdf).

10 It is also noteworthy that it was revealed that when the Corinthian Colleges filed for bankruptcy they had been able in 2013 to pay their outgoing CEO a compensation package worth over $3 million (Lewin, 2015).

11 Alan Greenspan was the third winner. He ignored warnings that his guiding the Federal Reserve's rapid extension of the money supply and credit would create a financial and housing bubble.

12 Another 2016 candidate, Hillary Clinton, has brought over strategists and advisors that served Barack Obama (Confessore and Chozick, 2015).

13 There would need to be a corresponding increase in domestic investments that created better paying jobs for both growth and improved living standards for more than a small, wealthy percentage of the population to benefit.

14 One reason for lower prices is that Canadian drugs prices are subject to government price controls.

5 Trading Favors within the Nexus

The wealthy call the tune, and the politicians dance. So what we get in this democracy of ours are astounding and increasingly obscene tax breaks and other windfall benefits for the wealthiest, while the bought-and-paid-for politicians hack away at essential public services and the social safety net, saying we can't afford them. ... In the mad rush to privatization over the past few decades, democracy itself was put up for sale, and the rich were the only ones who could afford it. The corporate and financial elites threw astounding sums of money into campaign contributions and high-priced lobbyists and think tanks and media buys and anything else they could think of. They wined and dined powerful leaders of both parties. They flew them on private jets and wooed them with golf outings and lavish vacations and gave them high-paying jobs as lobbyists the moment they left the government. All that money was well spent. The investments paid off big time. America's public officials have rewritten the rules of American politics and the American economy in ways that have benefited the few at the expense of the many.

(Herbert, 2011B)

Introduction

This chapter will demonstrate that the pattern identified in the quote above has continued through 2015. It focuses on corporate welfare fueled by the existence of industry nexuses and policies influenced by limited, biased discourse culminating with extensive trading of favors among nexus members. Most of these trades effectively result in an upward redistribution of income and wealth, and technically, according to the US legal system, are not considered to be corrupt. The trades have been facilitated through organized, systematic, conceptualized, and financially motivated subversions of fiscal responsibility and free market principles. Among the negative outcomes is that either taxes must be increased to pay for the corporate welfare, or spending reduced for needy programs including health care, education, food stamps, and transportation. Polls indicate about three fourths of Americans want corporate welfare eliminated, and each year Congress – including those proclaiming to be fiscally responsible and against government interference in business ventures – promise that they will work to reduce or eliminate this welfare. However, the annual dollar amount of corporate welfare doled out to major industries continues to increase. Noting the typical personality traits of the key players in the flow of corporate welfare provides some indication of why they so willingly trade favors, to the detriment of most Americans. Research indicates that very wealthy individuals, which of course include the top management of major corporations, possess little empathy towards poorer Americans. Pertinent findings from studies conducted by prominent psychologists include that "people with the most social power pay scant attention to those with little such power" (Goleman, 2013). Industry nexus members tend to focus their interests on those they value most, namely others within the nexus or those they consider as their economic peers.

With income inequality and differences in political power being at their highest levels in a century, the empathy gap between the nexus members and average Americans is widening. Whether in the private sector or high public office, the more economically and politically powerful are likely to express disregard for those lower in socioeconomic status to the point of being dismissive of less fortunate people's low standard of living. Adam Smith believed business owners/entrepreneurs possessed "sympathy" (which to him meant empathy) for the working class. What has emerged during the past few decades is a different breed of owners who, in the midst of the highest degree of income and wealth inequality since the 1920s, are unabashedly shameless at accepting millions, and in cases billions, of dollars in corporate welfare. Labeled by Sigmund Freud as "the narcissism of minor differences," these personality traits affect public policy making and business investment decisions. For example, nexus members of Congress who shamelessly vote for policies that provide their campaign contributors substantial corporate welfare eagerly propose reducing public funds for health care and nutrition programs sorely needed by less fortunate citizens (Goleman, 2013).

The lack of remorse and unwillingness to accept responsibility for the negative effects from their decisions, combined with other personality traits identified in studies by psychologists that include being grandiose, deceitful, skilled in flattery and manipulation of other powerful people, and being heavily egocentric describes many major industry nexus members. These traits are being manifested most visibly by the professional sports teams' nexus as they continue to bully cities into providing public funds for stadiums and arenas that will enhance their income and wealth substantially. George Monbiot, British writer and political activist, referring to research findings[1] concluded that "if you have psychopathic tendencies and are born to a poor family you're likely to go to prison. If you have psychopathic tendencies and are born to a rich family you're likely to go to business school" (Monbiot, 2011). To that I would add "or go into politics where the art of sophistry is given its full expression."

Corporate welfare takes many forms while the trading of favors is ongoing – fueled by the relatively short and expensive presidential and congressional election cycles. According to a Cato Institute report "[t]hese welfare payments come in every conceivable shape and size, including government grants, contracts, cut rate insurance, loans, and loan guarantees" (Cato Institute, 1999). Direct and indirect subsidies to corporations, and federal tax breaks to corporations (and to the richest Americans) that include tax havens are the two most common forms. Some may not consider lucrative government contracts awarded without competitive bidding in some cases as corporate welfare since technically the business receiving the contract provides something of benefit in return. However, in cases where fraud and excessive cost overruns are involved, one could consider to be corporate welfare these costs as well as the difference between what is paid to the recipient of the no-bid contract and what would have been paid to the lowest-bid contractor chosen from a bidding process. Some of these cases are discussed later in the chapter, in particular the defense industry's case.

The examples of corporate welfare included in this chapter will not provide all details of the favors traded since unfortunately some of these remain unknown. For example, we do know that then-President Bill Clinton on his last day in office pardoned Mark Rich, who "was indicted on 50 counts of wire fraud, tax evasion, racketeering, and other charges but we don't know what Clinton received in return" (Kim, 2013). We can estimate that for the 2016 presidential and congressional elections an estimated $8 billion will be provided to candidates, much from major industry nexus members. What that will buy in return remains to be seen. If the following egregious examples of ongoing corporate welfare are any indication, few industries that provide campaign funding and promises of employment (or donations to foundations) will be left off the dole, regardless of how little they need any financial assistance.

When Walt Disney World was built on land southwest of central Orlando, Florida, a law was passed that applied only to the lands Disney purchased. It had been granted its own governing jurisdiction. Disney could then establish its own tax rates. This autonomous city, as a "taxing district," could write its own city codes and exert control over all the land within this district (Elderd, 2014). Those deemed outsiders by Disney would be unable to purchase property to establish legal residence. Consequently, all members of the board of supervisors for this legal entity represent the interests of the Disney Corporation. Disney, which has shown annual profits of about $5 billion, also successfully lobbied the state of Florida (as has the International Speedway Corporation which owns a dozen racetracks used for NASCAR events) to receive a tax break that would come on top of federal tax breaks it receives that combined have produced hundreds of millions for the multibillion dollar corporation. This request was made during a year in which Florida's budget deficit was about $2 billion (Melone, 2012).

No analysis of wealthy recipients of corporate welfare could be complete without including Wal-Mart, owned by a family whose collective wealth is among the five largest of the world's families. The retail giant receives hundreds of millions of dollars of subsidies from local governments throughout the country. One study found that 244 Wal-Marts around the country have received over $1 billion worth of government favors (Quigley, 2014). This amount pales in comparison to what Wal-Mart receives in corporate welfare from tax havens. It was reported that the retail giant holds over $75 billion "through a web of [more than 75] units in offshore tax havens around the world" (Drucker and Dudley, 2015). Tax laws thus permit Wal-Mart to avoid paying the United States annually almost $600 million. Wal-Mart is not alone. Corporate giants such as Google, Apple, and Starbucks also receive what amounts to corporate welfare thanks to their ability to avoid paying income taxes through federal tax laws that permit corporations to engage in "cross border tax avoidance" simply "by attributing profits to mailbox subsidiaries in low-tax jurisdictions like Bermuda" (Drucker and Dudley, 2015). Tax breaks were included in 2013 even as the federal budget was heading towards a "fiscal cliff" due to partisan disagreement over budget items. In the final budget agreement there was plenty of corporate welfare for special (nexus) interests, including continuation of tax breaks for Hollywood movie studios if they produced their movies and television programs within the United States.

At the state level Disney and Wal-Mart are not the only recipients. A Wisconsin example is of note because Governor Scott Walker has been the main benefactor of campaign funds from the Koch brothers whose well-funded political agenda is consistent with libertarian (read "free market") values. Walker created a jobs agency (The Wisconsin Economic Development Corporation) soon after he was elected, then doled out without any formal supervision almost $125 million to business interests – some of which are less than reputable. Included among the recipients was one currently defunct company that received an unsecured loan worth $500,000, despite its owner having had to appear in court to answer charges of not paying taxes the previous year. Evidence indicates that lobbyists for this company included someone who had been convicted of a felony for fraud conspiracy (Stein et al., 2015). Public–private cooperation has contributed to economic development and job creation throughout all wealthy countries. However, the Wisconsin case is clearly corporate welfare and hypocritical since the public funds are approved to be distributed by a self-proclaimed fiscal conservative whose administration appears quite insensitive to the many needs of less fortunate Wisconsin citizens, but quite open to wealthy nexus members that include the owners of the Milwaukee Bucks (discussed later in this chapter).

The case of two other friends of the Clintons, disgraced ex-governor of Virginia Republican Bob McDonnell, and his successor, Democrat Terry

McAuliffe, illustrates both sides of favors traded. Gifts and loans were provided by wealthy private members of Virginia's business community to these political leaders. McDonnell received gifts worth over $150,000 and loans from a contributor to his campaign, in return this generous contributor receiving the then-governor's support for his dietary supplement company (*New York Times*, 2013B). McAuliffe provides a unique case of a public official who also operated a large business called Green Tech Automotive, an electric car company he founded that he touted would create many jobs. Hillary Clinton's brother was director of fundraising for the company. The corporate welfare McAuliffe's company received came in the form of permanent residence visas for the 50 foreigners who invested at least $500,000 in "start-up money" – a deal which prompted an SEC investigation (Gabriel, 2013).

The Wisconsin and Virginia cases illustrate both the link between state governors and some of the most prominent nexus members on the national level. Virginia also shows that when trading of favors involves doling out corporate welfare some members of both political parties are willing participants. The remainder of this chapter will provide more examples of favors traded that generate corporate welfare. The focus will be on this welfare provided through tax breaks and outright subsidies to very wealthy individual or family owners of corporate entities as well as to major corporations in the following industries: defense, agriculture, energy, education, health and pharmaceuticals, finance, and professional sports. It would take an encyclopedia to provide an in-depth account of every corporate welfare example involving major nexus members. The examples presented are particularly flagrant ones that have all the appearances of being highly unethical, and perhaps illegal. These examples will serve to illustrate the egregious degree to which the doling out of corporate welfare is pervasive.

Tax Breaks and International Tax Havens

Among the contributors to the multibillion dollar flow of corporate welfare to many of the country's wealthiest individuals and largest corporations is the federal tax code which features a complex range of deductions, credits, and tax exemptions heavily biased to favor the wealthiest corporations and individuals. One observer describes the code as "the King James Bible of welfare for the rich and corporations. Special breaks in the tax code are the reason that there are thousands of lobbyists in the halls of Congress, hundreds of lobbyists around each state legislature and tens of thousands of tax lawyers all over the country" (Quigley, 2014). The tax rate actually paid by the richest 400 individual taxpayers, each of whom earns more than $200 million, is below 20% – and is also below that of those individuals whose income is only a paltry few million dollars (Stiglitz, 2013). Not to be outdone currying favor with multibillion dollar corporations and individuals, generous tax breaks are doled out by many states, counties, and cities across the United States that provide corporate welfare estimated at being over $80 billion annually (Story, 2012). The driving force that has stimulated elected officials to approve tax codes that generate such corporate welfare has been campaign contributions from the wealthiest and most politically and economically influential donors. One estimate of the total amount of individual taxes the very wealthy do not pay thanks to special tax breaks is almost $125 billion, roughly the estimated amount of corporate welfare in the form of tax breaks received by major corporations which take advantage of the offshore tax loopholes (Stiglitz, 2013). One study of major tax legislation revealed that each new proposed bill "contains new welfare for the rich and corporations" (Quigley, 2014). Continuing a trend that began during the early 1980s under the Reagan administration, the share of total tax revenue paid by corporations continues to decline. In one recent year while the total amount of income and payroll taxes amounted to almost $2 trillion, corporate taxes collected were under $250 billion (*New York Times*, 2013C). Another disparity that, while not corporate welfare, is a valuable benefit accorded to major corporate managers who by objective accounts engaged in some form of criminal activity is that almost none are imprisoned – witness the aftermath of the 2008 financial and real estate crises. When multibillion dollar fines are imposed on corporate giants such as JPMorgan Chase, which reached a $13 billion mortgage settlement with the federal government, they do not admit guilt, no official is imprisoned, and they can take a tax deduction for a large portion of the settlement. In the case of JPMorgan Chase their saving (one might consider it corporate welfare) was about $4 billion (Quigley, 2014).

It is a testimony to the nexuses' effectiveness since the corporate welfare attributable to tax breaks and tax havens is legally sanctioned by Congress. Popular tax havens where corporations can establish a "subsidiary" (which may be a mailbox) in one haven and then transfer their billions to another haven are Bermuda, the Cayman Islands, Ireland, the Isle of Man, Puerto Rico, or Singapore. While the official marginal corporate tax rate for the United States is almost 40% the existence of tax havens and lax rules and loopholes make a mockery of this rate for the richest corporations. One critic argues that the tax rules for major global corporations exemplify "corporate socialism" with either greater budget deficits, higher taxes imposed on the remaining taxpayers, or reduced public programs or services (Napach, 2012).

Two other tax breaks afforded to corporations that provide them corporate welfare are the repatriation holiday and the bonus depreciation. The former was actually introduced in an attempt to reduce the amount of tax avoidance global corporations were able to enjoy. The holiday reduced the tax rate to just over 5% so as to entice repatriation of what was estimated in 2005 to be about $300 billion held overseas. The discourse focused on the job creation and increased domestic investment that this new law would provide. What occurred instead was money repatriated by corporations at the very low tax rates, rather than being invested to create jobs, "was mostly used for dividend payments, share buybacks (which tend to raise executive pay) and severance pay for employees laid off in corporate restructuring" (*New York Times*, 2013C). In 2013 it was revealed that over three fourths of repatriated dollars came from tax havens – so that the corporations that engaged most aggressively in avoiding taxes reaped the most corporate welfare. Even worse, in anticipation of more such tax breaks in the future the flow of profits shifted to tax havens actually increased (*New York Times*, 2013C).

The "bonus depreciation" was a domestic tax break introduced in 2007 that generated significant corporate welfare under which depreciation of plant and equipment could be written off faster than those assets actually depreciated. It was intended to be a temporary break, the impetus for which was to stimulate the economy after the 2008 recession. However, Republicans have been seeking to extend this break even though a survey of leading corporation tax accountants indicated that such a break did little to stimulate the economy – and was unlikely to do so in the future. If this break becomes permanent the corporate welfare received could amount to almost $300 billion through 2024 (Super, 2014).

Major global corporations such as Amazon, Apple, Facebook, General Electric, Goldman Sachs, Google, Hewlett-Packard, LinkedIn, Microsoft, and Procter & Gamble have reaped corporate welfare by making aggressive use of tax havens and other tax avoidance tactics. Microsoft was able to avoid paying over $6 billion in taxes by establishing subsidiaries in havens that included Bermuda, Ireland, Puerto Rico, and Singapore (Napach, 2012). Like other global companies that take advantage of these legal tax havens, the value added to Microsoft's products within these havens tends to be overstated so that higher profits in these havens can be declared. As mentioned in Chapter 4, General Electric had been outdoing these other global giants in avoiding taxes until Apple's tax accountants devised even better schemes that included stockpiling "some $100 billion in Ireland without paying taxes on much of it *anywhere in the world* and, apparently, without breaking any law" (*New York Times*, 2013C). One estimate is that the world's most profitable technology company was able to avoid paying US taxes on its $44 billion income received from outside the United States between 2009 and 2012.

America's global corporations also receive corporate welfare from the much criticized Export-Import Bank, described by one critic as a "case study in corporate welfare featuring private firms' profits being enhanced with public funds" (Rufermarch, 2015). Another critic argues that the bank (whose charter Congress did let expire in mid-2015), and the benefits it provided to primarily large corporations, exemplified "crony capitalism" (Rugy, 2015). The program has existed since the 1930s. It was intended to promote domestic employment by facilitating US exports through loans, guarantees, and insurance benefits backed by federal tax dollars. In cases where a default from the foreign company on the trade occurred, the US trading firm received payment anyway – which can be considered a form of corporate welfare. Among the reasons for criticism is that the program, according to trade economists' analysis, does not generate a net increase of either jobs or exports. Other criticisms focused on the fact that a lion's share of the profits earned from trade activities backed by the Export-Import Bank were received by the largest corporations. For example, in 2012 over 80% of the loan guarantees were to customers of Boeing, while in 2013 more than 90% of the loan guarantees involved only five companies – among them Caterpillar and General Electric (Rufermarch, 2015). Other major beneficiaries included the financial industry's JPMorgan Chase and Citibank, each of which received fees and interest from being involved in the Export-Import Bank's guaranteed program (Rugy, 2015). The Congressional Budget Office estimated that the annual cost to taxpayers to cover anticipated losses the bank would have incurred for the 2015–25 period, had the bank's charter not been discontinued, would have averaged about $200 million a year (Rufermarch, 2015). Nevertheless, there remain Congressional advocates for the bank who will try to have its charter re-established. They fear that discontinuing the bank's charter "is a critical blow to [domestic] manufacturers" and that revocation, in effect, will be "undermining thousands and thousands of jobs" (Puzzanghera, 2015). Critics argue that taxpayers will be spared from having to continue funding this corporate welfare.[2]

A particularly egregious part of the federal tax code is the reclassification of some income received by hedge fund and private-equity fund managers' income as a "capital gain" or "carried interest" that provides this group, some of whom have had annual incomes that exceeded $1 billion, with billions of welfare dollars. Critics argue that defining their income so creatively rather than as ordinary income "makes little sense: in economic terms, the fund managers (also known as investment advisors) perform a professional service, much like lawyers or doctors, and receive remuneration for their labor" and is a testimony to the power Wall Street financial institutions exert through their nexus over Congressional lawmakers (Dodd, 2007). For a hedge fund manager whose annual income was $100 million this loophole would provide them with nearly $20 million more income/welfare than had their income been taxed at the 39.6% rate for normal income (Baker, 2014). When one liberal economic analyst inquired of a conservative economist how such a tax break could be justified the response was "that the fund managers are rich and powerful people. I assured him I knew this, but I wanted to know what sort of economic rationale there could be for this sort of tax break. He said there isn't one" (Baker, 2014).

Trading Favors: Defense, Where Cost Overruns and Reconstructing War-Torn Areas Yields Corporate Welfare

The rationale given by the defense industry for the lucrative contracts they receive that smack of corporate welfare is that they provide national security and job creation. While these justifications are seemingly difficult to refute, a closer look at some contracts reveals that some of the revenue they receive in the form of corporate welfare does little to enhance national security, and that per million dollars defense industry projects tend to create fewer jobs than a comparable amount of spending would create were it to be for alternative projects such as rebuilding the crumbling infrastructure of the United States. While the jobs to spending ratio for the defense industry is quite modest, the ratio of defense industry lobbying dollars to the value of the contracts they receive is massive. Analysts have demonstrated that defense industry giants such as Boeing, General Dynamics, Lockheed Martin, Northrop Grumman, and Raytheon (as well as some nondefense contractors) score high on the "Lobbying Index" that identifies the ratio of a corporation's profitability to the money it devotes to lobbying expenditures as a percentage of their total assets (Nesto, 2012). To help maintain this favorable return the defense industry has doubled its annual lobbying expenditures since 2000.

Even the smaller defense contractors can receive a lucrative return on currying favor expenditures, even if they produce a shoddy product that fails to meet contract specifications – as was the case of a DHB Industries product. The multimillion dollar corporation, whose primary client is the government, produces bulletproof vests some of which are worn by combat soldiers. During 2005 about 18,000 of these vests were recalled, some of which were being used in Iraq – the second such recall by the military that year. Meanwhile the corporation and its CEO, David Brooks, were being investigated by the SEC (*New York Times*, 2006). Brooks could be the poster boy for how defense contract corporate welfare can enrich the CEOs of industry producers. Brooks had earned $525,000 in 2001 before the Iraq War began, but in 2004 his reported income was $70 million with an additional $185 million earned from the sale of his DHB stock.

While fiscal conservatives are outspoken and highly critical of reports indicating excessive and questionable spending on poverty and environmental programs, they conveniently look the other way when similar reports that focus on unnecessary and even fraudulent defense contracts are made public. This has been the case for some weapons that the military either did not request or no longer wished to receive. One of these involved the production of some F-35 fighter planes the Pentagon did not request, but that congressional friends of the defense industry believed were worth more than the $500 million it appropriated for construction of the planes and some projects within the community in which the planes were built (Parker and Weisman, 2014). Another almost as expensive case concerned construction of a $350 million structure that could be used to test rocket engines at Mississippi's Stennis Space Center. However, even after the structure has been completed it will not be used because NASA has indicated they do not need to use it (Salant, 2014). No protests have been launched by the defense contractors who will be paid handsomely to construct this monument to the defense nexus' ability to generate wasteful spending while providing corporate welfare.

The M1 Abrams tank is the costliest example of a weapon being produced that the military stated it did not want any more of between 2014 and 2017, according to testimony made by an Army general at a congressional hearing concerning the defense budget. The general pointed out that there existed "more than enough combat tanks in the field to meet the nation's defense needs" (Griffin and Johnston, 2012). One indication to support that testimony was provided by the Army depot near Reno, Nevada, that serves as a "parking lot" for over 2000 idle M1 Abrams tanks. In fairness, production of the tanks does provide employment for an estimated 16,000 individuals at more than 800 subcontractors located across the United States, with General Dynamics being the main contractor. Ceasing production would generate savings of about $3 billion. Four congressional nexus members who collectively have received over $5 million in campaign contributions from General Dynamics' sources as well as the benefits provided by the corporation's lobbyists led the charge to block attempts aimed at "freezing refurbishment of the M1," as proposed by the Defense Department (Mehta and Mulvany, 2012). There was a strong correlation between "spikes" in the campaign contributions and lobbying expenditures and the start of congressional committee hearings and votes on the defense budget. How were the different positions of the US Army and Congress reconciled? The budget that was approved included over $180 million for production of 70 more tanks. Who would likely be chosen to receive the contract to build these unneeded tanks? According to former House of Representatives member Buck McKeon, a recipient of General Dynamics campaign contributions, "General Dynamics would probably get the contract for it anyway because they are kind of the ones that are out there leading the way on this" (Griffin and Johnston, 2012).

Self-proclaimed fiscal conservatives do not mind looking the other way when reports surface concerning outrageous cost overruns for defense department contracts. Weapons producers have a history of bidding low so as to be awarded the contract in question. In cases where the cost overrun is egregious and the weapon produced fails to come close to the requirements stipulated in the contract the producer is not held accountable, let alone punished – and that contractor gets back in line for more contracts. Thus, when defense contractors such as Lockheed Martin were responsible for billions of dollars in cost overruns producing a Navy helicopter they remained one of the major contractors for subsequent weapons – even though the *Wall Street Journal* reported that the cost overrun was almost 90% of the contract cost (Edwards, 2009). While construction of something never built before, whether a weapon, mountain highway, or the latest product for your cat featured in *Sky Mall* magazine, the following examples go well beyond what knowledgeable analysts believe they should cost. The bill for parts supplied by Bell Helicopter in 2012 came to $13.4 million, but a watchdog group reported this cost should have been less than $4.5 million (Salant and Capaccio, 2014). The difference between a "fair price" (covers cost plus a reasonable return for the seller) and the price charged in the contract was 300% or more for a number of parts. A Cato Institute report focuses the "main blame" on Congress for tolerating defense contractor cost overruns that a 2008 Government Accounting Office review of 72 weapons systems found to be about 40% on average (Edwards, 2009).

These cost overruns pale in comparison to the costs incurred from still another war begun on dubious grounds and the postwar reconstruction of that same country.[3] The corporate welfare reaped from postwar reconstruction was given its fullest expression in the aftermath of the Iraq War – the costliest effort to rebuild a nation ever undertaken by the United States. One critic's research led her to conclude that "U.S. corporations [such as Halliburton, Bechtel, Parsons, PPMG – among others] that were in Iraq to take advantage of the reconstruction were part of a vast protectionist racket whereby the U.S. government had created their markets with war, barred their competitors from even entering the race, then paid them to do the work, while guaranteeing them a profit to boot – all at taxpayer expense" (Klein, 2007, p. 449). Except for access to Iraq's vast oil reserves American firms were "[f]reed of all regulations, largely protected from criminal prosecution and on contracts that guaranteed their costs would be covered. … [In response] corporations did something entirely predictable: they scammed wildly" (Klein, 2007, p. 451). Former US Senator from North Dakota, Byron Dorgan, used an example to explain the "elaborate subcontracting schemes" as follows: "The contract goes to a subcontractor, which goes to another subcontractor, and a fourth-level subcontractor. And the payment for air-conditioning turns out to be payments to four contractors, the fourth of which puts a fan in a room. Yes, the American taxpayer paid for an air-conditioner" at great expense (Klein, 2007, p. 451). According to another report:

> Tales of waste, fraud and mayhem by private contractors have been commonplace during the more than 10 years of military operations in Afghanistan and Iraq. There was a warehouse constructed in Afghanistan at a $15 million cost that never will be used by the United States. Another $36 million was wasted building a never-used headquarters at one military base despite reports that the leading general at the base had made a request to halt the project. As with

most defense department contracts, it is not clear how much of this $50 million plus expenditure could be considered corporate welfare. A recent congressional study commission has put a "conservative" estimate on "waste" to be between $31 billion and $60 billion out of the $206 billion paid to contractors since the start of the two wars.

(*New York Times*, 2011B)

One author documents many examples of boondoggles for which by all appearances welfare was being received every step of the way – and despite the efforts of the Special Inspector General for Iraq Reconstruction: "[t]here were almost too many failed projects to document" (Van Buren, 2011, p. 214). In his *We Meant Well: How I Helped Lose the Battle for the Hearts and Minds of the Iraqi People* (2011), Peter Van Buren gives his eye witness account of numerous cases of costly boondoggles that only the combination of a government and military administrators could concoct. There were newspapers written by the army published that few people read, computers and internet service provided to a zoo so that resident veterinarians could establish technology links with their US counterparts. Among the topics that perhaps were discussed using this costly technology (dollar amount unknown) was whether or not alcohol should be fed to bears each day so that they would be "docile toward visitors" (Van Buren, 2011, p. 212). Perhaps the Iraqi veterinarians could have used their new-found technology to chat with their American counterparts about the zoo's daily practice of throwing into the lion cage a live donkey to feed the hungry felines (Van Buren, 2011, p. 212). Other profitable (for those corporations doing the reconstruction) boondoggles were roads built that were not used (partly due to fear that insurgents would use them to harm citizens and US soldiers) after they had been built (cost not known); an English Academy intended for Iraqi bureaucrats that was not used soon after completion – cost of at least $13 million; $40 million spent to construct a prison that never was used; and the more than $170 million for a hospital that did not have a patient for years after it opened (Van Buren, 2011, pp. 212–14). Reviewers praised Van Buren's work for exposing the waste, fraud, ineptitude, and corruption pervasive throughout the Iraq reconstruction effort. To those assessments needs to be added "with considerable corporate welfare reaped in the process."

It likely never will be known what the relationship was between the Iraq War and reconstruction-related corporate welfare doled out and the roughly $8.7 billion of Defense Department spending using oil revenue funds designated for the reconstruction of Iraq that is not fully accounted for – with "no records at all" for $2.6 billion of this amount (*Los Angeles Times*, 2010).[4] "Improper accounting practices" and weak "financial and management controls" were the causes according to the Special Inspector General for Iraq Reconstruction. This sum represents the "largest theft of funds in national history" according to this group's director Stuart Bowen

(Goodwin, 2011). A report revealed eye witness accounts of Iraqi contractors receiving millions of dollars "shoved into 'gunnysacks'" with no paperwork seemingly involved (Goodwin, 2011).

How much corporate welfare was paid in the construction of the new US embassy built in Baghdad, the world's largest that sits on 104 acres, features over 20 buildings, and employs more than 3000 people, is not clear. The cost overrun, according to a congressional report, could be more than $140 million. A large consulate employing over 1200 people was also constructed in Basra, while the new US consulate in Erbil will employ even more. At least jobs are being created, supporters might argue. While military activities have been reduced substantially, one knowledgeable observer commented "many other aspects of our relationship are going to ramp up" (CNN, 2009). What may have been ramping up are our control over the oil supply and the amount of corporate welfare some members of the defense industry and oil industry nexuses will receive. "Of course it's about oil; we can't really deny that," said General John Abizaid, former head of US Central Command and Military Operations in Iraq, during 2007. Former Federal Reserve Chairman Alan Greenspan agreed, writing in his memoir, "I am saddened that it is politically inconvenient to acknowledge what everyone knows: the Iraq war is largely about oil." Then-Sen. and now Defense Secretary Chuck Hagel said the same in 2007: "People say we're not fighting for oil. Of course we are" (Juhasz, 2013). The revolving door swung in the process. "Upon leaving office, Bush and Obama administration officials have even worked for oil companies as advisers on their Iraq endeavors. For example, former U.S. Ambassador to Iraq Zalmay Khalilzad's company, CMX-Gryphon, 'provides international oil companies and multinationals with unparalleled access, insight and knowledge on Iraq'" (Juhasz, 2013).

A common theme throughout Naomi Klein's *The Shock Doctrine* (2007) focuses on major US corporations benefiting from unstable political situations worldwide, often instigated by US intervention. Klein even devotes an entire chapter to profiteering by some major US corporations during the Iraq War and after, with a large portion of their profits stemming from their gaining greater control over the flow of Iraqi oil. One company close to the heart of the Bush administration which was awarded almost $40 billion in contracts for projects related to Iraq during the 2002–12 period was Halliburton, of which Dick Cheney had been CEO prior to becoming Bush's vice president. Halliburton was awarded many of these lucrative contracts without having to engage in a competitive bidding process. Some of these billions were for "support services" for the "unprecedented levels" of privatization programs that replaced what had been military operations (Young, 2013). One project involved so many "alleged kickbacks" that Halliburton later faced a lawsuit from the US Department of Justice.

The total cost to the US taxpayers of the war was estimated to be over $2 trillion if veterans' benefits now and in the future are included, with billions of corporate welfare channeled to major defense industry nexus members and their corporations. More sobering were the findings of a bipartisan study done by the Commission on Wartime Contracting in Iraq and Afghanistan. The Commission reported that "the level of corruption by defence contractors may be as high as $60 billion" (Young, 2013). These findings are supported by the author of *Halliburton's Army* (Chatterjee, 2009), who summarized his book as a "sordid tale of politics and profiteering, courtesy of the Bush administration and a compliant military" (CorpWatch, 2009). The book documents how Halliburton's stock rose after Cheney assumed the Vice President's office from about $10 per share to $80, perhaps due to speculation concerning profits the corporation would receive from its lucrative Iraqi contracts. Halliburton's profitability, and untold billions in corporate welfare, can be heavily attributable to Cheney being a major defense industry nexus player, a nexus through which he orchestrated the awarding of many lucrative reconstruction contracts not only in Iraq, but in other unstable poorer countries. However, ultimately Halliburton came under congressional scrutiny for doing substandard work in Iraq, and an SEC investigation for allegations of "corruption, negligence, fraud, and corporate crime" that led to dozens of their workers (albeit none of the leading executives) having to serve jail terms for theft of government contract funds (CorpWatch, 2009).

How did Halliburton respond to these allegations? It took advantage of another source of "corporate welfare" in the sense of providing protection for profits earned – it moved its legal address to Dubai, but still remained eligible to bid for more government contracts. The federal law (loophole) permitting this specifies a corporation that does change its legal address remains eligible to be awarded a government contract if it has "substantial business in its new home – thus nominally demonstrating its move wasn't solely for tax reasons" (*Bloomberg Businessweek*, 2014). This process, known as inversion, enables Halliburton to remain eligible for corporate welfare from government contracts as well as potentially lessening its corporate tax liability. Of course, Halliburton defended its move by pointing out that "we clearly see there are greater opportunities in the eastern hemisphere than the western hemisphere" (Learsey, 2007). Since Dubai is known for its shopping centers, perhaps Halliburton decided to spend its billions of Iraqi profits in style.

The focus on Halliburton should not be interpreted as their being the only defense contractor guilty of seemingly illegal practices while reaping corporate welfare. Accounts of waste and fraud combined with corporate welfare (they go together as well and as often as apple pie and milk) have been made for decades. One 1990s book, *Take the Rich Off Welfare*, stressed that there was "waste beyond your wildest dreams" when major defense department contracts were concerned, including tens of billions awarded that were unaccounted for due to "financial management troubles" (Zepezauer and Naiman, 1996). Even more sobering was the authors' reporting that according to public records between 1980 and 1992 every one of the 10 leading defense contractors had been "convicted of or admitted to defrauding the government" – including Boeing, Grumman, Raytheon, and General Electric. GE pleaded guilty to 108 counts of fraud involving one contract alone (Zepezauer and Naiman, 1996). Among other sources of corporate welfare received by these, and some other current defense department contractors, are purchases of their products directly from foreign governments who receive "aid" from the US State Department in the form of credits requiring them to purchase US weapons. All this would make the defense industry eligible for being ranked number one on the list of top 10 most egregious corporate welfare recipients. However, it would face stiff competition from the agricultural industry for that dubious honor.

Trading Favors: Agriculture, No to Food Stamps but Yes to Corporate Welfare for Agribusiness and Millionaire Congressional Farm Owners

While reports of the demise of the traditional family farm are widespread, the agricultural industry remains very healthy – particularly agribusiness corporations. Contributing to the demise and health trends is the US Department of Agriculture whose farm subsidies have accounted for the largest fraction (about two fifths) of all corporate welfare spending. Two reporters best described the US farm support program as a "Depression-era program intended to save [American] farmers from ruin has grown into a 21st-century crutch enabling affluent growers and financial institutions to thrive at taxpayer expense" (Lynch and Bjerga, 2013). The federal agricultural subsidy system rewards those with greater revenue and assets with more corporate welfare (Slivinski, 2007). The cost of these rewards has risen so fast that USDA crop insurance payments were almost seven times greater in 2014 than they were in 2000 (Lynch and Bjerga, 2013). The favor traded in return comes in the form of ever-increasing and quite generous agribusiness political campaign contributions and perks generated by lobbying efforts. Among the lobbyists providing such a favor was a group of more than 40 members who combined their defense of maintaining the farm program with over $50 million in lobbying expenditures for the 2012 election (Lynch and Bjerga, 2013).

Numerous studies and watchdog groups note that 10% of the recipients of agricultural subsidies receive anywhere from 50% to 75% of all subsidies in a given year – with the average handout being about $450,000 (Egan, 2011). Among the grateful recipients of subsidies, some of which is widely considered to be corporate welfare, are agribusiness giant Archer Daniels Midland, Caterpillar, Chevron, International Paper, and RJ Reynolds Tobacco, plus a few wealthy celebrities who own farm land. This is not surprising because the farm programs reward large industrial farms rather than assisting or protecting family farms, over 60% of which received no subsidies between 1995 and 2012 (Environmental Working Group, 2013). So much for the discourse that agricultural subsidies are needed to help the small farmer. Even worse, the design of the various programs in place over the past few decades gives the large industrial farms more ability to expand their operations. Little wonder that the Organic Consumers Association, citing a *Washington Post* report during the George W. Bush presidency, concluded that "Mr. Bush signed a farm bill that represents a low point in his presidency – a wasteful corporate welfare measure that penalizes taxpayers and the world's poorest people in order to bribe a few voters."[6]

A program truly dedicated to helping family farms would heavily subsidize budding organic vegetable and fruit producers rather than the producers of the products that receive, by far, the most subsidies: corn, wheat, cotton, and soybeans. US agricultural policy makers could learn from countries such as New Zealand where abolishing all farm subsidy programs actually improved productivity and profitability (DeHaven and Edwards, 2012), and of course eliminated any vestiges of corporate welfare. The political reality, however, is that American agribusiness firms enjoy receiving the corporate welfare without having to meet any needs test. The US farm program is filled with hypocrisy that makes the notion of agribusiness operating within a "free market economy" a farce. Regardless of the discourse from Democrats (let's help the small farmer) and Republicans (let's be fiscally responsible) every successive farm bill passed by Congress hypocritically "expands the lavish welfare system enjoyed by well-off farm businesses" (DeHaven and Edwards, 2012). A corporate welfare queen of hypocrisy was former Tea Party member of Congress Michelle Bachman. Her self-proclaimed "rigid ideology" of fiscal (and evangelical social) conservatism complete with strong anti-tax discourse apparently met "mushy reality" when it came to her family farm reaping more than $250,000 in farm support/welfare payments between 1995 and 2009. Perhaps applying for and receiving welfare from the "nation's most indefensible socialist scheme" (Egan, 2011) was one of her evangelical Christian social conservatism beliefs.

The corn and ethanol subsidies and a range of other federally designed programs have evolved over the past three decades. The one constant has been that whether the program is described as providing subsidies, loan guarantees, tax credits, crop insurance, or import tariffs corn producers have collected more federal dollars, and corporate welfare, than producers of any other agricultural product. The payment trend has continually been upward even during periods when corn producers' income was well above average. Beneficiaries include not only agribusiness giants such as Archer Daniels Midland and Cargill, but smaller corporations and some members of Congress who own a large farm producing large amounts of corn attracted by an easy harvest of federal dollars. Despite many well-argued calls for eliminating corporate welfare received overwhelmingly by the largest corn producers Congress has continually found ways to maintain the flow.

The Cato Institute has aggressively called for the elimination of corporate welfare, particularly for wealthy agricultural producers. A 1995 study identified clearly how trading of favors works in Washington DC. It involved the CEO of Archer Daniels Midland. He traveled to Washington DC in 1986 with the corporation's top lobbyist to meet with Secretary of Agriculture Richard Lyng. Since the price of corn was rising, but gasoline prices were falling from their late 1970s high point, thereby making ethanol uncompetitive, a creative solution was proposed to the Secretary. Ethanol would be made "pseudo competitive" thanks to what they proposed should be "USDA gifts of free corn" (Bovard, 1995). Just two days after the meeting a new USDA program was announced that gave Archer Daniels Midland almost $30 million in free corn while a few other large ethanol producers would also receive a gift commensurate with their size. One critic representing the gasoline industry described the program as "corporate food stamps" for the agribusiness giant (Bovard, 1995).

Until 2014 there were no substantive changes in the subsidy program, save for import restrictions against foreign-produced ethanol that, of course, propped up both ethanol and corn producers. This was in spite of scientific challenges to the claim that ethanol use would be more environmentally friendly than is gasoline. During 2007 the amount of federal funds received by corn and ethanol producers was over $4.5 billion. Industry and congressional discourse included that ethanol was environmentally friendly since purportedly less greenhouse gases would be emitted, thus combating climate change, if it replaced fossil fuel-based gasoline. This assertion was challenged. Princeton University researchers found that by subsidizing ethanol use the net effect was more, not less, greenhouse gas emissions due to changes in land use (Prante, 2008).

Over the next few years Taxpayers for Common Sense actively argued against the various programs that provided subsidies and tax credits for corn and ethanol production that maintained a steady flow of corporate welfare. From 2004 through 2011, when it was discontinued, the primary subsidy program for ethanol was provided by the Volumetric Ethanol Excise Tax Credit. This creative subsidy replaced the traditional ethanol subsidies, but the cost to US taxpayers rose from about $1.5 billion in 2004 to more than $5.6 billion in 2010 (Taxpayers for Common Sense, 2011). The main recipients were not needy farmers. Rather, those who blended gasoline and ethanol such as Shell Oil received a large portion of the benefits/corporate welfare. When widespread criticism against this tax credit arose Congress approved the Renewable Fuel Standard that required the use of blended fuels – one effect of which was to create a substantial increase in the demand for ethanol. Critics countered that all of these taxpayer supports should be eliminated because greater ethanol use increased the price of corn, and the many products for which corn is a primary ingredient, while having negative environmental effects. Aspiring presidential candidates anxious to curry favor among Iowa's voters continued to support the programs for corn production. One case in point occurred at the Iowa Agricultural Summit in March 2015, where one critic noted that Republican presidential aspirants openly "embraced the renewable-fuel standard, one of the worst examples of corporate welfare in America" (Pyle, 2015).

Thus it should not be surprising that once one subsidy program is phased out another is quickly introduced. Following the end of the Volumetric Ethanol Excise Tax Credit in 2011 another subsidy program was proposed for ethanol use-related "infrastructure" such as blender pumps at gasoline stations, storage tanks, and biofuels pipelines designed for the more corrosive ethanol–gasoline blend. Known as the Rural Energy for America Program, some analysts predicted that the subsidy would "just be another huge bill for the taxpayer" (Taxpayers for Common Sense, 2011). This last subsidy was phased out in 2014. However, within one month new subsidies were proposed for ethanol blender pumps. Also in 2014, facing criticism due to the absurdity of providing billions of corporate welfare dollars while farm profits were reaching a record, subsidies were eliminated – but not the continued flow of corporate welfare not only for corn, but for all eligible agricultural producers. The new programs are not found in any description of a free market economy. One insured farmers' incomes for years where harvests were poor, while the other provided federal funds should the price of the eligible farm product fall. The total estimated cost to taxpayers has since been less than before the programs were introduced, thanks to record harvests. However, large corporate producers of corn and ethanol did not see any complete curtailment of the corporate welfare they have been receiving for decades.

The familiar pattern with trading of favors among industry nexus members goes well beyond the corn/ethanol industry. Examples of such behavior in the sugar, cotton, pork, horseracing, fast food and junk food industries exist as well. Corporate welfare is received in a range of programs that include direct subsidies, government grants or contracts, low interest loans or insurance rates, loan guarantees, and indirect subsidies such as import restrictions on foreign producers of the industries' products. Every government agency seems to offer welfare in some form to some of these industries.

The *sugar* support program illustrates the nexus pattern of controlling discourse that leads to corporate welfare for its members. Perhaps no industry has received as much bipartisan federal support as Big Sugar. For example, American Crystal Sugar Company donated over $1.3 million to 221 members of Congress for the 2014 election, following $1.4 million spent on lobbying in 2013 (Meyer and Cooper, 2014). Going back to 1995 when Congress was debating whether or not to reduce or eliminate the corporate welfare flow the industry launched a major lobbying effort with substantial financing from Florida's giant sugar farms, the Fanjul brothers who then realized increased profits of about $60 million thanks to generous price supports and import quotas. The power of campaign contributions and other benefits was such that when the final vote occurred in the House of Representatives the existing sugar support bill was retained by a margin of three votes. Later it was revealed that "4 members of Congress who were original co-sponsors of the legislation to kill the sugar subsidies voted against their own bill" – and that the ratio of campaign contributions to those voting to retain the supports to those voting against the supports was ten to one (Moore, 1999).

In 2013 a test of whether the touted free trade benefits of the North American Free Trade Agreement (NAFTA) would be permitted to demonstrate themselves became costly to US taxpayers – compliments of the sugar price support program. Due to a substantial increase in sugar imports from Mexico the domestic price of sugar in the United States declined. No problem for sugar producers. Part of their subsidies included price guarantees that enabled them to store sugar as collateral for a government loan, then if they could not sell the sugar at a favorable price the sugar became US government property while the sugar producers kept the loan funds. The taxpayers suffered since the government had to pay for storage of the excess sugar (excess meaning that if a reduction in the supply sold in the market at a free market price would have caused sugar producers to incur losses – as would occur in any industry operating in a free market).

During the year the USDA chose to "prop up" sugar prices by purchasing about 400,000 tons of "excess" sugar the industry producers had put up in return for over $850 million in loans. This is a sweet deal for giants such as American Crystal, Amalgamated Sugar, and the US Sugar Corporation, but a sour one for candy and other producers who use sugar as a main ingredient. One CEO of a confectionary company lamented that "the USDA has made up its mind that Big Sugar is going to trump the American consumer" (Wexler, 2013). The National Confectioners Association, whose members include Mars and Hershey, estimated that this program required consumers to pay an extra $2.5 billion in a typical year to provide the sugar industry its support/corporate welfare. Part of the higher sugar price could be attributed to the import and tariff quota imposed against foreign sugar – a policy that increases the price of domestic sugar vis-à-vis foreign sugar, something that is not supposed to occur in the free market economy fiscal conservatives argue should exist.

The congressional debate 2013 which focused on increasing corporate welfare for the agricultural industry while reducing food stamps provided an illustration of the cotton industry nexus power and blatant hypocrisy. Not only has the *cotton* industry been subsidized by about one quarter billion dollars a year, but there is also another $147 million paid to Brazil. That payment is required by the World Trade Organization (WTO) because the

United States, with its many free market economy proponents in Congress, violates the WTO agreement it signed concerning the limit of agricultural subsidies. Thus, taxpayers pay what amounts to corporate welfare to the cotton industry, about 80% of which is collected by the wealthiest cotton farm owners. One member of Congress, Tennessee Representative Stephen Fincher, spouted evangelical verse when arguing against food stamps when he pontificated that "[t]he role of citizens, of Christians, of humanity, is to take care of each other. But not for Washington to steal money from those in the country and give to others in the country" (Collins, 2013). Left out of this sermon was the fact that as of 2013 farmer Fincher had received about $3.5 million in subsidies for his cotton farm operations.

Federal funding for pork producers seems to have no limit, as it actually includes some government funds which could be considered "pork for pork shit." Large hog farms (actually factories when you consider the poor pigs are confined to metal bins so small they cannot turn around) generate an enormous amount of smelly excrement that the EPA rules had to be treated. In response, industry lobbyists proposed that the taxpayers help foot the bill. Congress agreed. Livestock producers could get up to $50,000 for treatment of hog waste – thus having taxpayers pay part of their costs rather than add the price to their products as all industries do if the economy is truly a "free market." The new bill lifted the upper limit for farms (2500 hogs or less) to be eligible for a subsidy and raised the subsidy cost by about six times to over $1 billion. Advocates for "small" hog farms that included some environmental groups called this program "a clear case of corporate welfare" (Lancaster, 2001).

The degree to which the excrement program would be deemed unjustified might have been outdone by the $1.8 million earmarked in the 2009 farm appropriations bill for pig odor research in Iowa – a year in which fiscal responsibility was prominent in Washington DC discourse. One would think that members of Congress, of all people, would know how pork smells. Apparently Iowa Senator Tom Harkin needed more proof. He defended the earmark he proposed when asked to explain on the Senate floor why it was not wasteful spending. Harkin replied that this spending was neither "wasteful" nor "frivolous" because "[p]eople constantly complain, with good reason, about big farms, factory farms and their environmental impacts so it makes good sense to fund research that addresses how people can live in our small towns and communities and livestock producers can do the same and co-exist" (Pelofsky, 2009). Another Senator, Tom Coburn of Oklahoma, who has been an outspoken critic of corporate welfare also seemed to be defending this pork. He took a jab at urban areas, claiming that the odors from farms are "pretty good" when compared to the odors one encounters in urban areas (Pelofsky, 2009). Last I checked there were no major urban areas in either Iowa or Oklahoma, but there remains plenty of eau de swine that Harkin now can better enjoy.

At least the subsidies (corporate welfare for those incorporated) for *racehorse* owners has touch of class compared to what's in the Iowa air. Self-professed fiscal conservative and current Senate Majority Leader Mitch McConnell, who has voted against numerous social program proposals, must have felt it to be his duty as a Kentucky citizen in proposing a tax break for racehorse breeders – few of whom qualify for the social programs McConnell has opposed. In 2008 McConnell introduced into the farm bill a tax break for horse breeders that after being enacted in 2009 provided over $125 million worth of welfare to some of America's richest individuals. In 2014 a provision that retroactively extends three-year tax depreciation for all racehorses was passed by the United States Senate as part of bill H.R. 5771, the Tax Increase Prevention Act of 2014. Naturally the National Thoroughbred Racing Association was grateful to McConnell for providing the welfare that was "so important to horse owners and breeders" (Blood Horse, 2014). Tax savings will be almost $100 million each year. Taxes may have been prevented from increasing, but not the budget deficit or corporate welfare. Democrats had attempted in 2011 to eliminate the "Bluegrass Boondoggle" which McConnell had defended years before as being "an issue of fairness given the limited racing life of many horses" (Dennis, 2011). It would be interesting for McConnell to define what he means by "fairness" given his willingness to muster Senate votes to reduce spending on or to eliminate public health care as well as food stamp programs.

Another recipient of corporate welfare comes in the form of social programs that some low-paid workers in the *fast food* industry receive, and which enable them to maintain a minimum standard of living. Some of their employers, such as McDonald's, have reported multibillion dollar profits in recent years. McDonald's has been found to have encouraged its employees (on its McResource helpline) to whom it pays a low, non-living wage to "sign up for food stamps and other government assistance programs" rather than pay higher wages. Once evidence of this encouragement of its own employees to seek federal funds hit the social media air waves a strong negative public reaction ensued (Walshe, 2013). McDonald's is not alone in having its low-paid employees receive public assistance. A joint study by University of California and Illinois researchers reported that over 50% of families of "front line fast food workers" were enrolled in at least one public assistance program as compared to only 25% of the entire US workforce. The same study estimated that the cost of these subsidies amounted to almost $7 billion annually (Walshe, 2013). Congressional budget conservatives have remained silent about this form of corporate welfare and many refuse to advocate an increase in the minimum wage, which even if it had only been indexed for inflation since its inception in 1968 would be almost $10 per hour, albeit still well below the estimated living wage of about $15 per hour.

Over the years provisions contained in the farm bill and the trading of favors that created some provisions illustrate the workings of the corporate welfare economy. When it was introduced in the 1930s the intent was to assist then struggling poor farmers. However, year by year the bill's provisions "slowly have been altered by agribusiness lobbyists. It is now largely corporate welfare" (Kingsolver, 2007, p. 206). Rather than boost incomes of poor farmers, including those seeking to farm in a more environmentally sustainable manner, corporate welfare and other favorable provisions have contributed to more family farms being taken over by large agribusiness corporations.

Each instance described below typically features significant campaign contributions and the perks received by Washington DC officials provided by lobbyists. In return the largest agribusiness corporations (along with some large individually owned farms) tend to receive about 75% of the federal dollars flowing to agricultural producers – a large portion of which could be considered corporate welfare. An example of favors traded that actually was a double trade involving two political interest groups occurred during 2001. Nexus members included Larry Combest, Head of House Agricultural Committee and cotton former, some of his House colleagues on this committee – among them a hog farmer, a rice farmer who received government subsidies, and another cotton farm owner who received about $75,000 annually in subsidies during the 2001–5 period (Morgan et al., 2006). When this seemingly biased committee finished with the proposed 2001 farm bill it included raising subsidies by $50 billion over the next decade, something George W. Bush said was in opposition to his fiscal conservative discourse. Allegedly Combest and Bush met, with Combest threatening to muster votes against Bush's proposal for greater power for him as president to negotiate trade agreements that Bush's corporate campaign contributors favored unless Bush supported the farm bill. Bush relented. This and other of Combest's many contributions to the cotton industry's own nexus were not overlooked. After he resigned from the House in 2003 he was given the "Harry S. Baker Distinguished Service Award for Cotton for his 'invaluable assistance' [i.e., promoting the flow of corporate welfare] to the U.S. cotton industry" (Morgan et al., 2006).

Another noteworthy trading of favors concerns the agricultural subsidies non-farmers received. While these handouts likely involve little corporate welfare, the generosity of Congress in continuing such payments while threatening to reduce food stamp funding (see below) provides insight into a majority of the members of this legislative body demonstrating the willingness to allocate federal funds without regard to need or adhering to the spirit of federal support for actual farmers. When direct payments were still part of farm bills some owners of farms could receive federal funds even if they neither grew any crops nor lived on a farm, but could be considered "actively engaged" in farming. That would explain why in 2012 over 18,000 people living in the 54 largest US cities collectively received almost $25 million in farm subsidies, and that over 600 recipients of the federal farm subsidies had grown no crops for a decade (Nixon, 2013). The degree to which the program was carefully monitored was called into question when a Government Accountability Office audit discovered $10.6 million had been paid between 2008 and 2012 to farmers who had been deceased for more than one year (*The Economist*, 2014). Finally, in 2015 at the behest of Congress the USDA did make a modest proposal to eliminate some categories of non-farmers (e.g., joint ventures and general partnerships) who would become ineligible to receive some of these handouts. Perhaps owners of these types of businesses fell behind on their campaign contributions. Undoubtedly if this becomes law members of Congress and President Obama will tout it as a "major reform."

Favors are also traded when the *junk food* industry's sales are part of the equation. Health experts openly question whether food stamp recipients, many of whom suffer from diet-related health problems that include obesity, should face restrictions on types of food that can be purchased using food stamps. Lobbyists at the national and state level representing major junk food (and processed food) producers, including Cargill, PepsiCo, Coca-Cola, and Kraft – plus giant retail food sellers such as Wal-Mart, have done their best to forestall any restrictions placed on food stamp purchases besides those existing restrictions that apply to alcohol and some prepared food products (Task, 2012). Not only are profits enhanced for those sellers of popular (among food stamp users) soft drinks and junk foods that have little nutritional value, but health care costs for these users, many of which likely are paid by Medicaid, increase. One health expert familiar with the profits these sellers receive from the food stamp program found that Wal-Mart, among others, has a strong interest in no restrictions on the use of food stamps since it receives "a large fraction of Food Stamp dollars, which contributes 25% to 40% of revenue at select stores" (Task, 2012).

One of the most significant trading of favors occurred in 2014 when the direct subsidy payment program was phased out in favor of other programs such as crop insurance that insured farmers against the loss of crops or income. The new program was trumpeted in Washington DC as being a major farm bill reform. As one reporter observed, rather than providing substantive reform that reduced payments to "well-heeled agribusinesses living off corporate welfare" the insurance program and other post "reform" programs had an effect that "actually locks that support in place through misdirection" (Dayen, 2014). The cost of the "reforms" was estimated to be an additional $7 billion over the following decade unless poor weather required higher payments. An attempt to reduce payments/corporate welfare (so that the wealthiest agribusiness corporations no longer were the beneficiaries of the largest amount of payments/corporate welfare) by requiring that eligibility for crop insurance be restricted to farmers whose income was below $750,000 passed the Senate – but was defeated in the House. A trading of favors followed as Congress was able to provide a smoke screen in the form of announced, highly touted reforms so that corporate welfare could continue to be provided "in a hidden, more politically palatable way, making it more difficult to ever dislodge them" (Dayen, 2014).

What was particularly deceitful to the public was the appearance that crop insurance would begin to be provided by private insurance companies so that when insurance payments occurred it would appear as if they originated from the private sector, but the government would be paying most of the bill. The reality is that the old subsidy program was traded in for a new crop insurance program under which corporate welfare also could be spread to financial institutions providing the crop insurance. The profitability for administering this program has been much higher than one would expect from a financial industry program. The average return was 30% and payments substantial – about $1.3 billion received for their expenses in 2011 (Dayen, 2014). It is a win–win situation for both insurers and farmers since both reap rewards, some of which are in the form of corporate welfare, regardless of actual crop yields.

A typical year will provide guaranteed profits for the insurance companies. Taxpayers meanwhile have spent well over $10 billion in some years to fund over 60% of insurance premiums owed by farmers, while the insurance companies ultimately received over $1 billion in profit. An agricultural policy analyst at the University of Tennessee saw the program for what it appears to be: "What we've got is a money-laundering operation. … It looks like we're doing a free market thing and it's not free market at all" (Lynch, 2013). It is hard to argue with such an assessment of a program fully backed by the government that was designed to generate a 14.5% rate of return for the insurers. To his credit House member Paul Ryan who chaired the House Budget Committee led the attempt to reduce subsidies to farmers who suffer "catastrophic losses" instead of engaging in "crony capitalism" (Lynch, 2013). Ryan must be pleased that there is nothing approximating crony capitalism or a favorable and guaranteed rate of return for needy food stamp recipients.

Part of the favor trading in Congress over the past few years when the farm bill is being debated has been the Republicans' threat to reduce food stamps unless their corporate welfare programs were maintained for agribusiness corporations and the financial industry's crop insurers. Given that choice enough Democrats chose to vote in favor of the proposed farm bills, trading what in effect were cuts in food stamp funding while the benefits to agribusiness, financial, and large retail sellers of food would continue to increase. As of 2015 it was publicized that the "subsidies" contained in the latest farm bill actually were higher than in previous years. One forecast was that the corn and soybean subsidy recipients were likely to receive from the "reform" programs over $4.8 billion in fiscal 2017, over double that paid to eligible recipients producing these two products in 2014 (Rogers, 2015). The amount of corporate welfare from the trading of favors, or congressional "back-scratching" as one true fiscal conservative House member describes it, like the revolving door between industry and Washington DC, continues to accelerate. This certainly has been true in the case of the oil and natural gas industry.

Trading Favors: Energy Industry, Led by Oil and Natural Gas Producers Who Have the Power and Ability to Turn Your Drinking Water Dark

The power of these two segments of the fossil fuel energy industry, particularly the oil industry, has been perpetuated partly because its proponents, including those it employs and its nexus members, plus some of the general public for decades have believed the interests of the industry are "indivisible from the national interest" (Hertsgaard, 2014). Members of Congress are eager to accept and spout as a main part of their discourse reports the oil industry prepares itself on key issues such as the continuation of the subsidies/corporate welfare doled out, climate change denial, the environmental impact of fracking, and support for projects that will receive some federal funds such as the Keystone Pipeline. The extensive power of the oil industry and the power it exerts within its industry nexus led one analyst to describe the United States as a "petro state" (Hertsgaard, 2014) in which oil interests sway debates over those subsidies, climate change, pipelines, and fracking legislation continually in the industry's direction – with corresponding legislation passed to protect the industry and enhance its profitability beyond what it would be without their being channeled corporate welfare. The industry nexus is tight, fueled by the national interest perspective and enormous amounts of lobbying and campaign expenditures. Many a military operation has been fought, typically with very costly, highly undesirable outcomes for taxpayers and the brave members of the military killed or wounded. Through it all the oil industry's power and profits have grown.

The oil industry (as well as natural gas and coal) benefits from a range of tax breaks that include tax exempt bonds to finance some types of projects; the nearly century-old expensing of intangible drilling costs; tax deductions for cleaning up oil spills (from which British Petroleum saved about $10 billion in taxes from its Gulf of Mexico disastrous oil spill and subsequent cleanup costs); generous depletion allowances; and low royalties which are purported to be an "incentive" for extracting oil on federal government property; and state subsidies. Also taking advantage of laws and government policies that generate corporate welfare for themselves are mining companies where public funds have been used to pay for the extensive environmental spillover costs due to some of their production activities. The extent of environmental damage caused by mining, public utility, and chemical firms has been so extensive that "Superfunds" have had to be created to pay for damage in what became abandoned hazardous waste sites – which number over 1500 throughout the United States. While funds to pay these costs come from fines and penalties on those private firms responsible for the hazardous waste, as well as from taxes on crude oil, certain chemicals and private firms, over the past 15 years an increasingly large proportion of funds come from "appropriations from the general fund" paid for by taxpayers (US Government Accountability Office, 2008).

Spillover costs to the environment from mining activities include rendering water supplies and land unsafe for use, increased risk of developing cancer, liver damage, and learning disabilities. The law creating this fund permits the Environmental Protection Agency to clean up hazardous waste sites while requiring those responsible to pay for the cleanup. Unfortunately, some firms ceased to exist long before the damage was found, and thus their owners are free from liability – but not so US taxpayers. The Bunker Hill Mining and Metallurgical Site that extracted lead and zinc from the Coeur d'Alene region of northern Idaho is a prime example of this problem. The Bunker Hill Company operated very profitably from 1885 until it closed in 1982. Although the owners paid for some pollution control processes, they aggressively resisted attempts by government agencies to evaluate the health effects of the mining operation. The EPA has estimated the total cost for cleaning up this 21 square mile Superfund site to be about $1.4 billion. A legal dispute continues as to who ultimately is responsible for paying these costs (Aiken, 1994).

Due to the profitability of the energy industry and that the programs generating the corporate welfare were introduced many decades ago to address potential problems that have long ceased to exist, a succession of US presidents have publicly stated that Congress should eliminate the corporate welfare (although they choose to use terms such as "billions in taxpayer dollars") doled out to the oil and natural gas industry, albeit in vain. Barack Obama considered such a proposal to eliminate about $9 billion of annual subsidies while preparing his 2012 budget proposal to be included in his State of the Union Address. He included one tax break that became law almost 100 years ago. When word got out the response throughout Congress was "little more than a knowing chuckle" that such a proposal had no way of being enacted (Froomkin, 2011). They were correct. As of 2015 estimates are that the amount of "subsidies" received by the oil industry from the federal government exceed $18 billion, up from under $13 billion in 2009 (Sheppard, 2014). In addition, state and local subsidies where a few local officials are also anxious to curry favor with the powerful industry also provided billions, including to Shell Oil which annually receives over $1 billion from such subsidies (Quigley, 2014). Finally, the tax exempt bonds issued at the state and local level averaged about $6 billion per year for the decade ending 2013. This benefit can be considered a subsidy as it reduces interest the oil corporations would have owed the state (Walsh and Story, 2013).

The rate of return reaped by this industry on their lobbying investment would make any financial analyst jealous. A 2011 estimate was that in return for the estimated $200 million the industry spent on lobbying efforts and campaign contributions they received an estimated $4 billion in corporate welfare (Froomkin, 2011). My MBA corporate finance classes at NYU never hinted that such returns were likely, although that was in 1969 before the corporate welfare economy (CWE) had been created by nexuses and an ever-increasing number of Washington DC officials willing to profess fiscal responsibility while creating legislation to guarantee an increased flow of corporate welfare. There has been a significant increase in lobbying and campaign contributions from the oil and natural gas industry – particularly since 2010 (Kretzmann, 2015). Between 1990 and 2014 the oil industry invested over $350 million in presidential and congressional candidates' campaigns, the leading contributors being the Koch brothers and ExxonMobil. To remind lawmakers not to forget its priorities, the industry has invested on average "$140 million a year on Washington lobbying since 2008" (Hertsgaard, 2014). The oil and gas industry has spent an average of almost $400,000 *per day* on lobbying aimed at both members of Congress and government officials (Klein, 2014, p. 149). Some consider this spending to be a form of "bribery" that is part of a "circle of legalized corruption" between the oil and gas (as well as the coal) industry and Washington DC, with the flow of industry spending during federal election cycles steadily increasing. For example, campaign contributions more than doubled from about $34 million for the 2010 federal elections to about $75 million for the 2012 election (Kretzmann, 2015). All estimates are that this record amount will be shattered during the 2016 election cycle.

Much of the spending is routed through the Super Political Action Committees established since 2010. Referred to by one critic as "money laundering machines," a few of these PACs were found to have spent in excess of $220 million on behalf of candidates their supporters enthusiastically endorsed. Not surprising, these few PACs have close connections with the fossil fuel industry from which they receive considerable funding (Kretzmann, 2015). Those members of Congress who receive funds the most from PACs with oil and natural gas industry ties need to either remain silent or deny the existence of climate change or face this financial support being withdrawn in favor of another candidate from their party (mostly Republicans) not ashamed to deny what almost every reputable scientist in the world has recognized.

To the extent that the industry nexus can influence environmental protection legislation to limit the costs energy companies must pay for damage they inflict, their cost savings could be considered a form of subsidy – and, at worst, another type of corporate welfare. Legislation has been enacted at the federal and state levels that substantially limits the responsibility oil, natural gas, and mining companies have to pay for the direct costs to the environment and human health caused by their production, transportation, and refining activities such as oil spills, gas leakages, chemical leaks into the soil, and railroad cars or trucks exploding. Such outcomes are to be expected, and those who take advantage of the energy provided could be charged higher prices or taxed to pay for some of the cleanup. However, corporate welfare can be considered relevant when energy corporations' profits are enhanced by legislation not requiring payment for environmental costs they create treating the environment within which we all live and which our grandchildren will inherit as a "free waste dump" (Klein, 2014, p. 70). The number of incidents in which these costs are created are staggering. For example, in 2012 the number of onshore oil and gas sites for which a spill was recorded exceeded 6000, which averages over 16 spills each day – a "significant increase since 2010" (Klein, 2014, p. 332).

Thanks to the industry nexus' political and economic power, there is little or no liability on energy companies for the massive environmental damage and cleanup costs due to industry activities. Two of the recent cases involving the oil and other industries that are particularly egregious and which clearly illustrate this pattern occurred in New Jersey and North Dakota. In both cases the appearance of corruption is strong. In New Jersey Governor Chris Christie, who is on record as saying during a campaign speech that "the rich are doing fine … the [Republican] party shouldn't cater to the wealthy at the expense of middle-income workers," apparently was only referring to paychecks and not to the natural environment in which those workers live. The environmental damage in this case was done by ExxonMobil. The corporation already had been found liable for massive environmental damages, and a judge was deciding whether or not the corporation should be assessed a fine of $8.9 billion for what experts testifying in court argued were "damages to the state's natural resources, primarily through the destruction of creeks, wetlands and aquatic life" (Campbell, 2015). This was in one respect a test case for a 2014 New Jersey initiative that taxpayers should "be compensated and natural resources restored where major polluters had caused damage" (Campbell, 2015). The state had worked with some large corporations, including Chevron, to work out what appeared to be fair settlements for environmental damages attributable to them in the state.

ExxonMobil's attorneys, however, fought the case for about eight years, but did not offer convincing evidence that the company should not be held liable. Enter Christie. Just becoming involved in this case gave the appearance that he was part of the oil industry nexus given that a Republican Governors group of which he was chairperson had received over $500,000 from ExxonMobil and its employees – donations that were made while the trial for environmental damage was in process. Before a judge issued the final verdict as to whether or not the fine should be $8.9 billion, Christie intervened in the case. According to a highly respected reporter covering the case, "Christie's chief counsel inserted himself into the case, elbowed aside the attorneys general and career employees who had developed and prosecuted the litigation, and cut the deal [a $250 million fine] favorable to Exxon" (Campbell, 2015). Perhaps Christie, not unlike some other 2016 presidential candidates, was making it clear to multibillion dollar corporations (and perhaps billionaires) that if he were to be elected they would have a true friend in the White House.

The North Dakota case involving oil industry corporations such as Halliburton offers indications of an in-state nexus: (1) it enabled some oil industry corporations to acquire leases to drill on land through rewritten rules that violated traditional property rights while reducing compensation property owners ultimately would receive as royalties for oil extracted from their property – then patronizing and insulting affected state residents who raised violation of their property rights objections, reduced property value, and environmental damage detrimental to their health accusations; (2) substantial environmental damages for which there was very little punishment imposed on the offending company; and (3) a legal process that seemed to make a mockery of justice despite there being egregious conflicts of interest as well as every appearance of corruption at the gubernatorial level (Sontag, 2014).[7]

The prominent members of the North Dakota nexus include Halliburton, among other oil industry corporations, Governor Jack Dalrymple, Lynn D. Helms, and former governor and US Department of Agriculture Edward T. Schafer. Dalrymple reportedly has received over $2 million in campaign contributions from the oil industry, of which over $500,000 came from oil-related executives, lawyers, and PACs. He held a "direct interest" in one oil project that paid him over $90,000, and owned oil stock in companies doing business in North Dakota. Someone who knew Dalrymple on a first-name basis told a reporter that "[i]n essence, Jack converted a quasi-public local institution into a personal, one-time profit maker and sold it to a multinational corporation ... I believe he used his public office for private gain" (Sontag, 2014). Helms served simultaneously as the state's director of mineral resources department and also as the chief regulator of the oil industry. Schafer once curried favor from the oil industry in a bus sponsored by the oil industry while on a state tour during which he argued in favor of lower taxes for the oil industry. Although that proposal did not fly, Schafer ascended to a board position for one oil company, the remuneration for which (including shares of stock) was about $700,000 in 2011 (Sontag, 2014).

State residents voice concerns and complaints about the process by which oil companies are granted leases on or near their property, environmental damage due to oil extraction activities (such as having black water due to nearby fracking operations come out of their kitchen sink faucet), or make corruption accusations on the basis of having obtained considerable evidence there were incidents of their being patronized, ignored, or shut out from obtaining a seat in state government.

In return some residents who voiced objections were mocked, being referred to as "pesky folks" while others were "ignored, ridiculed or threatened."[8] A ConocoPhillips official clearly stated the industry intent, claiming that his corporation will be acting "for the common good" once they succeed in "being freed of the artificial boundary lines" under previously existing laws that afforded much more protection to private and community property rights (Sontag, 2014). Even former presidential candidate Mitt Romney got in the act. Perhaps trying to curry favor among multibillion dollar corporations he believed would become contributors to his 2012 presidential campaign Romney openly mocked a prosecutor of a case involving an oil company facing accusations of improper behavior in North Dakota (Sontag, 2014).

The cases of environmental damage due to fracking and other oil extraction methods in North Dakota are numerous and substantial. They include the September 2013 oil spill in Tioga that was the "largest on-land oil spill in recent American history" (Sontag, 2014). Later that year an oil train derailed causing a fiery explosion, and there were subsequent derailments and fires over the next two years (Gallucci, 2015). Other incidents include many birds dying due to oil drilling activities that, when discovered, the driller tried to cover up; damage done by oil filter socks that contained radioactive materials illegally disposed of by the company responsible; and state approval of an oil waste pit that would be located in an area that would threaten the local water supply.

Citizen attempts to protect themselves have met a stone wall amidst conflicts of interest and charges of corruption leveled against elected and appointed officials. North Dakota has no law prohibiting an elected official to both receive campaign contributions from the oil industry while simultaneously holding a position on an oil regulatory commission. Thus, it is not surprising that when oil wells spill toxic pollutants the state's leading officials who regulate the industry tend to not assess fines. As evidence mounted that one of these officials, Governor Jack Dalrymple, "had a corrupt relationship with the oil industry" (Sontag, 2014) it eventually was reported to the FBI. Citizens uncovered that one large oil deal arranged by state officials making lease agreements with landowners was of considerable benefit to industry giants such as ExxonMobil, Marathon Oil, ConocoPhillips, and Continental – all of which had contributed to the governor's re-election campaign. Dalrymple is not alone among governors who receive campaign contributions from industries with business interests in their respective states. However, none of them chair their state's Industrial Commission. The state of North Dakota is an oil industry nexus' dream since an elected official can own stock in a company they are assigned to regulate, and the industry can make contributions to their election campaigns. Citizens sought to bring Dalrymple to trial, using a statute in state law that prohibited officials from receiving "anything of pecuniary value" from any company, or individual, who were involved in a "pending proceeding" (Sontag, 2014). Not surprisingly, a state judge refused to hear the case.

North Dakota is not alone in having an in-state energy industry nexus. Evidence exists that in states with Republican attorneys general a "secretive alliance" has been formed with some energy producers in an attempt to further reduce regulations pertaining to their responsibility to respect environmental quality and the health and property rights of citizens. Of course the favors in return are record amounts of campaign contributions to such friendly attorneys general. Investigations by *New York Times* reporters found that not only in North Dakota, but in other states, the attorneys general has shamelessly "shut down investigations, changed policies or agreed to more corporate-friendly settlement terms after intervention by lobbyists and lawyers, many of whom are also campaign benefactors" (Lipton, 2014B). In Oklahoma a letter was sent to the EPA from state Attorneys General Scott Pruitt contesting EPA findings about air pollution emitted from a natural gas drilling site in the state – a letter written by lawyers representing one of the largest oil and gas companies in Oklahoma, Devon Energy (Lipton, 2014A). This is one more example of how the pursuit of corporate welfare contributes to industry nexus relationships that are incestuous and damaging to nearly all citizens.

The environmental impact of hydraulic fracking will impact far more than the drinking water of North Dakota. Over 15 million Americans live within one mile of a well drilled using this extraction process. Many municipalities throughout Texas, Wyoming, Pennsylvania, among other states are exposed to what scientists have discovered to be toxic water, leading one to wonder how this condition could have arisen given Congress passed the Safe Drinking Water Act in 1974 specifically designed to prevent toxic chemicals from getting into drinking water systems. Citizens should be able to use the legal system as a recourse when their water becomes unsafe to drink. However, enter the oil industry nexus and Congress, plus US presidents not averse to complying with oil industry interests, even at the expense of public health. These political bodies took action that enables the court system to protect oil companies engaged in fracking, thereby saving these firms from paying multibillion dollar fines for environmental damage. It would be difficult to find a more egregious example of the oil industry nexus enhancing its profits through a form of corporate welfare that comes at the expense of Americans' health.

The story begins in 2005 when Vice President Dick Cheney, formerly vice president of Halliburton, formed an energy task force. Halliburton, which had patented the process of hydraulic fracturing decades before, wanted to expand its fracking operations without fear of public opposition. What could reduce their ability to reap more profits was the 1974 Safe Drinking Water Act. Cheney's task force, like so many task forces set up to reach a predetermined conclusion, declared that fracking is a safe process for oil extraction. Congress then passed what became known as the

"Halliburton loophole." Staff members from Halliburton were involved in the EPA review process that contributed to the decision that fracking would not endanger fresh water supplies. The outcome was that Halliburton and other companies engaged in fracking became exempt from the regulations specified in the 1974 Act. They did not have to reveal to the EPA or any municipality the chemicals they used in their fracking operations. Washington DC officials had provided another form of corporate welfare, this time to protect profits earned from "high risk fossil extraction" by providing Halliburton and other oil companies "freedom from fines for polluting water" (Klein, 2014, p. 328).

No such protection, of course, was provided to those who now had their water contaminated. Citizens fought back, trying to protect themselves. The case of Dimock, Pennsylvania, is a sad testimony to the power of the oil industry nexus and willingness of Washington DC elected officials and regulators to be bought off. Dimock residents were suffering health problems from drinking their water which they argued was contaminated due to fracking operations. It was reported that the EPA's investigators had examined Dimock's drinking water and discovered "significant damage to the water quality" which was similar to findings in Pavillion, Wyoming, and Weatherford, Texas (Bacon, 2013). The EPA's finding had been undertaken after a similar conclusion was reached by the Pennsylvania Department of Environmental Protection. No problem for the oil corporations responsible. The EPA ignored the findings and closed their investigation. Rumor has it that the EPA's report was prepared in consultation with officials from the same oil companies doing the fracking. Citizens from Dimock took their case to EPA offices in Washington DC, but were ignored. One resident who joined this group claimed the EPA went on record and told them the water was safe to drink (in a report that came out during the 2012 election year), but then told them off the record they should not drink their water. Someone with enough expertise to understand fracking and how it could potentially affect drinking water could look at the EPA's PowerPoint presentation[10] describing its Dimock study. It would then become clear that there was a link between fracking and water contamination affecting the drinking water (due to higher methane concentrations caused by fracking) and that the EPA, according to whistleblowers within the agency, had political pressure put on it during that election year to cover up this potentially explosive (for the oil industry) finding (Horn, 2013). In the face of mounting evidence that fracking does contaminate drinking water and thus provides a significant health hazard the Congress rejected a proposal to repeal the "Halliburton loophole" in January, 2015.

Each year there is more scientific evidence indicating the damaging environmental effects from energy industry extraction, transportation of the resources extracted, and emissions from use of what is extracted. Meanwhile the "rising tide of climate science and citizen activism" has increased (Kretzmann, 2015). In response the energy industry nexus through Super PACs and individual corporation accounts has used its economic and political power to block or remove environmental legislation that would reduce its profits or have sought to defund environmental agencies that regulate it – while, of course, maintaining the corporate welfare they receive. The industry has learned that the best investment it can make in achieving its goals is to spend more lavishly each year on campaign contributions and lobbying. The favor they get in return from grateful Washington DC and state political officials is to virtually guarantee the industry little or no penalty when one of their extraction or transportation projects results in significant damage to the natural environment or citizens' health. Another favor friendly members of Congress grant is to quash every piece of proposed environmental legislation. Members of Congress who lack the strength and conviction to represent the public interest fear that during the next election campaign a vindictive energy industry will use its muscle to deny them re-election. As one analyst observed, these members of Congress "know for sure that if they try to break with the pack, they will be targeted by this now enormous fossil controlled Death Star of Dollars, and they're not willing to risk it" (Kretzmann, 2015).

Trading Favors: For-Profit Colleges and Universities Where Wall Street Investors Have Learned Much More than Deeply Indebted Students

While much of the profits earned by the typical multibillion dollar agricultural or energy corporation certainly could be considered as well deserved from the products and services they provide in both domestic and international markets (while the rest can be considered corporate welfare), very little of the profits reported by the for-profit colleges and universities can be considered likewise. This multibillion dollar industry seems to receive more corporate welfare as a percentage of the total revenue profits it reports than any other industry. Even worse, much of the education and training these institutions provide has been characterized as a sham, which is not surprising when their mission (profits), the percentages of total spending the typical for-profit devotes to educating students as opposed to recruitment and marketing, the high rates of student attrition and low rates of success in the job market, and the salaries paid to their chief executives as compared to non-profit academic institutions are taken into account.[10] There is a sharp divide between the education provided students in a typical non-profit liberal arts college or major university and that received by the typical student enrolled in a for-profit academic institution. One prominent academic summed up the typical for-profits education academic program as one that provides "stripped down curricula" where a majority of students "are taught online, often by poorly qualified professors who have limited contact with the students," and the outcome of this so-called education is often "nearly worthless degrees" (Etzioni, 2010). Case in point: at the Art Institute of Seattle faculty were encouraged to inflate grades to keep students from failing to enable the for-profit institution "to keep collecting federal aid money" (Hechinger, 2010).[11]

If all of these accusations are correct how have the for-profit colleges and universities been able to achieve such high enrollment rates and generate sufficient revenue to cover their expenses while lavishly rewarding their executives and stockholders? The answer is the combination of recruitment fraud, corporate welfare, and their own nexus which has thwarted legislation from Washington DC that could have ended federal support for these institutions and thereby lessened the student loan crisis and the pervasive anguish suffered by many people who took the bait and enrolled in one of these profit-driven institutions, incurring considerable debt in the process.

Recruitment fraud accusations have been made based upon interviews with current and former students of the for-profit institutions as well as undercover reporters posing as potential students, and a whistleblower who had worked as an admissions supervisor at Education Management Corporation (EDMC), the second largest owner of for-profit education institutions. Each account details the same story. The recruitment tactics used, often on unsuspecting military veterans or poor minorities who unfortunately had been poorly educated in high school, reveal "fraudulent and invasive recruitment tactics" used to lure them into enrolling, and then to put themselves deep into debt. Even some faculty at for-profit institutions have objected to high-pressure marketing to students to take out loans they were unable to afford (Hechinger, 2010).[12] Some of the information such as total cost, quality of education, and previous job placement results and remuneration students who complete some of the training programs were told they could expect to receive was "blatantly misleading" (Garrett, 2010). For example, a representative of a Washington DC program told an undercover reporter posing as an applicant that someone who completed their barber training program would enter a field that paid up to $150,000 to $250,000 per year – information that probably has not yet been received by those working at Super Cuts.

Even more damning was data provided by the whistleblower who went so far as to file a lawsuit that allegedly EDMC's "marketing materials deceived prospective students by falsely inflating job placement statistics at its many campuses around the country" and that EDMC "manipulated the job placement rates by counting students working in a job that they did not need the degree for" (Greenblatt, 2012). The accusation that EDMC's business model was intentionally based upon what represented a "wretched fraud" was concurred with by US Senator Dick Durbin after he reviewed the same data the whistleblower had provided to ABC News.

Durbin concluded "[i]t's just plain fraud. ... These students get sucked in by these ads, sign up for debt, sign up for courses that lead to nowhere" (Greenblatt, 2012). One sad case involved a person who paid $70,000, mostly with student loans, for a degree as a video game designer. A year after the $12 per hour job she finally found was eliminated and the reality of debt and having obtained what the person described as a "worthless degree" set in. She took a job at a topless club in an attempt to earn sufficient income to repay the debt incurred (Hechinger, 2010).

Tuition fees at for-profit institutions tend to exceed those of area community colleges and state universities. One study found that the certificate and associate degree programs for-profits offer (programs which tend to be offered at community colleges) cost about four times as much (*New York Times*, 2012). Consequently, there is a relatively greater need among young people who enroll at the for-profits to incur student loans in addition to Pell Grants. One study found that about 90% of the students attending the for-profit colleges took out a Stafford Loan, and that the amount of debt they had to assume was greater than it would have been had they attended a non-profit academic institution that offered a similar (likely to be of higher quality) degree program (Field, 2010). Other studies indicate that at community colleges nationwide fewer than 15% of students take out loans while at four-year public colleges and universities about half the students do likewise (*New York Times*, 2012).

The combination of poorly prepared young people with a low chance of graduating incurring considerable debt to receive a low-quality degree that is highly unlikely to help them qualify for a job which pays a sufficient income to enable them to repay their debts is a recipe for a high rate of default on students' loans. This is what has occurred. These types of loans cannot be written off if one declares bankruptcy as can some business and real estate loans "even when for-profit schools didn't deliver what they promised and didn't provide an education that would let the borrower get a job that paid enough to pay back the loan" (Stiglitz, 2012). For example, in 2011 about 650,000 students entered into "repayment" of their federal student loans. By 2013 the default rate for the for-profits' students was 44%, while they accounted for only 12% of this group of students. This rate far exceeded default rates from students attending non-profit colleges and universities (Wright and Gallegos, 2014).

Such unfavorable outcomes have stimulated government investigations. No problem for the for-profits. Some aggressively provide information to former students regarding how they can just stay ahead of being considered as having defaulted, including seeking an extension on their loan. While in business Corinthian Colleges, Inc. allegedly passed out certificates to McDonald's to entice some of its students who had been delinquent in making student loan repayments to request that their payments be postponed. The for-profits' objective was to have enough students be considered not having defaulted on loans so that the institutions would avoid any federal financial penalties. Unfortunately, an extended loan only serves to postpone, but not improve, the debt repayment burden. When defaults do occur, it is taxpayers who absorb over 95% of the financial loss, but the for-profits owners wind up making out like bandits. The for-profits retain nearly all the revenue paid to them from what had originated as a federally guaranteed loan, but have no liability when students default on those loans. For example, the University of Phoenix reported one year that its profits were almost $4 billion, and that over 85% of those profits came from the Department of Education – with some having been paid from loans that have a good chance of going into default, or from loans on which there already had been default (Greenblatt, 2012). EDMC reportedly received over 80% of its revenue from federally funded financial aid programs (Hechinger, 2010). The total cost to US taxpayers exceeds $30 billion annually. While taxpayers also foot the bill for loans defaulted by those who attended non-profit academic institutions, there was no profit/corporate welfare reaped by anyone connected to these institutions. A representative example concerns someone who finished a graduate program at the for-profit Argosy University with over $240,000 in student debt. Unable to find a job that will generate sufficient income to repay this debt the person was able to qualify for a taxpayer-funded program that will pay for the portion of the debt that will be forgiven.

The for-profits, however, continue to receive billions in corporate welfare for the substandard education product provided. The for-profit corporate owners continue to have an incentive to encourage their students to assume a heavy loan burden, knowing there is little risk involved to their profitability from high default rates since taxpayers will have to pay when loan defaults occur. Under this business model and aggressive recruiting practices the federal aid provided to those attending the for-profits rose from under $5 billion in 2000 to over $25 billion by 2009 (Hechinger, 2010), while the average profit margin earned by publicly traded companies operating the for-profits was almost 20% for that same year (*New York Times*, 2012). EDMC, of which Goldman Sachs became the biggest stockholder by 2010, was reporting profits that exceeded $2 billion annually a few years ago before it began suffering losses – perhaps due to the considerable adverse information reported about the low probability someone completing their programs would receive a good rate of return on their investment. At their peak value the now defunct Corinthian Colleges, Inc. was valued at around $4 billion (Weise, 2014).

In summary, taxpayers provide billions of dollars, much of which can be considered corporate welfare, to privately owned institutions which purport to offer (but seemingly do not) quality academic programs that typically do not improve graduates' chances of securing a good-paying job – as evident by the much higher student loan default rates and weak job placement results of those who attend a for-profit college as compared to non-profit academic institution rates. The documented reports of recruitment fraud and high default rates that require billions of taxpayer dollars with corporate welfare included would seem to invite serious investigation and subsequent regulation by an increasingly "conservative" Congress outspoken against wasteful spending. Not so. There was a Department of Education proposal in 2012 that included more stringent rules that the for-profits would have had to abide by to justify continuing to receive federal funds. However, "a swarm of industry lobbyists" pressured the department to propose soft revised legislation, and those paying for the lobbyists got the results they wanted (Greenblatt, 2012). Perhaps the bankruptcy case of Corinthian Colleges, Inc. that could cost taxpayers about $200 million to make up for student loan defaults will stimulate some congressional response. Given how beholden many members of Congress have been shown to be towards multibillion dollar corporations seeking to protect the flow of corporate welfare they receive the odds established by a Las Vegas bookie would not be strong in favor of that occurring. The discourse from a strong supporter of multiple nexuses, the *Wall Street Journal*, "falsely blamed the Obama administration" when Corinthian Colleges, Inc. closed its doors in April 2015 (Weise, 2014). This closing occurred after eight years of its being under Department of Education pressure to cease engaging in unacceptable recruiting practices and to disclose more accurate information to the government. Eventually Corinthian was sued by the Consumer Protection Bureau for operating an "illegal predatory lending scheme that lured students with false job promises, saddled them with high-cost debt, then harassed them when they couldn't repay their loans." The *Journal* argued that the federal government was guilty of "choking off federal student aid" (Tone, 2015), while failing to mention that over 80% of Corinthian's revenue in 2014 was in the form of federally funded student aid programs which was about $1.4 billion (Weise, 2014).

Trading Favors: Finance Industry, Where Millions of Campaign and Lobbying Dollars Buys You Billions of Corporate Welfare

Even Charles Koch, one of the billionaire conglomerate owners and ALEC leader, has publicly called for ending corporate welfare for "big banks," referring to them as being "among the greatest proponents of corporate welfare" (Mider, 2015). Koch failed to mention where oil industry corporations rank on the corporate welfare recipient list. Looking back at the 2008 financial crisis and the aftermath we can learn a few things regarding how and why so much corporate welfare flowed to the industry. The finance industry nexus features substantial campaign contributions and lobbying expenditures, plus the possibility for lucrative employment opportunities – particularly for federal government officials responsible for recommending policies and regulations and the enforcement of those regulations. As the investment banks have gained control over trillions of dollars and more members of Congress are willing to be influenced by those able to finance their campaigns substantially a recipe for corruption and capturing of regulators has been created. When the finance industry appears guilty of criminal behavior or pursuing practices that once again put the banking system in a precarious position those in Washington DC with strong ties to the industry look away. One revealing instance occurred in the wake of the 2008 financial crisis. Two chief executive officers of supreme nexus member Goldman Sachs were required to testify before Congress. After public accusations were made by critics that the information they provided was misleading at best, and false at worst, there were no consequences faced by either Goldman Sachs or the officers who testified (Blodget, 2011). It is as if some Washington DC officials have become paid employees of Wall Street banks with the banks controlling the laws to which they are subject, feeling confident that they would be bailed out should they once again create another financial crisis as they did in 1987 (Savings and Loan crisis) and 2008. Knowing that many voters are aware of this Barack Obama campaigned using the slogan "Main Street, not Wall Street" which resonated widely. Then after assuming office he surrounded himself with Wall Street insiders and approved the bailout scheme so favorable to banks. The more than $25 million he received in campaign contributions for the 2008 election seemed to outweigh his campaign rhetoric.

The Dodd–Frank law passed in 2010 that purported to require the Wall Street banks to modify practices in order to substantially reduce the chances of another finance industry meltdown not surprisingly has had only a modest impact. Within a year extensive lobbying and campaign contributions "merely reinforced the longstanding cozy relationships" within the nexus and nearly every Republican member of Congress. Even worse, "Wall Street's lobbyists and executives ... [kept] busy cozying up to regulators at the Securities and Exchange Commission, the Federal Reserve, the Federal Deposit Insurance Corporation and others to make sure the regulations still being written in the wake of Dodd–Frank come out just the way they want them" (Cohan, 2011). It would not take long before this bill would be watered down so that modified practices on Wall Street not unlike those leading to the 2008 crisis would emerge, with new financial regulations sanctioning these practices.

One reason the new regulations were so friendly to the finance industry is that Wall Street institutions and their lobbyists were essentially writing the bills, while overall lobbying expenditures were nearly double those of previous years. In 2013 it was discovered that the House Financial Services Committee approved "over the objections of the Treasury Department" an 85-line bill of which 70 lines included recommendations provided by Citigroup which was "in conjunction" with the position of other Wall Street banks (Lipton and Protess, 2013). An examination of the relationship between how members of Congress voted on the new finance industry legislation revealed that those voting in favor received about double the campaign contributions received by those voting against the watered-down regulations. In passing this bill, a critic from the Americans for Financial Reform argued, Congress "restores the public subsidy to exotic Wall Street activities" (Lipton and Protess, 2013).[13]

There is a history of lax regulation of finance industry practices, low fines Wall Street firms have been required to pay relative to the profits they earn from practices that proved so costly to nearly all Americans and to the federal budget, and virtually no cases of the chief officers of these financial giants being found guilty and required to serve time in prison over the past few decades. This should not be surprising, since for years members of Congress and their staffers felt entitled to play by a different set of rules when engaging in stock market transactions than all other citizens. In 2011 a study published in the *Journal of Business and Politics* revealed that some members of Congress apparently had been engaged in insider trading, based upon a comparison of the rates of return they made trading stocks as compared to the rate earned by the average investor. For example, between 1985 and 2001 House members made almost 7% more than the average. Senators also did better than the market average return. The journal concluded that these congressional members "were almost certainly relying on insider information to fatten their stock portfolios. ... This is corruption, pure and simple" (LiveLeak, 2011). Apparently, trading of favors within the nexus extended to trading of stocks by some congressional members based upon insider information. This stands in sharp contrast to the 2004 case involving Martha Stewart who was convicted and sentenced to five years in jail for engaging in insider trading activities, and what penalty the rest of the American public would be subject to if found guilty of insider trading; no one in Congress has been punished for similar activities.

Later that year a bipartisan ethics bill being considered that would ban the practice of insider trading was facing opposition among House Republican leaders. After a *60 Minutes* report on the alleged insider trading activities of some congressional members and members of their staff, including the infamous Spencer Bachus who chaired the Financial Services Committee, an "explicit ban" on such trading was passed (*New York Times*, 2011A). The following year (2012) the Senate passed the Stop Trading on Congressional Knowledge (STOCK) Act which became law. A year later the appetite in Congress to improve the stock portfolio rate of return for their staff members stimulated passage of a new law that would ease the ban against their staffers lest they be reduced to earning a rate of return comparable to that earned by the average American investor. The STOCK Act had strong and relatively transparent disclosure requirements (e.g., posting trades online) so that data was easily searchable, sortable, and could be downloaded on one's computer quickly, thus enabling someone to easily monitor and detect if insider trading activity was practiced by any member of Congress or their staff. The new law eliminates disclosure requirements for congressional staffers (Carney, 2013), although members of Congress and the executive branch are still subject to the STOCK Act – one assumes to emphasize their dedication to public service.

Even when there is guilt beyond a doubt of criminal behavior by the largest financial institutions the worst penalty they face is a fine that is a minimal percentage of the profits they earned from the illegal activity. In such cases, no high-ranking bank officers have been punished. When evidence that nexus members at the Federal Reserve Bank were complicit in being aware of the wrongdoing and taking no action there were no subsequent penalties imposed on anyone at the Fed with knowledge of the situation. The Libor case in which banks manipulated a key interest rate before the 2008 financial crisis illustrates this point. There were over ten banks involved, including two Wall Street giants – JPMorgan and Citigroup. The scandal ultimately cost five of these banks, including the two Wall Street banks, a collective fine of $5.6 billion for "breathtaking misconduct" and a conspiracy among these banks that was of "breathtaking flagrancy," but no penalties were imposed on bank officials nor were any other bank practices required to be changed (Viswanatha, 2015). The investigation also focused on regulators, particularly the Federal Reserve Bank of New York, as to whether they were aware of the illegal activity, for if so they were complicit in permitting these banks "to report false rates in the run–up to the 2008 financial crisis and afterward" (Protess and Scott, 2012). It turned out that internal documents within the New York Fed reveal it was aware that these banks were manipulating the rates. At the time key nexus member Timothy Geithner was chief of the New York Fed. The documents indicated the existence of a very "cozy" relationship between the New York Federal Reserve bank officials and some other regulators that resulted in their "looking the other way in order to spare the banks too much pain at a time when the financial crisis was still brewing. Even worse, the Fed chose not to take any actions it had the authority to do even after becoming aware in 2007 that banks were lying about their borrowing costs when setting Libor" (Gongloff, 2012). None of this, of course, prevented Geithner from being appointed Secretary of the Treasury in 2009.

A case such as this emphasizes the need for a strong consumer watchdog to monitor the finance industry. The Dodd–Frank reform bill included creation of such an agency, the Consumer Financial Protection Bureau. It was charged with protecting consumers from illegal financial industry practices, and was given jurisdiction over virtually all financial institutions in the United States. By 2013, when finance industry lobbyists were unable to sway the Bureau to see things their way Republican members of Congress sought to shut down what would appear to anyone familiar with finance industry illegal and reckless practices to be a vitally needed institution to protect us from a repeat of the 2008 financial crisis. The

Republicans used a "backdoor" method, the filibuster tactic, to delay the appointment of the Bureau director (*New York Times*, 2013D). Ultimately their efforts failed, and Richard Cordray became the Bureau's first director. The attempt to reduce the ability of a federal agency to monitor the finance industry attests to the power of the nexus and trading of favors that benefits its members – with the assistance of many friends in Congress, but at the cost of the effects resulting from future abuses caused by the finance industry through their economic and political power.

Firms responsible for rating Wall Street products also were investigated after the 2008 financial crisis and were found guilty of civil fraud for the inflated credit ratings they gave to nearly worthless mortgage investments in the run–up to 2008. Of course, there was strong evidence of a cozy relationship between the ratings agency and the banks whose products it rated. After being found guilty Standard & Poor's began negotiating a settlement with the Justice Department which was demanding a fine of over $1 billion to settle the case (Protess, 2014). No Standard & Poor's official faced any criminal charges. This settlement procedure was similar to lawsuits against Wall Street investment banks that led JPMorgan and Bank of America to pay fines of $13 billion and $16 billion, respectively. As with previous settlements concerning those responsible for the 2008 financial crisis immunity was provided to bank officials, so that by mid-2015 no leading Wall Street official has faced any criminal charges for their part in the ratings scam (Protess, 2014). During 2014 the Justice Department decided to reopen cases in which settlements had been reached with some Wall Street banks and consulting firms, including those involved in the Libor case. The department found guilty and fined some of them for engaging in illegal practices after more evidence was discovered. The pattern of banks resuming similar practices to those for which they had been found guilty is at the heart of accusations of repeat offenses. Research by a law school professor revealed a pattern of repeat offenses by some of the nation's largest banks. However, "[t]op executives are not expected to land in prison, nor are any problem banks in jeopardy of shutting down" (Protess and Silver-Greenberg, 2014).[14]

During 2015 the same large banks already found guilty in the Libor case pleaded guilty to having committed a felony by engaging in a conspiracy to rig exchange rates. The banks were placed on "corporate probation" and the fine was increased to about $9 billion, which must be compared to the estimated revenue of $85 billion revenue the banks collectively received from the 2007–13 period in question from their foreign exchange dealings (*New York Times*, 2015B). No bank officers will face criminal charges. When the fine is compared to the revenue the criminal activity generated and the virtual immunity bank officials have from personally having to face criminal charges and the possibility of a jail sentence (where are you, Martha Stewart?) the likelihood of this conviction and penalties imposed being a deterrent to repeat offenses in the future is equal to the probability of a resolution uttered by a drunken person at a New Year's Eve party being kept.

The dollar value reaped by individuals from a tax break which benefits only the owners of hedge funds, as well as private equity, venture capital, and real estate firms, may be the single most lucrative favor granted to any individual from all of the favors traded among members of the finance industry or to any other industry nexus member. In 2014 the average pay, including the base salary and a bonus, for a hedge fund manager at funds that managed in excess of $4 billion was about $2.4 million. Among all those eligible for a special tax break nearly 70% are in the upper 1% of income earners (Harjani, 2014). The discourse that generates this tax break that costs the federal treasury between $11 billion and $13 billion annually in forsaken tax revenue is considering income these individuals receive as "carried interest" subject only to the 20% capital gains tax rate versus the 39.6% rate an individual who earned over $400,000 would be required to pay (de Rothschild, 2013). Since 2007 some congressional members have attempted to eliminate this break by requiring that carried interest be considered as ordinary income. Naturally a massive lobbying effort was launched by the same firms whose officers benefit greatly from the tax break. They have been successful in persuading friendly members of their nexus and others in Congress to reject each of a series of similar proposals designed to eliminate their personal corporate welfare.

It is in keeping with the theme of this book that financial reform designed to prevent the abuse of the economic and political power held by Wall Street banks was heavily influenced by former Senator Christopher Dodd. He chaired the Senate Banking Committee responsible for the legislation that would provide federal support to the failing real estate industry after the 2008 crisis. It was revealed that Dodd received a mortgage from Countrywide Mortgage, a company at the center of the real estate industry scandals, that required Dodd to pay no fees and a lower interest rate on a home he refinanced (*New York Times*, 2008). The nexus had the right person in the right place to prepare a reform bill.

By 2013 aggressive lobbying by the five Wall Street banks[15] that control over 90% of the risky derivative contracts and their main lobbying group, Securities Industry and Financial Markets Association, had succeeded in convincing federal regulators to relax a new rule that required making public all derivatives contracts. The intention was to make transactions more transparent to regulators so as to lessen the chances for a repeat financial crisis and calls for billions in bailout dollars. The chair of the Commodities Future Trading Commission argued that modifying the rule would mean that derivatives trading was no longer going to be a "closed, dark market," but consumer advocacy groups such as Americans for Financial Reform disagreed (Protess, 2013). The criticism was that softening the rule would enable the banks to return to engaging in derivatives trades using practices not unlike those that were used and blamed for contributing to the 2008 crisis. The president of this consumer advocacy group argued that "[t]he banks have all these ways to reverse the rules behind the scenes" (Protess, 2013). After the chair of the Commodities Future Trading Commission at that time stepped down, among those considered to become his successor was a former Goldman Sachs employee.[16]

More lobbying pressure encouraged Congress to continue gradually to eliminate key provisions of the Dodd–Frank bill, thereby enabling the Wall Street banks to resume highly profitable and highly risky practices. The finance industry's friends in Congress echoed Wall Street's lobbying rhetoric as they expertly controlled the discourse throughout the process. The first part of the strategy was to have Congress repeal Section 716 of the bill intended to "regulate the most exotic and custom derivatives," particularly custom credit default swaps which have been cited as a prime cause of the 2008 financial crisis (Konczal, 2014). The rule prohibits banks receiving federal insurance through the Federal Deposit Insurance Corporation from trading the riskiest and most volatile types of derivatives. Otherwise federal funds, which in this case would be a form of corporate welfare, are at risk to bail out these banks should the derivatives market collapse. Section 716 would require the riskiest derivatives trade to behave according to the discipline of market rules without a guarantee of taxpayer money subsidizing huge losses incurred by the banks engaging in these trades. According to Nobel Prize winning economist Joseph Stiglitz this provision would achieve this intent: "[b]y quarantining highly risky swaps trading from banking altogether, federally insured deposits (and our basic payments mechanism) will not be put at risk by toxic swaps transactions" (Konzcal, 2014). Despite the arguments presented in favor of requiring investment banks to pay for all their losses should the derivatives market collapse the finance industry nexus ultimately influenced Congress to give them an early "Christmas present" in December 2014 when it eliminated Section 716 of the Dodd–Frank bill (Dayen, 2014).

The rolling back of these key Dodd–Frank provisions was inserted at end of the 2014 session into the Fiscal Year 2015 Omnibus Appropriations Bill under a Republican threat to not pass the entire budget bill and thus shut down the government unless their special interests that included the finance industry were satisfied. JPMorgan CEO Jamie Dimon allegedly made last-minute personal phone calls to some members of Congress urging them to support the spending bill that included the provisions to weaken Wall Street regulations. The Christmas present was actually a trade highly favorable to those who supported the rollback. Included in the bill was a rider that permitted more campaign contributions to be made to national political parties. No congressional Democrat or Republicans would admit to being responsible for inserting the provision.

Still not satisfied with its ability to pursue even greater profits with public finances and painful costs that would ensue if another recession were precipitated by trades of risky, lightly regulated financial instruments Wall Street pushed to extend the deadline to 2017 for ending trades involving collateralized loan obligations – "a type of debt security made up of several high-risk commercial loans, which have been bundled together and sliced into tiny, bit-size pieces for sale to investors" (Sanati, 2014). This time the Wall Street banks lobbied the Federal Reserve to give them an extension so as to reduce their possibly incurring losses were they required to comply with the initial 2015 deadline. Two of the five major banks were granted an extension, while three others who already had received the extension requested a further extension to 2019 (Johnson, 2015). Step by step the practices of the finance industry were returning to the pre-2008 practices, backed by federal insurance and sanctioned by Congress and the Federal Reserve. One critic lamented about a return to the same type of "[g]reed, stupidity, and slack government oversight [that] fueled the mortgage bubble. The same thing seems to be happening today, but this time with leveraged loans and junk bonds" (Sanati, 2014).

Analysts and critics reacted to the continual rollback of financial industry reform provisions designed to require Wall Street banks to incur losses if their risky ventures went awry rather than be propped up again by taxpayer subsidies. *Yahoo Finance* editor-in-chief, Aaron Task, provided an accurate assessment of what some consider to be the institutionalized corruption within the finance industry nexus. "This is exactly what Wall Street wanted and, as often is the case, what Wall Street wants, Wall Street gets from Congress" (Campione, 2014). Harsh critics such as Senator Elizabeth Warren stood on the Senate floor and asked her colleagues whether or not Congress "work[s] for the millionaires, the billionaires, the giant companies with their armies of lobbyists and lawyers? Or does it work for all of us?" (Campione, 2014). Simon Johnson, former Chief Economist of the International Monetary Fund, maintained that the discourse used by House Republicans that the rollback would create jobs and fix some technical issues was a smoke screen. He argued that "they are determined to strip away all meaningful restrictions imposed on Citigroup, JP Morgan Chase, and other megabanks – and to roll-back Dodd–Frank as far as possible, until it becomes meaningless or they are finally able to repeal it completely" (Johnson, 2015). Nobel Prize-winning economist Paul Krugman offered a more harsh assessment of Wall Street's finance industry giants. "The Masters of the Universe, it turns out, are a bunch of whiners. But they're whiners with war chests, and now they've bought themselves a Congress," particularly Republicans in whom they "invested heavily" – with the outcome not being "about free-market economics; it's pure crony capitalism" (Krugman, 2014E).

In early 2015 the House of Representatives set about reducing more regulatory measures targeted to reduce negative economic effects from risky finance industry practices. This time the focus was placing more restrictions on federal agencies charged with protecting the public from industry abuses, including the recently established Consumer Financial Protection Bureau. The House also went after the Dodd–Frank bill by introducing a bill designed to slow the rate of enforcement of some requirements placed on the finance industry. Those opposed admitted that they were "badly outgunned by an army of Wall Street lobbyists, and complained that the Obama administration has been too weak in its response" (Weisman and Lipton, 2015). Outgunned in Washington DC refers to money, as Wall Street was reported to have spent about $1.2 billion for lobbying and campaign contributions, with key nexus member Jeb Hensarling who chairs the House Financial Services Committee receiving donations from "political action committees run by Bank of America, Citigroup, Goldman Sachs and JPMorgan Chase" (Weisman and Lipton, 2015). One could conclude with confidence that the finance industry will invest even more heavily in the 2016 presidential election campaign to elect a Republican who will be expected to reward his generous supporters by repealing Dodd–Frank that will generate even more corporate welfare for the industry. This nexus activity could be described using a line uttered by Kevin Costner in the movie *Dances with Wolves* when he swapped his army jacket with a Lakota Sioux for his ceremonial vest – "this is a good trade" (of favors), although the social values traded in the movie differ dramatically from the favors traded within the finance industry nexus.

Professional Sports

In this highly visible and rapidly growing industry the doling out of corporate welfare received by team owners, some of whom are billionaires, is easier to identify than what accrues to major corporations in other industries. However, in specific cases when the issue is of city or state subsidies (corporate welfare) to subsidize new construction or renovation of the facility in which the local professional team plays its games rarely will there be a referendum held so that the public can demonstrate their willingness to pay the extra taxes required. Sleight of hand methods are used to circumvent the public, or even the budget process, so as to impose a tax burden on city, county, and perhaps state residents that will translate into greater profits for the team owners, especially if they choose to sell the team. In addition, teams receive corporate welfare in other forms, including tax breaks. A Forbes study estimated that between 1986 and 2012 US taxpayer subsidies to holders of municipal bonds sold to finance "sports structures" cost about $4 billion (Kuriloff and Preston, 2012). The imposition of higher taxes and federal[17] and local tax breaks that generate the corporate welfare occurs within a nexus that typically includes the commissioner of the local team's professional league, team owners, the local mayor and city legislative body, and occasionally the state governor and state legislative body. In addition, since the professional sports industries (particularly Major League Baseball) have enjoyed unusual privileges not granted to any other industries due to special antitrust treatment that has to different degrees over the years treated professional sports more as a game than as a profit oriented business, Congress on occasion has joined the nexus.

Today, however, all professional sports except for baseball face the same legal rules as any other business. Individual teams are subject to being taxed on their earnings. There are some exceptions permitted concerning tax obligations, labor contracts, drafting of players, and open cooperation in the interest of enhancing competitiveness among teams. In 2015 the NFL league office dropped its tax exempt status, which means that it will be required to pay an estimated $10 million taxes on the more than $325 million in revenues it received. Oddly enough one spokesperson for the NFL told a *Washington Post* reporter that the NFL office "has always been a non-profit because it does not engage in income-producing or profit-making activity" (Harwell and Hobson, 2015). This is a fascinating testimony considering the league president earns over $40 million annually and it is predicted that the expected combination of annual revenue the NFL receives from television contracts, sponsors, ticket and apparel sales, among other income generators will be $25 billion by the year 2027 (Ejiochi, 2014). The commissioner did not predict what percentage of that estimated amount this non-profit could expect to earn in the form of corporate welfare.

The economic rationale in cost–benefit studies that purport to demonstrate that construction of a new sports arena or stadium will "pay for itself" has been proven false in virtually every case study since the late 1990s, with taxpayers making up the difference.[18] Assumptions are made that overstate benefits while costs, including the opportunity cost of using the land on which the new facility is constructed for another income and tax-generating purpose, are either downplayed or ignored. The "feel-good" ego gratification benefit of having a local sports team undoubtedly exists, but is difficult to quantify. The issue is that some profits received by private owners of teams have come at the expense of diverting public funds that could fill far more pressing needs in cities than does the corporate welfare for what are in some cases billionaire owners. Fans attending the games that derive much of this benefit could be asked to pay higher ticket prices rather than requiring all residents to pay the costs – as is the case for virtually any private business. Only in cases where a significant number of fans from outside the local area choose to spend their money attending games, versus spending by local fans who can be assumed to spend their entertainment budget on another source of entertainment if there were no local professional team – making the net economic effect of spending on the sporting event not greater than what otherwise would occur without a local professional team. Further, studies also find that despite claims to the contrary typically "sports facilities attract neither tourists nor new industry" (Zimbalist and Noll, 1997). What the new facilities do generate is significant corporate welfare for the owners, particularly if they choose to sell the team for a price enhanced by having the new facility complete with luxury boxes to offer as an income-generating asset for the new owners. A Cato Institute study best sums up the many findings as to the likely economic impact to a community from construction of a new professional sports arena. According to its authors, "our conclusion, and that of nearly all academic economists studying this issue, is that professional sports generally have little, if any, positive effect on a city's economy. The net economic impact of professional sports in Washington, D.C., and the 36 other cities that hosted professional sports teams over nearly 30 years, was a reduction in real per capita income over the entire metropolitan area" (Coates and Humphreys, 2004).

The power of professional sports team owners to obtain corporate welfare was given its fullest expression in Cleveland, a city with a poverty rate in excess of 35%. The billionaire owners of the Browns, Cavaliers, and Indians jointly proposed a "sin tax" on Cuyahoga County residents for purchases of cigarettes, beer, and liquor. County residents voted in favor of the referendum, while the poorer city residents voted to reject it. The measure passed. Estimated revenue from these taxes will exceed $250 million over the next 20 years and will be invested in the three sports facilities used by billionaires' teams. That amount is on top of the $800 million in public funds already having been spent on these facilities. Technically the facilities are publicly owned, but if that were literally the case how does one explain that the naming rights to the stadiums were sold by the Browns for $100 million, the Indians for $58 million, and for an undisclosed amount paid to the Cavaliers for naming rights to their arena (Powell, 2015A)? The city of Cleveland did not receive any share of this revenue.

To bully Cleveland into adopting the sin tax instead of passing a proposal that would have placed a $3 surcharge on each ticket purchased to see the three teams play the owners launched a $3 million lobbying campaign touting the need to "Keep Cleveland Strong" and not to impose the surcharge because that would adversely affect the ability of the average fan to attend a game. Not mentioned in that discourse was the Cavaliers' intention (that later was carried out) to raise their ticket prices 15% for the 2015–16 season. Assuming the tickets cost over $20 the average Cavaliers fan, of course, will now be worse off. Still not satisfied the Cavaliers want more local funds for renovating their arena. Nexus leader Adam Silver, commissioner of the NBA who lends the weight of the league office when billionaire owners seek to extract corporate welfare from cities, offered a carrot by promising that "the league would love to have the All-Star Game in Cleveland" (Powell, 2015). The implication, of course, is that it would be possible only if Cleveland residents would provide even more corporate welfare for the Cavaliers' billionaire owner. Since the cheapest seat at the 2015 NBA All-Star Game exceeded $1300 the Cavaliers' owner might believe it was a good thing that Cleveland Cavaliers fans will not be required to suffer further by having to pay another $3 per ticket surcharge if they wish to see the NBA's finest should Cleveland host the all-star game.

The NBA has hurled threats at cities to either provide public funds for a new arena or face the consequence of their team moving to another city. In 2007 former commissioner David Stern arrogantly warned Seattle that if the SuperSonics relocated because Seattle would not comply with the team's demand for public funding of a new arena, then "there's not going to be another team there, not in any conceivable future plan that I could envision" (ESPN, 2007). Much to its credit Seattle refused to be bullied and the team relocated to Oklahoma City. After deciding to make the move the team's owner stated he was going to "begin a comprehensive discussion with the city and business leaders and understand exactly what the relationship will be" (ESPN, 2007). Of course, relationship in this case served as a euphemism for how much corporate welfare will be given at taxpayer expense to cover some of his basketball team's expenses, and not what it means on the "Dating Game."

Another nice relationship is the one between the owner of the New York Knicks and New York City. The Knicks play in Madison Square Garden which was described in 2007 as a "palace of a feudal state, and its lords fly the flag of entitlement" (Dwyer, 2007). The team's billionaire owner, James Dolan, pays no property taxes for his team's use of Madison Square Garden while the electricity rates are kept low courtesy of subsidies paid for by other users of city electricity. Eight years later Dolan, who along with some family members, still owned Cablevision that Forbes estimated to be worth almost $5 billion, received a property tax exemption for the New York Knicks estimated to be worth $54 million (Powell, 2015B). For Dolan, however, his tax exemption almost makes him look a food stamp recipient when compared to the corporate welfare handed to Steve Ballmer. During 2015, which could be called "The Year of Tax Exemptions for NBA Owners," Ballmer paid $2 billion of his estimated $21+ billion fortune for the Los Angeles Clippers, but then received a "goodwill tax exemption" which sports teams are eligible to receive. This exemption could amount to a $1 billion federal income tax break over the next 15 years (Udland, 2014). Now there's a good relationship.

While the Knicks are a woeful team and the Los Angeles Clippers have always fallen short of expectations, the San Francisco Warriors were NBA champions in 2015. Team owners plan to build a new arena that will be part of the surrounding economic development project. In keeping with NBA tradition it might be expected that the owners would attempt to secure some form of corporate welfare for the project. Not so. There will be no public subsidy. It is a sad testimony to the pervasive doling out of corporate welfare to professional sports team owners when this project aptly was described as an investment that was "unusual in the world of sports finance; the Warriors say it's unprecedented for an NBA franchise" (Walker, 2014). Unusual may be an understatement as illustrated by the findings from a study done by a University of Michigan professor concerning how one-sided the public–professional team owners relationship has become. She discovered "that the average public–private partnership has worked out to cost cities 78% and teams 22%. In 2010, she found, 121 professional sports facilities in use for all five major sports leagues required $43 billion in investments in new construction or major renovations. About half of that investment came from the public" (Walker, 2014). Those seem to be bad relationships.

Unfortunately for Milwaukee County taxpayers the Warriors' exemplary behavior was not contagious, as demonstrated by the nice relationship new billionaire owners of the Milwaukee Bucks was able to establish with Governor Scott Walker, the Wisconsin State Legislature and Milwaukee officials. During a year when the state budget included a $250 million cut from the University of Wisconsin, widely recognized to be one of the world's top 25 research universities, a comparable increase in taxes of about $400 million, including interest over the 20-year life of the payments, was required of city and state taxpayers to pay for the bonds. Proponents ignored research done by local professors that supported many previous findings that sports arenas funded publicly have not proven to positively affect the local economy (Walker, 2013). This extra tax burden will strain the budget of a city with many pressing social and economic issues. To gather public support the new Milwaukee arena proposal was part of a grandiose downtown development plan presented with great fanfare, with no mention in the discourse of research findings by a prominent sports economist that includes some case studies demonstrating that "professional sports have been historically unreliable when it comes to promises to make such local development investments" (Walker, 2013). The irony of this situation is that Governor and 2016 presidential candidate and self-professed fiscal conservative Walker has pledged not to raise taxes, but somewhere in that pledge the fine print must not have included unless doing so would provide some corporate welfare to billionaires (who potentially provide major campaign funding to presidential aspirants such as Walker). He declared the arena deal to be a "high priority" item.

After the deal was approved according to the new owners' terms and backed by the muscle power and threats to move the team provided by the NBA more facts were revealed, including how extensive was the trading of favors. The cost of the corporate welfare to the public was revised upwards to $500 million. The Bucks' owners had traded favors by giving shares in the team to leaders of the local African-American community and "prominent Wisconsin Businessmen and Republicans, including the developer John Hammes" who happens to be presidential aspirant Walker's national finance co-chair, and who has ties to a political action committee that has contributed $150,000 to Walker's campaign (Powell, 2015C). Most of the negotiations between the team and government officials were behind closed doors, with calls for a public referendum in Milwaukee County dismissed by Milwaukee business people who have shares in the team for not being practical. The local African-American business leaders given shares in the team reportedly pressured African Americans in the local government to support the corporate welfare deal. The deal included more favors, or "gift-giving" as one reporter described it, that included the sale of 10 acres of downtown publicly owned land to the developer of the arena-entertainment grand project for the price of $1; a parking garage that will cost the city of Milwaukee $35 million from which the Bucks' owners receive 50% of the revenue; and, as did the Cleveland sports teams' billionaires, the Bucks' owners receive all the revenue paid for naming rights for the new palace – estimated to be worth over $100 million (Powell, 2015C). The greed of the Bucks' owners stands in sharp contrast to NBA superstar LeBron James's sense of civic patrimony. Through the LeBron James Family Foundation, James, with the help of some private business firms, will donate over $40 million to provide a free college education to more than 1000 students to attend his hometown's Akron University.

One last part of the Milwaukee Bucks' deal is that the owners, in refusing to commit to keep the Bucks in Milwaukee for the 30 years for which they leased the arena, did agree to pay what could be about $175 million to cover some of the arena construction cost if they sold the Bucks to billionaires who chose to move the team to another city willing to pay corporate welfare for an even more lavish arena. Someone calculated that given the current market price of the NBA and the worldwide growing popularity of the sport the $175 million payment to the city would be a modest percentage of the profits the hedge fund managers would reap were they to sell the team for what likely would be well over $1 billion now that the new arena with parking lot revenue, etc. was part of the deal. Of course the new billionaire owners could then relocate the team in their own quest for more corporate welfare. That deal almost certainly would occur without any public referendum in the to-be-named city as to whether or not public funds should be doled out to billionaire sports team owners instead of for the pressing local needs Milwaukee currently has that include rebuilding decaying infrastructure and buildings whose foundations are eroding from water damage, improving recreation areas in need of repair, among many other needs in the inner city.

To the extent that expenditures are statements of priorities taxpayers providing billions of subsidy (corporate welfare) to NFL teams would classify as a top priority in cities across the United States. One stadium finance expert who has analyzed financing of professional sports stadiums for the past 15 years stated, "I still cannot believe cities and states are lined up begging to give money to these very profitable [teams]" (CNN Money, 2015). Not only does the University of Phoenix receive billions in corporate welfare from its for-profit education programs, but it also received about $300 million in taxpayer money to help fund construction of its University of Phoenix Stadium. Corporate welfare for stadium construction also has been doled out to the Dallas Cowboys. As of 2015 the franchise is estimated by Forbes to be worth about $4 billion, making it (along with the New York Yankees) the professional sports industry's wealthiest franchise (Ozanian, 2014). The year after a new stadium was built the franchise's value rose 12%, thanks in part to its new stadium some of which was funded by tax-free funds borrowed from the City of Arlington. Forbes referred to the new Cowboys Stadium as a "gold mine" (Kuriloff and Preston, 2012). It should be noted that the corporate welfare received in various forms by the Dallas Cowboys stands in sharp contrast to the New York's MetLife Stadium, the most expensive sports stadium ever constructed, which the Giants and Jets jointly built with no taxpayer subsidies.

A case that exemplifies every theme of this book occurred in Minneapolis where a broad nexus employed the same tactics adopted by other professional team owners to secure funding for a lavish new place to play their team's games. Minnesotans had demonstrated their lack of support for public funding for any stadium in 1997 by voting overwhelmingly in favor of a charter that would require a vote be held before the city of Minneapolis would provide substantial (over $10 million) public funds for a new stadium. This ultimately proved not to be an obstacle since in 2014 with a political sleight of hand revenue from a new sales tax will be channeled to a stadium authority that, in turn, would then spend the public money to fund part of the new project (discussed further below). Therefore, no vote approving "public funding" was required.

The nexus driving the process consisted of the NFL commissioner, Minnesota governor, Minneapolis mayor, and the team owners – the Wilf family whose wealth had been derived from their real estate business in New Jersey. Tom Brady was faced with potentially having to serve a suspension that would have cost him about one fourth of his 2015 season salary for foolishly getting rid of his cell phone while being one principal figure in the underinflating of footballs incident during the 2014 NFL playoffs. The Wilfs, however, faced no penalty or even public censure from the NFL for their lack of business ethics when they were "excoriated" in a New Jersey court for having engaged in what the judge called "racketeering" as they "fleeced" and "robbed" their business partner, and had also "lied, deceived and falsified financial accountings" (Powell, 2014). Such a judgment might have made some other NFL owners proud that the Wilfs had become part of their fraternity.

Once the Wilfs bought the team they made the usual threat that unless a new stadium deal could be reached (of course with the expectation that some public funding be provided) they would move the team to another city. An NFL lobbying blitz ensued, including the NFL commissioner meeting with the state governor. The report was that the threat was repeated that the NFL would permit the Vikings to move unless their wish was granted. In this case no mention of "relationship" was part of the discourse. Within a few weeks there was a deal to build what has been described as "the people's stadium" although one critic's calling it a state of the art "Taj Mahal" seems to be more appropriate (Powell, 2014). The Minnesota "people" get to pay almost half of the estimated $1 billion cost. New taxes would be imposed.

The economic assessments of the deal by those not paid by the team or the NFL were consistent with such assessments for similar projects. One critic described the deal as a "folly" and cited that "scores of times" analysts conclude that the "evidence is overwhelming" that "public subsidies for professional sports are one of the worst returns on investment a state can make" (Schultz, 2014). The mayor of Minneapolis and a former city councilman agreed, pointing out that "the economics of public stadiums are terrible" and that for Minnesotans they received "one of the worst deals ever for the public" – which will be an even worse deal if the state of Minnesota grants the NFL tax breaks which the league is asking for should it choose to have the 2018 Super Bowl played in the new Vikings stadium (Powell, 2014). Were this sad story to be a fable the moral would be "If you [e.g., a powerful nexus for a professional sports league] pull often enough on the state and municipal levers, the gold of public subsidies inevitably tumbles into your hands" (Powell, 2014).

Major League Baseball features similar examples with billions of corporate welfare being provided. In Atlanta the mayor refused to provide public funding for the Braves, who promptly entered into a nice relationship with nearby Cobb County which will require public funds the county can commandeer to cover $300 million of the expected $672 million cost for the new stadium scheduled to open for play in 2017 (Nash and Deprez, 2014). The Detroit Tigers' billionaire owner was able to receive $115 million in public funds to cover part of the estimated $360 million cost of building their new stadium in 2000 (Kuriloff and Preston, 2012). He may have been kicking himself after he learned about the percentage of public funds used to fund the construction of the Florida Marlins Sun Life Stadium. The new lavish facility that opened in 2012 cost about $630 million, and the team was only required to pay about 20% of the cost compliments of corporate welfare provided by Miami and Dade County residents. The usual threat to relocate was made by the team and MLB to relocate unless a better relationship could be reached. Questions arose concerning the financial disclosure circumstances surrounding the deal that sparked a Securities and Exchange Commission investigation. There also was a public backlash leading to a recall vote that ousted the mayor who had voted in favor of providing the corporate welfare to the Marlins' owner Jeffrey Luria. Luria had the dubious distinction in 2013 of being ranked by ESPN as the most dishonest professional sports team owner (ESPN, 2013).

Gradually, there is a growing taxpayer resistance and city officials' skepticism regarding the illusionary promise of positive economic returns from doling out corporate welfare for construction of stadiums or arenas used by teams owned by billionaires, as well as for hosting grandiose sports events such as the Olympic Games. The city of Las Vegas recently rejected a request to publicly fund a soccer stadium for a yet-to-be-found Major League Soccer team (the proponents had argued build it and someone will come). In Chicago the mayor rejected the idea of issuing one-half billion dollars in bonds to fund the renovation of Wrigley Field. Apparently citizens of these localities do not wish to forge a new, expensive relationship with local professional sports teams. Citizens of Boston rose up and drove Boston officials to withdraw the city's bid to host the 2024 Summer Olympic Games. Apparently these citizens like relationships within the city exactly as they are.

Chapter Summary

The nexus discourse shaping trading of favors patterns leading to corporate welfare given to some of the richest American individuals and corporations has become pervasive. The amounts doled out have increased. The next chapter focuses on the costs of this profligacy and suggests what disgusted citizens might do to eliminate the pattern.

Notes

1   See Babiak and Hare, 2006, and the behavioral economics research of Nobel Prize winner Daniel Kahneman.
2   Many conservative Republicans complained that the bank mostly helps large corporations, such as Boeing. Note that taxpayers are at risk for any losses the bank cannot cover on the roughly $112 billion it had in mid-2015 in outstanding assistance.
3   Before the second Gulf War began I was in Cairo having lunch with Mona El Barradei whose brother would be awarded a Nobel Prize for his work, including as chief inspector in the search for weapons of mass destruction in Iraq. He happened to be in Cairo that same day. I asked her if the weapons inspectors had found anything resembling weapons of mass destruction there, and she informed me that he had told her no such weapons had been found. That finding, of course, did nothing to stop the Bush–Cheney administration from initiating one of the costliest wars, and reconstruction programs, ever involving the United States.
4   Due to accounting procedures used by the Pentagon and its not complying with the letter of the law concerning being audited it will remain unknown exactly how much of the more than $8 trillion spent by the Pentagon since 1996 has been waste, corporate welfare, and destination unknown. See Lyster, 2013.
5   See https://www.organicconsumers.org/old_articles/ofgu/subsidies.htm
6   See ibid.
7   This section draws heavily from the Sontag report as published in the *New York Times*. See Sontag, 2014. Full citation is included with all sources.
8   Dalrymple is reported to have said that "Outsiders ... simply need to be educated out of their fear of fracking: There is a way to explain it that really relaxes people, that makes them understand this is not a dangerous thing that

we're doing out here, that it's really very well managed and very safe and really the key to the future of not only North Dakota but really our entire nation" (Sontag, 2014).

9   See   http://desmogblog.com/sites/beta.desmogblog.com/files/Dimock%20 report.pdf

10 That some members of Congress are incapable of recognizing this low quality may be attributable to the lack of rigor and critical thinking contained in their respective education experiences.

11 Unfortunately, I have worked at non-profit academic institutions where peer pressure for upward grade inflation was considerable. Some of us who refused to engage in this academic fraud were treated like pariahs.

12 Senate held a hearing in August 2010 that focused on evidence obtained by the Government Accountability Office study that found recruiters at 15 of the for-profits colleges "misled investigators posing as potential students about the cost and quality of their programs" (Hechinger, 2010).

13 In this same report it was noted that within a week after the vote on this bill occurred some first-term Democrats were in New York on a trip during which they met CEOs from Goldman Sachs and JPMorgan and discussed, among other topics, the Dodd–Frank law. The members of Congress were assured that "America has the widest, deepest and most transparent capital markets in the world. ... Washington has been dealt a good hand" (Lipton and Protess, 2013). The speaker failed to mention that it was the law-making process within the finance industry nexus that was not particularly transparent.

14 Globalization is having an effect here, for like manufacturers banks can establish offices around the world and engage in illegal practices from locations where laws and enforcement are even more lax than they are in the United States.

15 These banks are Bank of America, Citigroup, Goldman Sachs, JPMorgan Chase, and Morgan Stanley.

16 The person later withdrew themselves from consideration.

17 Two sports analysts note that "[t]he 1986 Tax Reform Act denies federal subsidies for sports facilities if more than 10 percent of the debt service is covered by revenues from the stadium. If Congress intended that this would reduce sports subsidies, it was sadly mistaken. If anything, the 1986 law increased local subsidies by cutting rents below 10 percent of debt service" (Zimbalist and Noll, 1997).

18 In addition to the excellent work done by Zimbalist and Noll, separate studies by economists including Grant Long, Robert Baade, and Victor Matheson come to a similar conclusion – namely that the municipality that uses taxpayer funds for constructing a new facility is making a poor investment.

6 Recognize the CWE Exists, Reject the CWE, Reestablish a Community-Friendly Economy

[We need to initiate a] process of rebuilding and reinventing the very idea of the collective, the communal, the commons, the civil, and the civic after so many decades of attack and neglect.

(Klein, 2014, p. 460)

Introduction

The previous chapters have demonstrated that since the late 1970s, the emergence of the corporate welfare economy (CWE) in the United States has been accompanied by a major shift in the distribution of political and economic power that has brought us to the point where we no longer have a functioning democracy. During this period some of the country's wealthiest individuals and corporations have received billions in tax benefits and other types of corporate welfare with nearly total immunity to legally mandated penalties that had been established to protect the public's economic and physical health. By tempting elected officials and regulators with the prospect of increasing their own fortunes and power, these wealthy individuals and major industry executives, with the help of their lobbyist army, have essentially "captured" the government, thus diminishing the effectiveness of regulations put in place to protect the interests of the public at large. Thus empowered, they have further increased their economic and newly acquired political power by influencing Congress or state legislatures to create policies that legitimize new tax breaks and corporate welfare in addition to the profits they would deservedly receive from their normal business activities. In some cases the regulations and fines for the harmful aspects of their corporations' production and distribution activities have been reduced substantially. Many political candidates, elected officials, and regulators have become beholden to unscrupulous benefactors – witness the 2016 presidential primary functions hosted by wealthy donors seeking to identify which horse to bet on, and the candidates, desperate for funding, pandering shamelessly to billionaires who have a narrow, self-serving, increase-profits-first agenda. The inevitable result is the dilution of the government's commitments to attend to the long-term interests of the public at large.

The individuals and industry nexuses described in previous chapters have taken advantage of the shift in power and the purchase of some major news media and funding of purported "research" institutions to shape and limit discourse so that virtually every issue is seen through the prism of profits. Highly reputable scientific findings that identify economic, health, and environmental hazards to the public from some of their industry's activities are strongly disparaged. Together with the diversion of government allocations from public services in favor of corporate welfare, the rejection of warnings about public health have resulted in environmental damages including the poisoning of some drinking water sources. Health concerns also ensue from the reduced requirements for the testing of some imported foods and domestically produced chemicals. In addition recently passed federal laws prohibit local communities from either banning or regulating risky production activities such as fracking or use of chemicals by industrial farms.

This chapter will argue that there is a path towards a new economy that will serve the best interests of the majority of Americans whom the CWE has not served and will not serve. The path begins with recognizing that the CWE does exist, and that the CWE is a far cry from the free market economy that its proponents claim it to be. The next step is to reject the CWE in the face of evidence that the CWE's limiting and shaping discourse and its inevitably corrupt favor-trading and collusion within the nexuses contribute to the poor economic, social, and environmental indicators described in previous chapters.

The last step is to reestablish a different type of economy that draws its inspiration in part from the period between late 1940s until the late 1970s. We can return to the inherent principles and priorities of that era, but with a different economy able to take advantage of the new technology – thereby keeping the best of our existing economy while replacing its worst aspects. The economy during this period emphasized the importance of private business activities, but was not stymied by corporate welfare. It emphasized community – at the local as well as the national level – and was wary of limiting regulations designed to curb the temptation to pursue profit regardless of the negative costs that might be imposed on the general public. Before describing some key components of what a new economy could feature we need to recognize what type of economy currently exists in our nation.

Recognize that the CWE Exists

The previous chapters have provided numerous examples of major industry nexuses that shape and limit discourse, with considerable evidence of favors traded among nexus members that include widespread distribution of corporate welfare on a scale almost unheard of prior to 1980. Some of the names, positions, and activities of the most powerful nexus members have been identified. Those interested in identifying more elected officials who belong to an industry nexus could check published records that show which Congressional members received how much in campaign contributions from which industries, then noting the voting record of the same member on policies that would provide or eliminate corporate welfare or reduce regulations applying to those same industries. One place to start would be at the website of the Center for Responsive Politics – OpenSecrets.org. The skeptical reader could go further and identify which of these same legislators passed through the revolving door to the corporate world, as well as noting appointments of private sector industry nexus members who joined the public sector – all the while furthering their own and their nexus' interests in securing more corporate welfare or substantially boosting the personal incomes of a very small percentage of the population.

The nexuses' ability to limit and shape discourse has been explained as well in previous chapters. This ability has been enhanced through the increased concentration of media ownership that adds to the power of each industry nexus to influence the reporting (or non-reporting) of policy issues as well as economic, social, and environmental indicators. The dominant analytic and policy discourse reflects the ideology of a very small percentage of wealthy Americans. This discourse continues to describe the US economy as if it were a free market economy (at least until some environmental regulation is proposed), but it seeks to rig the economy in favor of the nexus. The free market evangelism that is part of the discourse rejects the possibility of exploring other approaches to economic activity. Discourse pertaining to specific economic, health, or environmental issues is limited and shaped in a manner to create policies that place profits as the only priority while discouraging or preventing any discourse that would indicate the policies' potentially adverse effects on the public.[1]

Less visible in its mechanics, but often disturbingly evident in its impact, is the existence of industry nexus' influence in high political places, an unofficial partnership that has been instrumental in the establishment of specific forms of corporate welfare. Evidence abounds that favors are traded among nexus members. The CWE has ushered in a pervasive range of lavish subsidies, tax breaks, debt forgiveness, loan and price guarantees, bailouts and other unique payments or benefits to specific wealthy individuals and corporations. It stretches across a wide range of industries and is now so widespread and systemic that its existence has simply become part of the American political landscape. These trades effectively result in an upward redistribution of income and wealth. Since these trades, although legal, are ethically questionable, they likely contributed to the United States' being ranked an uninspiring 17th (1st being the least corrupt) in the 2014 "Corruptions Perceptions Index" done by Transparency International (2014).

Over the past three decades the CWE has stimulated excessive government–industry collusion and fostered concerted efforts to stifle dissenting voices. The CWE's existence is evident in grants, lax regulations, and other favors that benefit relatively few Americans. The CWE's existence is evident in statistics that reveal massive inequalities in the distribution of income in our country. It is evident in the experience of many Americans, who find that basic comforts and financial security seem to be slipping out of their grasp. It is evident in the superficial level of our current public and political discourse. The CWE's existence is evident in the diversion of our once representative government from its mission to ensure the well-being of all its citizens. It is time to consider rejecting the CWE in favor of new economic policies.

Reject the CWE

Millions of Americans do continue to enjoy material goods and services born out of technological achievements which have softened the negative impacts of the CWE for many people. Since most of them do have their basic needs met and some creature comforts, widespread public motivation and collective action towards rejecting the CWE has been stifled. However, after recognizing the CWE's existence as well as becoming aware of the growing negative impacts the CWE is having on a majority of Americans one could be convinced that the philosophy, institutions, policies, and outcomes the CWE is generating should be rejected.

The degree to which income inequality has increased as the CWE has risen is one of the strongest reasons to reject the CWE. This inequality has been going up faster in the US than in any other wealthy nation with the possible exception of the UK. Among the group of 33 countries the IMF refers to as the most "advanced" (wealthiest) only Singapore and Hong Kong have a more unequal distribution of income than the US (Blow, 2013). This inequality is boosted by corporate welfare in the form of profits and special tax favors for wealthy individuals, as is being reported virtually every week along with specific points such as the percentage of wealth owned by the richest 1% being about 33% in 2015 versus a mere 25% in 1980; that at the very top of the pyramid about 10,000 individuals representing one hundredth of 1 percent of the population have a combined net worth that exceeds $6 trillion – which is about the same total net worth of the lower 66% of the population. The wealthiest 400 alone are worth about $2 trillion, more than the wealth owned by the bottom 150 million Americans. The US's distribution of income and wealth more closely resembles that of a Third World country than that of every other country on the IMF's most advanced country list. As the income and wealth distributions have become more highly skewed the manner in which our democratic institutions operate has been undermined as evidenced by the pattern and extent of contributions and favors traded among industry nexuses members. Such favors include tax laws under which the pay of some CEOs exceeds that which their corporation pays in taxes. In the mid-1960s corporate CEOs earned on average about 20 times what their workers averaged. Today that ratio exceeds 300 to 1, and average workers have less job security and a smaller percentage of workers have guaranteed pensions than did workers a few decades ago. It is noteworthy that no strong relationship between increasing the CEO's pay package and subsequent greater profitability of that corporation has been identified in numerous studies.

A second reason to reject the CWE is that one part of this economy's philosophy glorifies the pursuit of profits as an end in itself with scant attention paid to the economic, social, and environmental costs, with the perpetual promise of good jobs being created. The reality is that about two thirds of jobs created in the past decade pay less than $10 per hour. CEOs who lower worker pay, produce buyout packages that reduce their workforce, or devote lower percentage of profits to reinvestment that would create more jobs receive high praise in some media. An illustration of this is the glowing praise some business journals heaped on the most recently appointed CEO of Harley-Davidson, considering him a success and worthy of his multimillion dollar income package because after having overseen a significant downsizing of the local workforce profits increased considerably. Even during the period (fourth quarter of 2014) when the US economy grew at its highest annual rate in a decade the average worker did not experience an increase in their real pay. From the middle of 2009 until 2014 the average hourly wage of college graduates in the 21–24 age group, many of whom bear a substantial student loan burden, declined for both men (from $18 to below $17) and women (from almost $17 to below $15.50) (Tritch, 2014). Poor job prospects are reflected by the historically low labor force participation rate, which partly explains why the job market (when pay for those jobs is considered rather than only the unemployment rate) for many Americans remains grim despite unemployment falling below 6% during 2015. Older workers are less likely than their parents to have a company pension, which helps explain why more senior citizens continue to work than in previous decades.

Another reason to reject the CWE is that while the plight of these unfortunate Americans has worsened there has been a noticeable absence of discourse and policy proposals at the federal level to assist them. One explanation could be the attitudes of those major industry nexus members who are among the upper 1% in terms of their wealth and income. Findings from a Russell Sage Foundation study of the perceptions held by "elites" (those in the upper 1% of wealth holders whose income averaged over $1 million per year) regarding existing economic and social conditions and what future policies should be to alleviate the problems were compared to the average findings of perceptions held by a majority of Americans. The majority results were compiled using the average of other similar surveys, including those conducted by the Pew Charitable Trusts' Research Center and Gallup, Inc. (*Daily Kos*, 2014). The findings reveal that Adam Smith's assumption that wealthy entrepreneurs would reinvest most of their profits because of the "sympathy" (empathy) they possessed towards those less fortunate has been replaced by a new ethos. For example, 33% of the upper 1% responded that social security should be reduced, versus 10% for the majority (note that many responded to leave it as it is or increase it); only 40% of the upper 1% believed the minimum wage should be increased to reduce the likelihood that working families would not fall below the poverty line, while 78% of the majority believed so; when asked if they favored US companies establishing overseas operations 78% of the upper 1% endorsed that move, while only 23% of the majority agreed with them; and on the question of whether a national health serviced should be financed mostly by taxation only 32% of the upper 1% favored such a policy as compared to 61% of the majority.

Another reason to reject the CWE is the elites' mindset that the best way to resolve our economic, social, and environmental problems is to encourage competition over cooperation and reduce most problems to monetary terms and value. Biased cost–benefit analyses are used to justify production and distribution activities that neither include social and ecological costs nor adopt the precautionary principle when these activities are deemed risky to our economic, social, or environmental well-being. Findings from studies indicate less concern among the elites for the negative environmental impact from some of their corporations' investments that are creating swelling environmental problems that negatively affect virtually all of us. Some of this investment is stimulated by the CWE providing corporate welfare and other incentives for more fossil fuel extraction with lax regulations, expansion of industrial farms and transportation of food products nationwide, greater depletion of groundwater, and more weapons production – all of which could be partially or fully replaced over time with alternative production and distribution methods far more likely to promote a sustainable economy. Proponents justifying the incentives that encourage such investment also will downplay the negative environmental costs while justifying the need to generate even more profits to provide for further expansion of these types of investment.

The problem with this mindset is forcefully argued by Naomi Klein in her superb book, *This Changes Everything* (2014). She emphasizes that "we cannot avert the ecological disaster that confronts us without loosening the grip of that superannuated zombie ideology" of neoliberalism (orthodox economics with a free market emphasis). This ideology held by the CWE's major industry nexus members promotes excess consumption of products including fossil fuels and many agricultural products manufactured using processes heavily dependent upon fossil fuel extraction, transportation, processing, and even more transportation to distribute the product. One reviewer pointed out that in the competition between the ideology driving this process, which emphasizes "hyper-corporatized, hyper-carbonized pursuit of short-term growth at any cost" (Nixon, 2014), and those offering alternative production and distribution methods, which are consistent with long-term economic and ecological sustainability, the main drivers of the CWE are currently winning control over the alternative proposals throughout the policy-making process. Recognition and rejection of the CWE will facilitate a movement towards this latter alternative.

One example of this mindset in practice can be found on industrial farms. Through shaping the discourse and lax enforcement the environmental costs created by industrial agricultural continue to mount. The individual industrial agricultural farms along with the economic and political power of the multibillion dollar agribusiness firms have been enhanced by farm subsidies and an interest rate policy that has enabled these firms to more easily acquire land from struggling small farmers. On land farmed by industrial farms using mono cropping the extensive use of chemically based fertilizers and pesticides contributes heavily to chemical runoff that is polluting our rivers, lakes, and oceans, including the Great Lakes, the Mississippi River, and the Gulf of Mexico. Toledo, Ohio, for example is caught in a cycle of worsening water pollution triggered by a "serendipitous slug of toxins" that has resulted in the "loss of drinking water for a half-million residents" (Wines, 2014). The more than 10 million residents who live along Lake Erie face a similar fate as more phosphorous in chemical fertilizers and pesticides than can be absorbed safely by the ecosystem runs off of farms into the water system (along with runoff from concentrated manure in livestock feedlots). The phosphorous in the chemicals contributes to excessive algae growth that, in turn, chokes off aquatic life and poisons the water. Another example of chemical runoff damage has been occurring in Florida where chemicals used to produce sugarcane find their way into the Everglades, which both destroys wildlife habitat and contaminates the groundwater (Meyer and Cooper, 2014). Federal laws such as the Clean Water Act were passed to limit water pollution, but the agricultural industry nexus has successfully lobbied against strict enforcement of the law.

Another negative impact to which the CWE contributes, and a further reason to reject this type of economy, is that the actions of entrepreneurs whose financially successful firms earn substantial profits has drifted far from what the philosophy justifying a free market economy assumed they would be. Many of the legendary American entrepreneurs fit the FME mold, including Henry Ford and Bill Gates. Even those great twentieth century entrepreneurs whose biographies paint a mixed evaluation of their contributions to their economy and society demonstrated far more civic patrimony and community interest than most of today's major industry nexus members. Andrew Mellon, for example, was considered to be "cold," and "devoid of insight, warmth, or empathy." However, he also was considered to have been one of the quintessential job creators of his age who "helped to found and develop aluminum and oil companies that helped build America" as well as being very generous in his civic patrimony activities that included funding the National Gallery in Washington DC, Carnegie Mellon Institute, and the Mellon Foundation with assets currently exceeding $6 billion (Cannadine, 2006, p. 597). He spoke out against budget deficits and stock speculation while championing domestic investments that promoted long-run economic growth and employment – albeit at the expense of the local environment.

The key point is that Mellon (and later his children) was generous with his wealth and spoke out against irresponsible financial speculation, while creating thousands of jobs locally. When the degree of financial speculation, investments in the political mechanism to secure corporate welfare, overseas investments (rather than into the community where the corporation is located), willingness to move their corporation or even their citizenship abroad (as well as extent of philanthropy) practiced by many of the CEOs and wealthiest individuals cited throughout this book are considered, it can be concluded that a new breed of entrepreneur has emerged with a very different commitment towards community. Some of the practices of this new breed, especially the modest to weak extent to which reinvestment of their profits in their workers and local communities is concerned, have contributed to the negative economic, social, environmental, and political corruption trends characteristic of the CWE.

Rejecting the CWE also can be justified by considering the declining standard of living for many Americans along with other unfavorable economic, social, and environmental indicators that have been adversely influenced by the CWE. The economic, social, and environmental problems identified throughout this book could lead one to agree that in many respects, as history has demonstrated, the United States is becoming a declining empire. Partly due to the CWE we now feature the same trends experienced by every major empire that eventually declined or even collapsed. It is worthwhile to repeat here these trends that were outlined in Chapter 2. They have included: (1) greater shares of spending generated through the finance industry speculation with less devoted to manufacturing and social services; (2) high, unsustainable levels of debt at the household, municipal, state (note Illinois), and federal levels; (3) extreme economic inequality with excessive conspicuous consumption by the wealthy class while the average family's standard of living declined; (4) costly military overreaching in search of cheap resources globally as the empire sought to dominate the rest of the world – which came at an increasingly higher domestic cost; and (5) corruption and political ineptitude, with considerable favoritism, fraud, graft, collusion, and the diversion of public funds into private pockets – with honesty less valued while lying and deception (note Chapter 4 concerning discourse) become the norm, even at the highest levels of government and the media – while some elected and appointed political officials become shamelessly sycophantic to some industry corporate welfare interest. For the United States can be added (6) production methods that rely on unsustainable use of water and extraction of fossil fuels along with consumption patterns that contribute to ecological degradation.

These trends, and still another reason to reject the CWE, have been bolstered by the CWE's philosophy towards globalization, the leading institutions enforcing globalization rules (the WTO, World Bank, and IMF) and the policies that have deregulated trade to the detriment of many American workers so that we can purchase things such as cheap textile products and all sorts of plastic items much more cheaply than anyone thought possible a few decades ago. However, the philosophy and rules WTO members such as the United States agree to abide by puts national democratic governments in a "golden straightjacket" when the desire to exert some control over the negative effects of globalization should be rejected in favor of a more "feasible" globalization philosophy and policies (Rodrik, 2002). The negative effects particularly relevant to Americans not prospering in the CWE include products sold without the consumer being aware that they were produced by labor under unsafe, unhealthy conditions; more job insecurity and slower increases in income for American workers – among workers in other rich countries; tax avoidance; and the facilitation of international financial speculation and the threat of another financial crisis. An alternative type of globalization policy would be one feature of a new type of economy that can be reestablished after the CWE has been rejected.

There are precedents for rejecting economies. Over the past 85 or so years, some countries have rejected their existing major economic philosophy and some of the corresponding institutions and policies in favor of an alternative type of economy. This occurred in the 1932 US rejection of what was a lightly regulated free market economy; similar rejections occurred throughout Europe over the 1932 to 1960s period and in China (1978); also, there was the widespread 1989 to early 1990s rejection of the Soviet-type of economy throughout Central and Eastern Europe. In each case public dissatisfaction with the political system's inability to correct the existing negative economic and social indicators occurring reached a breaking point that stimulated a democratic or not-so democratic revolution in favor of an alternative type of economy. The alternative choices these countries made were not simply between a "free market economy" versus "socialism." This overly simplistic discourse has been used by CWE elites, although in this case discourse emphasizing that the US economy is an FME has been a smoke screen while CWE activities rig outcomes in the nexuses' favor, free from actual competitive forces and citizen discontent, or what some current North Dakota officials describe as "pesky folks," who protest negative environmental impacts and loss of property rights from fracking policies highly favorable to oil and gas industry interests.

The CWE has existed for decades. The worst characteristics of the CWE are steadily becoming more extreme, as indicated by the following instances, all of which came to public attention in late summer and early fall, 2015. During this period it was widely reported that nine Americans had died and about 700 others suffered serious illness after having consumed peanut products tainted with salmonella. The CEO of the company that had produced these products had known that they were unsafe, but did nothing to prevent their distribution or alert the public of the danger. That it was considered unprecedented that this CEO was sentenced to 28 years in jail is a testimony to the protection afforded to corporation executives who knowingly endanger the public. During this same period it was revealed that Volkswagen had intentionally perpetrated a massive fraud to evade detection of illegal emission levels. As further evidence of the protection of irresponsible CEOs, it is considered unlikely that the CEO of Volkswagen will serve time in jail. The same is true of the General Motors CEO, who presided over the production and sale of over 2.5 million automobiles containing a defective ignition switch that was blamed for causing over 120 deaths. Evidence indicates the company knew of the faulty ignition switch but failed to recall the defective autos and replace the switch. Although the corporation paid a fine, none of the GM officers or other employees who were actually responsible for this callous endangerment of consumers were indicted. Evidence suggests that Exxon employees knew as far back as the 1970s that greenhouse gases spewed by petroleum use were contributing to climate change, but made no public revelation of findings that might jeopardize their bottom line. No Exxon executives are expected to face criminal charges, despite decades of concealing this information while denying that Exxon products were damaging the environment. More than 20 for-profit colleges and universities face charges of fraud, but federal government tax dollars continue to support and perpetuate them. Meanwhile, corporate welfare continues to flow to such an extent that even conservative columnist Nicolas Kristof noted that "the only kind of welfare that carries no stigma in America is corporate welfare" (Kristof, 2015). A final – and ironic – example is that of the current construction of a steel mill owned by the Koch brothers, outspoken opponents of corporate welfare. Financing for the mill includes funds from a bond issue paid by Arkansas taxpayers, loan guarantees from a German government agency, and recycling credits that will benefit the Koch investors. As one analyst argues, "the Kochs didn't just take advantage of corporate welfare; their involvement was the impetus for [this] corporate welfare" (Nocera, 2015).

Despite growing evidence of negative outcomes created by the CWE, Americans, with the exception of some progressive movements, continue to accept this type of economy. Some of these movements focus on the basic morality, or lack thereof, of the CWE. For instance, the public funding of stadiums has generated protests that argue it is immoral to ask people to pay taxes and do without while making professional sports team owners and their players much richer. Protesters point out that most other entertainment businesses manage to survive through self-financing. Why have more people not joined such protest? What is required to mobilize citizens to reject the CWE? The questions point toward the path to a new economy that is emerging in the United States.

Reestablish a Community-Friendly Economy

Effective rejection of the CWE and a commitment to reestablish a new economy will not occur until there is widespread protest against the CWE that creates a national movement with an agenda for reform. Political thinkers and historians such as Alexis de Tocqueville and Sheldon Wolin have analyzed the US political system. Some of their findings, with which the description of the CWE provided throughout this book are consistent, offer insights into why a mass protest has not yet occurred here despite the increasing negative effects of the CWE. The prediction of de Tocqueville was that the United States was characterized by "soft despotism" such that the citizenry was easily manipulated, but those being manipulated were either unaware or unwilling to admit it. He further argued that our political system will make people feel helpless and become passive, and that these feelings were an intentional by-product of the system's design. Wolin (2010) coined the term "inverted totalitarianism" with totalitarian tendencies used to describe the US government that has been seized by corporations and the wealthiest Americans, disenfranchising most Americans in the process.

A growing number of groups are trying to overcome de Tocqueville's soft despotism effects and are protesting against various negative effects of the CWE, including the widespread feelings of being disenfranchised that Wolin identified. These groups include those interested in political and economic reform such as Occupy Wall Street, Campaign for America's Future, Bold Progressives, People for the American Way, End Citizens United, and the Center for Responsive Politics, as well as groups focusing on environmental reform that include Greenpeace, Environmental Action, League of Conservation Voters, and Food and Water Watch – among other national and local groups committed to reform. By remaining separate groups each risk remaining a reform movement that exists only at the margin without changing the CWE's political power distribution and effectively achieving comprehensive reforms. Each group would continue to lack the political power to promote substantive political, economic, or environmental reforms. What is needed now is for greater political activism that includes political mobilization through unification of these and other groups with a common desire to substantively reform our increasingly corrupt system of governance and the CWE.[2] Unification could spearhead a peaceful political revolution in which the populace becomes more vigorous, active citizens rather than remaining passive consumers, dedicated to protecting ourselves against the growing abuses of the CWE. Ultimately this movement could gain political power at the local, state, and national levels from which to engage in further political reform such as overturning Citizens United, while promoting economic and environmental reforms.

Given its diverse interests this coalition would recognize the political–economic–social–environmental complexity of policy issues. Combining the separate protest groups' respective missions could establish the basis for thinking about a new economy whose new philosophy, institutions, policies, and indicators for evaluating progress would be far more capable than the CWE of alleviating the pressing political, economic, social, and environmental problems we now face. The next step would be the more daunting, but not insurmountable, task of establishing substantive economy-wide reforms based upon the new philosophy. Should the coalition who gain sufficient political power choose to adopt a philosophy upon which to reform the economy based upon the essence of the pre-1980s philosophy that guided our economy better than the CWE they would be well advised to consult with economic and environmental experts who have written extensively about implementing the types of reforms suggested below, among their other suggested reforms.[3] The remainder of this chapter suggests as a starting point some economic and environmental reforms as well as indicators for evaluating the degree to which the new economy is achieving goals consistent with the new philosophy. These reforms could be part of a broad reform program to reestablish a community-friendly economy with priorities and values similar to those that existed before 1980 as well as greater concern for environmental sustainability. Some suggested reforms are substantive, others marginal. Substantive reforms are major fundamental changes, such as basing most economic activity on renewable, decentralized sources of energy. Marginal reforms would be those that correct problems with the current excesses of the past 35 years and return to 1960s era principles to reestablish balance, such as reinstating all provisions of the original Glass–Steagall Act to reduce risk throughout the finance system by making it work as it did before some of its major provisions were repealed starting in the late 1990s.

Every economy is based upon a philosophy that shapes the society's values while defining its primary goals, principal institutions, normative patterns of social organization and behavior governed by common rules that coordinate production and distribution activities and policy measures for achieving the economy's goals. Indicators then are chosen that would demonstrate if those goals have been achieved. The philosophy for the new economy must contain restraints on unfettered market forces so that the worst values of the CWE can be encompassed to avoid a continuation of the nihilistic behavior of leading industry nexus members that has been damaging to a large majority of Americans. Such restraints were prevalent during the late 1940s to 1980 US economy. The philosophy would emphasize that a distribution of income, wealth, and political power as highly skewed as it has become under the CWE must be prevented in the interest of all citizens, and that failure to do so will mean a continuation of the upward redistribution policies and concentrated government–wealthy private sector relationships that have prevailed for the past few decades. The new philosophy would place greater emphasis on poverty alleviation while raising the standard of living for the bottom 80% of the population. The philosophy also would oppose all corporate welfare, tax havens, special tax breaks, or subsidies for either wealthy individuals or large, highly profitable corporations, recognizing that subsidies in their current form are unethical, in some cases immoral, as well as being a misallocation of taxpayer funds and induce perverse behavior such as extensive lobbying by wealthy corporations to secure such subsidies. The philosophy would be the foundation for eliminating what one harsh critic summed up as what has become systemic throughout Washington DC: "Among the most outrageous [federal] expenditures is corporate welfare. Desperate businesses now overrun Washington, begging for alms. Believing that profits should be theirs while losses should be everyone else's, corporations have convinced policymakers to underwrite virtually every industry: agriculture, education, energy, housing, manufacturing, medicine, transportation, and much more" (Bandow, 2012).

A good starting point for policy reforms would be to implement proposals to eliminate corporate welfare using as a basis those already proposed by John McCain and Ralph Nader to establish a national commission that would determine which subsidies can be considered corporate welfare and which tax loopholes egregiously fail the test of both horizontal and vertical equity. The corporate welfare reform would be part of comprehensive finance industry reforms that need to go well beyond a reintroduction of the provisions specified in the Glass–Steagall Act. Some might propose that investment banks be required to put a large "casino" sign on their headquarters and be required to operate as such. No taxpayer funds or federal insurance would cover their bets, so the investment banks would need to have sufficient funds readily available in case the bets placed through purchase of their risky financial instruments led to large losses for those who willingly purchased those financial instruments, who would bear the full loss. Other reforms should be based upon recommendations by expert economists such as Simon Johnson, Paul Krugman, Joseph Stiglitz, and some analysts at the International Monetary Fund. These include collecting and making transparent more data that could identify growing risks throughout the financial system; strengthening regulatory agencies' ability to supervise the industry; and "clarifying who is responsible to prepare for and manage financial system-wide crises" (International Monetary Fund, 2015). Other reforms should center on restoring the local financial institutions and corresponding banking rules that, while boring, provided services throughout the 1940s to 1970s period that witnessed no major financial crises requiring public bailouts or high rates of foreclosures on homes.

Comprehensive finance industry reform would interrelate with reform of the current rules and institutions pertaining to globalization that have proven harmful to many working class Americans while providing tax havens and more incentives to invest individual wealth and corporate profits overseas, while avoiding paying taxes in the United States. Some analysts have argued that globalization has gone too far in the process of deepening the degree of economic integration, particularly freer trade and investment. This has occurred because in addition to harming many workers it has interfered with the desire in many countries to preserve the culture of their nation as well as to make political decisions at the local level designed to preserve the economic base of the community. One expert international political economy analyst recommends that we return to the pre-1980s form of globalization when countries were not bound by the "golden straightjacket" imposed by the WTO free trade and greater mobility of capital rules and were able to preserve their local cultures and job markets (Rodrik, 2002).

Among the needed domestic economy reforms would be to reduce income insecurity and associated stress for many Americans with policies that would firmly establish long-term financial sustainability for the social security, Medicare, and Medicaid programs. The specific means for doing so undoubtedly would stimulate contentious debate. Social security sustainability is easier to fix financially than these health care programs. This could be achieved through a combination of the following modest changes to taxes and benefits, although the aggressive ideological opposition to what has been America's most successful anti-poverty program needs to be overcome. On the expenditures side, monthly payments could be adjusted according to a sliding scale so that those of us whose income is deemed sufficient or more than sufficient could have our monthly payments reduced by a modest amount (1–2%) with this percentage rising perhaps up to 20% or above for those whose income exceeds $1 million annually. On the tax side a combination of modest changes could help resolve some of the predicted financial shortage problems (that will arise without funding and expenditure reforms). Gradually increasing the payroll tax from its current 12.4% to about 14%, or keep it where it is and raising the upper limit of income subject to the Federal Insurance Contributions Act (FICA) tax could be set so that about 92% of all income earned would be subject to the tax, as it was in the 1960s and 1970s, or tax all wages earned.[4] Other changes could include a gradual increase in the full retirement age, and replacing the current cost-of-living-adjustment measure of inflation, the Consumer Price Index, which assumes people purchase the same market basket over a few years, with a measure that accounts for changes in spending patterns in favor of goods and services whose prices go down with less spent on those that increase in price. For the Medicare and Medicaid programs one reform could be raising the 1.45% tax on all income earned by upper income groups up to about 2% or slightly higher, depending upon estimates of additional revenue generated from the calculations made by actuaries and medical economics experts.

One of the most pressing needs is to boost employment opportunities and incomes of families with income earners currently receiving an hourly wage of about $10 with few or no benefits. Considering the plight of this group and that worker pay increases have lagged far behind their productivity increases over the past few decades a starting point would be to raise the minimum wage. Rather than require a blanket, nationwide increase to $15 per hour phased in over a five-year period many economists suggest to compare the current minimum wage to the median wage of workers in the relevant geographical area, then raising the minimum wage in that area to bring it up to about 70% of the area's median wage. Doing so would reduce the chances of substantial increases in layoffs for those currently on minimum wage. Otherwise employers would be much less likely to be able to adjust to such a sudden, dramatic increase that might put the minimum wage close to or even above the existing median wage, as opposed to the ability of employers to afford retaining their workers in states where the current minimum wage is well below 50% of the median wage. Another adjustment would be to index the minimum wage to inflation so as to avoid the political process having to debate future increases, and thereby deflating the influence of lobbyists hired to argue against any increases. For families still in need a negative income tax boosting payment levels above those currently in place for the Earned Income Tax Credit program would contribute further to reducing income inequality while promoting higher standards of living for those in need.

Another reform that would improve the income levels and overall standard of living of a vital segment of the population would assist recent college graduates, particularly those burdened with debt from their student loans. As occurred during the 1950s and 1960s, and the early part of the 1970s until the first oil crisis, providing more high paying employment opportunities that included full benefits to these graduates would boost the standard of living of the younger generation and facilitate repayment of a much higher (than currently anticipated) percentage of their student loans. More higher paying employment opportunities would be likelier if there were a return to the 1960s attitudes of corporations towards rates of domestic investment and a modification of the current rules pertaining to globalization, along with reduction or elimination of incentives for corporations to invest and keep their profits abroad.

Given that the rate of homeownership is lower in 2015 than it has been since the 1970s this younger generation, and others with modest incomes, need assistance to own a home and thereby stabilize communities. Towards that objective the Department of Housing and Urban Development needs to be given the support it enjoyed pre-1980 before the workforce was cut in half. In recent years as banks have been unwilling to finance modest loans (about $50,000 or below) landlords with better credit ratings have moved in to purchase the same homes and become slumlords by renting them at very high rates, while some of the non-bank financial institutions charge unsuspecting low-income borrowers exorbitant mortgage rates and fees which raises the probability of foreclosures.

Job creation reform would be aided by recognizing, and funding accordingly, publicly funded investment in research and development that could benefit private sector firms and the general public. In the CWE the discourse on this topic has included the myth that the government is ineffective at "picking winners" that can prosper in the marketplace, and that the private sector is much better at doing so (Mazzucato, 2013). This ignores that much of the risky, expensive research and development that generates inventions has been funded by our government throughout the post-1940s period. During the pre-1980s era when private business firms took advantage of those inventions by successfully innovating in the marketplace to grow their business and earn profits they paid their share of taxes and reinvested in the domestic economy while creating good-paying jobs to the extent that many Americans experienced upward socioeconomic mobility. Under the CWE the trend has been that firms still innovate successfully and earn in some cases billions of dollars in profits using inventions the government funded, such as the case of Apple and its iPhone. However, Apple pays next to no taxes on those profits and relative to the size of those profits creates fewer jobs in the United States than the pre-1980s corporations. Other government-funded research has contributed directly to the development of products that are central to our everyday lives such as the internet, the Global Positioning System (GPS), and many medical procedures and types of equipment.

What are needed to varying degrees across the country are profitable domestic investments that generate above living-wage incomes for workers. Public investment could be in the form of rebuilding infrastructure, while the private sector could aim towards replacing overseas with domestic investments. Historically per million dollars invested in defense spending, construction of new stadiums, creation and sale of the latest financial asset, or expanding industrial farms will create far fewer good-paying jobs than would a comparable dollar volume of investments at the community level for ventures such as infrastructure repair for improving the capacity to produce products for the local and regional markets. Investments that promote community development would also assist with job creation for the younger generation.

A vital component of community development would be agricultural policy reforms that would include the phasing out of subsidies, some of which are corporate welfare, currently reaped primarily by large industrial farms using mono cropping primarily to produce corn, soybeans, wheat, cotton, rice, or sugar. Subsidies could be shifted towards expanding the existing movement that includes local fresh farm markets, restaurants offering farm to table menu items, and community supported agriculture (CSA) where farmers offer shares in the form of boxes of produce delivered on a regular basis to their members. The CSA assists farmers with their cash flow, marketing of their food, and developing a personal relationship with their customers, while also promoting integrated farming. Benefits to CSA members include receiving very fresh food and knowing their producer and how the produce is grown (or livestock raised) without having to decipher what is included on a food product's label – some of which (as discussed in previous chapters) can be deceiving and deceitful.

Expanding the local food production and marketing movement would stimulate increased local (and where feasible also organic) agricultural production and processing of local foods to reestablish a strong agricultural component to local communities. This movement, epitomized by Milwaukee's "Growing Power" organization, recognizes the many benefits of local agricultural development. These include job creation, more availability of better quality, healthier food products, and improving the health of local ecosystems while contributing to deceleration of the industrial farms' negative environmental effects – particularly greenhouse emissions and water pollution.[5] Integrated farms offer many advantages. They utilize a combination of agro science, agricultural engineering, ecology, conservation, plus business and economics principles to establish a more sustainable method of whole farm management. This type of farming also offers an alternative to industrial farm methods by combining production of fruits, vegetables, livestock, and livestock products (e.g., eggs) while utilizing both modern and traditional practices that are environmentally friendly.

Community support that would promote local agriculture and community development would include subsidies for local and organic fruit, vegetable and livestock production as well as for a conventional farm to transition into an integrated farm. The greater community could contribute by shopping for their food (as well as other locally and regionally produced goods and services) locally as often as feasible. Not only will this result in people consuming less food that has more potentially harmful artificial additives than they assume, but local farmers will be less likely to suffer when grocery chains choose the cheaper, mass-produced new "organic" produce offered by industrial farms instead of the locally produced products. One critic eloquently described how some Appalachian farmers and their communities have suffered as their local organic produce was no longer purchased by food wholesalers following the arrival in Appalachia from industrial farms of "pallets of organic tomatoes from

California … coming in just a few dollars cheaper" (Kingsolver, 2007, p. 210). While food and other products likely will cost more than if purchased from a national chain or large supermarket or retail establishment the quality of the product should be higher. In addition, when money is spent at locally owned businesses a much higher percentage of each dollar remains in that community than if spent at national chain stores. Typically well over 50% of each dollar spent locally will remain in the local economy while well under 50% remains when spending is at businesses not owned locally. As a result more local spending creates more jobs, builds community, enables production and consumption of healthier food, improves the ecosystem services by reducing environmental costs,[6] and in the case of livestock creates a more humane treatment of those animals.

Implementing some or all of the recommended policies aimed towards reestablishing a community-friendly economy will require an enormous investment as well as tax reform. Some of the funds would become available from what otherwise would have been doled out either as corporate welfare or through providing tax havens and special tax breaks for the wealthiest individuals. Additional funds could come from a global progressive tax on net wealth which would be calculated according to the total value of all assets owned by individuals including their real estate, bank accounts, insurance and pension plans, as well as stocks and bonds (Piketty, 2014). Since the distribution of wealth has become more highly skewed in the CWE and much of the wealth is not currently subject to taxation this could be another source of needed funds for transitioning to the new economy. Tax reform that eliminated loopholes for upper income groups and other modest reforms that stayed true to the principles of horizontal and vertical equity would add to the available revenue for transitioning to the new economy. An additional source of funds would be from savings due to reduced taxpayers' costs for environmental cleanup expenses as production methods shifted while extraction industries were required to pay the full cost of their damages – unlike ExxonMobil in Chris Christie's New Jersey.

Some believe the most pressing problem facing our country that is partly attributable to the CWE is environmental degradation and climate change. Environmental reforms would begin by adopting a new philosophy towards resource extraction and energy creation. The "extractivist mindset" (Klein, 2014, p. 447) that dominates the fossil fuel industry needs to be replaced with a philosophy based upon the precautionary principle when environmental policy decisions are concerned. Many excellent sources can be the basis for the new philosophy, including Jared Diamond's *Collapse* (2005), Herman Daly and Joshua Farley's *Ecological Economics* (2011), Daniel Goleman's *Ecological Intelligence* (2009), and Naomi Klein's *This Changes Everything* (2014). What these works have in common includes recognizing that we live in a finite world and have arrived at a point where production processes are taxing the ability of the ecosystem to continue supporting life. Lake Michigan's growing pollution problem and the loss of aquatic life due primarily to agricultural chemical runoff is not an isolated case. Continuation of industrial agriculture and the unsustainable, irresponsible extraction of minerals and energy sources using current methods will hasten the demise of our ecosystem. The guiding principles going forward for achieving environmental sustainability have been spelled out clearly by ecological economics expert Herman Daly (Daly and Farley, 2011). These include the need to limit the scale of production and live within the ecological limits of nature, which is paramount, to do so in the most efficient manner, and recognize that social justice needs to be achieved as the scale of economic activities would be reduced – thereby the existing distribution of wealth would become a more controversial issue. To achieve some of these objectives will require thousands of creative alternative means to generate energy and provide productive resources. It will also require reform of the EPA.

The EPA's credibility has come under scrutiny partly due to the appearance that the agency has been influenced by the oil and gas nexus. The agency's claiming responsibility for Colorado's Animus River becoming polluted with toxic water with high levels of arsenic and lead caused by a spill from an abandoned gold mine during the summer of 2015, poisoning the wells relied upon by about 1000 homes, will only increase criticism (Turkewitz, 2015). Whether or not the Kinross Gold Corporation that had last worked the mine will bear any of the cleanup costs remains to be seen. Meanwhile, southwest Colorado remains under constant threat from future cases of water pollution from the hundreds of other mines that have been closed down. Needed reforms of the EPA include making it more independent from Washington DC political influences, better funded, staffed by more independent scientists not beholden to corporate interests, and by giving a much freer rein to promote ecologically sustainable production practices.

The development of local integrated farms promotes such practices, including more biodiversity through preservation of woodlands and wildlife, as well as better maintenance of soil fertility. These farms also can help to reverse the startling decline in the number of pollinators nationwide, a decline hastened by the practice of mono cropping on industrial farms and the heavy use of pesticides. Evidence indicates higher yields per acre on integrated farms that embrace promoting agricultural biodiversity than yields on industrial farms. Greater biodiversity can also increase a farm's resiliency to climatic catastrophes, reduce contamination to soil and water from pesticides, reduce soil erosion, and enhance habitat for many forms of living creatures. A fascinating case study of a community that made a commitment to local development with an emphasis on its agricultural community that has achieved its goals is illustrated by the case of Samso, Denmark (Spear, 2014). This island successfully transformed its economy centered around the introduction of a range of renewable energy sources (wind, solar, geothermal, biomass) that has become an open laboratory for interested reformers who come from all over the world to study Samso's accomplishments.[7]

If the community-friendly economy were to be adopted how should we evaluate if it is meeting its goals? The most widely publicized indicators that have been used to evaluate the outcomes of the CWE are the rates of GDP growth, inflation, unemployment, interest, as well as the appreciation of stock prices, and profitability of corporations. For those wedded to GDP growth being *the* indicator for measuring an economy's ability to provide for its citizens, and who think that the new economy would hinder this growth rate, history reveals otherwise. The US economy had an annual average rate of GDP growth of about 3.6% between 1950 and 1979, versus about 2.7% between 1980 and 2014. GDP growth that was equal to or greater than 4% for five consecutive years has occurred only once since the mid-1940s, and that occurred between 1962 and 1966. Twice after that the growth rate was 4% or higher for four consecutive years, one of which was during the early 1950s. While GDP growth rates and the other major indicators should all continue to be measured and reported, the new economy should adopt additional indicators that would measure changes in the number of jobs created at different income levels, the percentage growth of income levels over time of the bottom 60% (or 80%) of the population, as well as changes in "progress" to be defined more broadly than simply growth of output and incomes – and in particular account for environmental damage from economic activities. Two particularly useful indicators focus on changes in income growth for below-average income earners and on a comprehensive measure of economic, social, and environmental outcomes.

The first indicator is the Ahluwalia–Chenery Index of Social Welfare. It was developed because of the misleading implication that improvements in overall income growth can be used to evaluate improvement in the earnings of everyone.[8] The index divides income earners into five groups of equal number (quintiles) ranging from the highest 20% of income earners on down to the lowest 20%, and then measures the income growth rate of each quintile. For example, income could grow about 7% over a one-year period, but the upper 20% of the income earners could have received well over half of the increased income, while the bottom 40% or 60% of income earners could have realized no increase in their income. Consequently, if each quintile is given an equal weight of 0.20 the 7% overall income growth rate hides this outcome. The Ahluwalia–Chenery Index assigns different weights to the income earned by each quintile rather than treating each income earner the same. For example, for its "poverty-weighted index" a 0.60 weight is assigned to the income earned by the lowest 20% of the population's income earners, and a 0.40 weight is assigned to the second lowest 20%. These weights are multiplied by the percentage increase in income received by those two groups, while a zero weight is assigned to income earned by each of the upper three quintiles. The resulting percentage indicates what percentage increase of the economy's income growth was received by the lower 40%. Over the past two decades this percentage has been at or close to zero. The advantage of adding such a measure as another indicator of macroeconomic outcomes is that it clearly identifies which income groups are receiving what share of any income growth. Policies that purport to be in the best interests of middle and lower income earners can then be evaluated for effectiveness using this index.

While GDP growth rates provide a good overall measure of economic activity, they do not account for numerous related outcomes. A second useful indicator is the Genuine Progress Indicator, which combines 26 different economic, environmental, and social measures into a single excellent indicator. Among the measures included are costs of crime, pollution, and commuting to work, income inequality, changes in leisure time, as well as depletion of resources and environmental cleanup costs. Due to its comprehensive nature it provides a broader, and truer picture of the effects of economic policies and as such should be used to supplement the standard GDP measures. For example, while the US GDP has risen substantially since 1980, "progress" as measured by the Genuine Progress Indicator has hardly risen at all.

Concluding Remarks

Detailed descriptions of community-friendly economies, including a more active involvement of workers owning and managing enterprises, can be found in *Think Like a Commoner* (Bollier, 2014) as well as in accounts of the growing cooperative movement nationwide.[9] Vermont also provides insight into what aspects of this type of economy would be like. The state has been able to put the political and economic power pyramid back to where it was in the 1960s, and as a result seems to manifest fewer indications that its residents are as alienated as many Americans in the 49 other states appear to be. The state maintains its rich history of communal governance over natural resources, and has in place local communal ownership and control over the negative features of privately owned firms' externalities. In doing so Vermont has been able to establish more self-regulation while freeing itself of being subject to the negative effects of corporate influence pervasive in the CWE. The state has been generating more positive economic, social, and political outcomes than most states dominated by CWE values and economic activities.

In many local areas people already have rejected the CWE and are attempting to reestablish the type of local economy that will be friendly to the community and avoid as best they can the negative effects of the CWE. We need a greater commitment to reduce the negative effects to our environment from extraction of resources and on budgets and incomes due to the trading of favors among nexus members, plus the growing alienation of workers and voters. This will require a nationwide rejection of the CWE and a mobilized effort to replace it with a community-friendly economy. Those who become involved in such a movement can expect a backlash once the size of the movement grows as more people begin to see through the lies that serve to create corporate welfare and tax breaks for the very wealthiest. The response likely would come from the industry nexuses' lackeys and blind zealots, including some in major news media, determined to continue receiving financial and power rewards at the expense of their own integrity, the interest of a majority of Americans, and democratic principles. However, economies that fail to provide for a majority of their nation's citizens are inevitably replaced. Our ability to replace the CWE, and in a peaceful manner, is an outcome devoutly to be wished.

Notes

1 Consider the case of cell phone tower locations. In 1996 the Federal Communications Commission enacted a regulation that prohibited local communities from including the consideration of health effects due to cell phone tower radiation when establishing zoning codes. No scientific findings regarding harmful health effects of cell phone tower radiation are permitted to be part of the discourse when a community makes a decision as to whether or not to grant a cell phone tower even though a growing number of studies give cause for concern. Local autonomy and property rights of individuals suffer as widely recognized and enforceable local community rights concerning ownership and control of our property and health were summarily superseded by a nexus-induced law that will boost profits at the expense of community rights, property, and free speech. Freedom of speech is also threatened when states such as Idaho pass an "ag-gag law" prohibiting undercover reporting intended to analyze the degree of inhumane treatment of livestock, with "guilty" whistleblowers subject to a prison term. A federal judge eventually overturned this law, ruling that it was not constitutional.

2 In Vermont some coalitions have been formed, such as the environmental group 350Vermont which acts with local works groups. Vermont, by virtue of being small with an active and knowledgeable citizenry, has long focused on environmental preservation, and local economies. Its citizenry has been and remains very interested in preserving landscape and their chosen way of life.

3 At this stage economists sympathetic to substantive reform, among them Dean Baker, Paul Krugman, and Joseph Stiglitz, should be asked to play a major role in policy making. Those leading a political movement to replace the status quo invariably are not those who should establish specific economic policies to achieve the movement's goals. This has been problematic in many countries, including the United States. Most people would readily admit they do not understand how a satellite can be launched or circle the earth, why a particular medicine can prevent a disease, or what the legal basis is for many federal laws. However, there are scientists at NASA, physicians at the FDA, and legal scholars on the Supreme Court that resolve such matters. It is noteworthy that there is not an independent federal government group of economic and financial experts with comparable authority over federal spending and rules associated with industry behavior, particularly the finance industry, with power comparable to that held by NASA, FDA, and Supreme Court officials.

Instead, economic policies are evaluated and voted upon by elected officials many of whom admittedly do not understand economics or finance, and who take their cues from leading Wall Street investment bank officials. An egregious example of this occurred during the 2012 presidential campaign when John McCain freely admitted he did not really understand economics. Then during the original bailout package policy debate in Congress McCain went to Washington DC and indicated he would play a leading role in the formulation of a bailout package designed to reverse downward economic activity while making the financial sector solvent. Few in our news media found this behavior problematic.

4   Note that due to the rising income inequality the percentage of income that falls below the maximum taxable earnings ($118,500 in 2015) has declined to about 85% in recent years.

5   For additional benefits of locally produced organic foods see https://www. organicconsumers.org/old_articles/ofgu/subsidies.htm

6   If purchasing more food locally results in fewer imports of produce by as little as 10%, the savings in gasoline would be in the hundreds of thousands of gallons due to less transportation of the food, and in the process would reduce CO_2 emissions.

7   For   more   information   see   http://ecowatch.com/2014/05/01/samso-renewable-energy-island-sustainable-communities/

8   For a detailed discussion of the index see Todaro and Smith, 2014.

9   For one account see Alperovitz, 2011. In this article Alperovitz describes the growth of cooperative businesses and credit unions, noting that "[a]s of 2011 more than 13 million Americans have become worker-owners of more than 11,000 employee-owned companies, six million more than belong to private-sector unions."

Appendix 1

The Beam in the Author's Eyes: Community Values Trump Free Market Values

The type of economy I would prefer for the United States is one that would combine the institutions and rules that existed between 1950 and 1980 – during which time the standard of living of nearly all Americans was rising, and that of the lower 50% was rising slightly faster than for the higher 50%. That would mean: (1) a return to the "boring" savings banks and other financial institutions that had to comply with the rules that existed prior to the late 1980s to early 2000s deregulation of the finance industry; (2) pre-1980 tax regulations (with an upper marginal tax rate of 35% – but with many of the current tax loopholes for individuals and corporations eliminated); (3) a greater degree of protection from foreign competition that existed pre "globalization" so as to protect the typical worker's income; (4) fiscal policy that required low budget deficits (less than 2% of GDP); (5) social security and health care revenue received so that payment obligations would be financially sustainable beyond my grandchildren's generation; (6) a public health care system that provides universal coverage *but* that would also require individuals pay above average insurance premiums for living lifestyles deemed unhealthy – and thus likely to require them to receive extensive and expensive health care; (7) institutions involved with production and distribution would remain predominantly privately owned, but with a stronger degree of public control sufficient to reduce market failures such as monopoly power, spillover costs, inadequate information, and poverty. In particular, polluters (both producers and consumers) would bear the full cost of the negative external effects caused by the good or service produced and consumed; and (8) no individual firm or the largest few firms in any industry would be considered too big to fail.

My preferred outcomes from this type of economy would include: (1) far lower rates of poverty and crime than currently exist; (2) greater security for Americans in terms of public pensions and health care benefits; (3) a far lower degree of income and wealth inequality than exists in 2015; (4) required ecological sustainability (as deemed so by environmental scientists) for industrial, agricultural, distribution, consumption, and waste disposal practices; and (5) evaluation of the effectiveness of economic policy according to the following two measures: first, a poverty-weighted index of social welfare that would measure how the lower 60% of income earners fared over time under the policy or set of macroeconomic policies pursued by the United States; second, the Genuine Progress Indicator.[1] This latter measure shifts away from emphasizing the annual percentage change in real GDP as *the* best barometer for measuring overall economic activity. As an alternative measure the Genuine Progress Indicator defines economic and social progress to mean the overall improvement in well-being of citizens. It is measured by using economic, social (particularly health), and ecological criteria rather than only GDP growth. Some of the criteria used to determine an index of "progress" include personal consumption data, income distribution, value of household and volunteer work, costs of crime and pollution, changes in leisure time, resource depletion, long-term environmental damage, the opportunity costs of defense expenditures, lifespan of consumer durables and public infrastructure, and dependence upon foreign assets.

If my preferred outcomes seem unattainable, note that the northern European countries have achieved these outcomes while ranking very high as compared to the rest of the world in terms of "happiness" and income security measures, while their multinational corporations' ability to compete in world markets ranks very high as measured by the Global Competitiveness Index (World Economic Forum, 2015). Further, one study (Blow, 2011[2]) that compares the United States versus 32 other rich countries indicates that US standard of living has become worse than in most other wealthy countries as demonstrated by the following indicators: income inequality, unemployment rate, level of democracy, a well-being of living standards index, food insecurity, life expectancy at birth, prison population, and high school student scores on standardized mathematics and science tests. Data was taken from a range of sources that include the US government, international organizations, and individual studies conducted by academic analysts. It is striking that the United States did not rank among the top 10 countries in *any* of these indicators. Even worse, we rank among the bottom quarter in nearly every one of these measures of social and economic standards, and among the worst 15% in terms of income inequality, unemployment, prison population, and high school students' mathematics test scores (Blow, 2011). The income inequality ranking (with the lowest degree of inequality being #1) of the United States in a recent study was 95th in the world (Coy, 2012). Another study by a London think tank, the Legatum Institute, ranked countries according to "prosperity (Helmen, 2013)." The Legatum Prosperity Index measured "prosperity" in 142 countries, using 89 indicators in eight categories that included education, government, and economics. The eight highest ranking countries were all social democracies mainly from Europe or Oceania, each of which offers its citizens generous welfare benefits financed by redistribution of income and wealth: 1 Norway; 2 Denmark; 3

Sweden; 4 Australia; 5 New Zealand; 6 Canada; 7 Finland; and 8 the Netherlands. These same countries all feature high degrees of civic literacy and civil liberties, and also place few restrictions on the flow of private capital. Meanwhile, in the free market paradise featuring policies some of which have been advocated or created by mystics such as Milton Friedman, Alan Greenspan, and Lawrence Summers the United States ranked 12th, down from a 10th place ranking in the 2011/12 study – although we did retain a number 1 ranking in growth of waste lines and purchase of ammunition for personal use.

Notes

1 For a description of the "Genuine Progress Indicator" see http:// genuineprogress.net/genuine-progress-indicator/
2 Sources: *The World Factbook*, CIA; Bureau of Labor Statistics; Economist Intelligence Unit; OECD UNICEF; King's College London; and World Economic Forum, 2013, "Global Competitiveness Report 2012/2013."

Appendix 2

Who Is Likelier to Accurately Predict Economic Policy Outcomes: An "Expert" Econometrician or a Chimpanzee?

According to psychologist Daniel Kahneman's research (Kahneman, 2011), which earned him the 2002 Nobel Prize in Economics, given the complexity of our world, particularly economic activity, many people choose to rely on "experts" for a simplified prediction of future economic conditions. These experts unfortunately develop a false confidence that their knowledge of past outcomes will enable them to accurately predict the future. As Kahneman argues, "[t]he illusion that we understand the past fosters overconfidence in our ability to predict the future (Slome, 2012)." Consequently, many economic predictions made by experts, particularly econometricians, are as likely to predict accurately economic outcomes from a given policy as a dart-throwing chimpanzee whose predictions are targets on the dart board that represent a range of outcomes.

This critique of econometrician forecasts, and criticism of existing standard of living indicators and associated reforms, is influenced by my own perspective and values concerning economic activity and outcomes from that activity. Presenting this perspective (see below) and values (see Appendix 1) will permit a reader to better understand the questions posed and interpretations offered throughout this book as well as the set of socioeconomic conditions and public policies I believe ought to exist. By not including this information a reader could become confused about the book's main objective as well as the influence on this objective from my personal values and analytical perspective. This occurred when draft chapters of this book were reviewed. One reviewer of some draft chapters was quite dismissive of the book's main theme because he/she was convinced I am an orthodox free market economist with a libertarian agenda. I would prefer to be considered a reality TV program junkie who advocated eating Twinkies. Another reviewer who read the same chapters believed me to be a socialist, albeit without explaining what "socialist" means.

To set the record straight, my way of thinking is that of a heterodox economist with sympathy for causes championed by European social democrats. My perspective when analyzing economic matters is that of a political economist, which stands in sharp contrast to the perspective held by orthodox economists. This perspective includes: (1) analysis of the political and economic mechanisms shaping our economy's goals and rules pertaining to production and distribution activities; and (2) recognition that the outcomes of these activities will be heavily influenced by the relative distribution of power held by individuals and economic institutions from that economy. This distribution affects the ability to translate one's economic power into political power to gain favors. An example of the excessive influence due to highly skewed distribution of income and wealth would be the ability of private owners of a professional sports franchise to influence state legislation to heavily subsidize the construction of more luxury boxes in a stadium or arena where this privately owned professional sports team plays its games.

If you prefer to accept the orthodox economists' belief in the superiority of free markets then ask yourself why these economists have not argued en masse for the elimination of tenure for all academic economists – a status protecting them from competitive market forces. If you think people are capable of always acting rationally when making purchase decisions survey fans of professional wrestling concerning their buying patterns, or consider someone who purchased a new home in 2007. Whereas orthodox economists tend to have faith that all members of an economy can benefit from a free market economy, evidence over the past 30 years is that countries (and some states in the United States) moving in a free market direction have witnessed declining living standards for a majority of their population. Whereas orthodox economists believe that free markets tend towards a stable equilibrium and endorse the efficient market hypothesis as it pertains to financial markets, I reject this position. I believe that lightly regulated financial markets tend towards considerable instability and, as one financial market expert argued, that the efficient market hypothesis theory is closer to rubbish than useful. While I agree with orthodox economists' belief that the rule of law will promote good outcomes in an economy, few of them emphasize how public choice theory (where self-interested groups lobby bureaucrats and elected officials for special favors not in the interest of the general public) affects the creation of these laws. Consequently, they have become blind to the emergence of the corporate welfare economy. Finally, orthodox economists pay far too little attention to the growing ecological problems, failing to recognize the full world "commons" we live in and the tragedy occurring due to economic growth rates and methods taxing, and in some cases destroying, ecosystems.[1]

I recognize the limitations of data, particularly that even the most sophisticated data does not measure quality, importance of place, loyalty, significance of tradition and culture. I enthusiastically endorse the cutting edge perspective of Nassim Taleb, author of *The Black Swan* (2007) and *Antifragile* (2012). He argues that the more data analysts acquire, the greater their ability to identify an even greater number of statistically significant correlations. The problem is that once such connections have been identified "[m]ost of these correlations are spurious and deceive us when we're trying to understand a situation. Falsity grows exponentially the more data we collect. The haystack gets bigger, but the needle we are looking for is still buried deep inside" (Brooks, 2013). Further, while orthodox economists purport to be value free with their use of "objective data," the reality is that they ask the question for which an answer is to be provided from using data, they choose the source of the data, and they interpret the data. Their values are inherent in the analysis every step of the way. Think about it – when was the last time an orthodox economist touted the response of Sweden's government to its mid-1990s financial crisis (when the managers of the banks were fired after the government temporarily nationalized the banks)? Also, have you read many orthodox economists' analysis of what we can learn from Chinese policy makers whose country's economy has averaged about 8% rate of GDP growth for over 35 years?

Taleb's critique of economists' predictions adds to the cutting edge work of Kahneman. His criticisms focus on how orthodox economists, when working with data, fail to account for random, uncertain events that occur in, and significantly affect, every economy (chimpanzees do not succumb to this accounting failure). He forcefully argues that randomness and uncertainty are the rule within social systems, not the exception. Some economic policy makers capable of adjusting policies in response to such randomness and uncertainty have been successful. This has been true in the cases of those who led the dramatic improvement of the Swedish, Japanese, and Chinese economies from a position of low development to a much higher level. Their policy makers accepted that randomness and uncertainty exist, and in response saw fit to "build a systematic and broad guide to non predictive decision making under uncertainty (Taleb, 2012, p. 4)." Orthodox economists try to combat randomness and volatility with orthodox macroeconomic fiscal and monetary policies. Unfortunately, as Taleb argues, doing so tends to make economies even more fragile and likelier to suffer even greater negative effects when the next unpredictable, random event occurs. Witness the dubious record of IMF and World Bank policies in poor countries and top-down macroeconomic policies proposed by orthodox economists. Taleb is skeptical of policy makers from such institutions because they do not have any "skin in the game" (little to lose if their forecasts and misguided policies fail) (Taleb, 2012, pp. 5–6).

The growing ineffectiveness of orthodox economic forecasts and policies also is attributable in part to the emphasis on econometric modeling. Intent on making economics "scientific," complete with determinate solutions, orthodox economists define "scientific research" as research "formulated mathematically" (Lawson, 2012, p. 26). As a result, increasingly formulaic, abstract mathematical models have been brought into play for analyzing these problems. I agree with Taleb's argument that such models fail to predict certain events such as a financial or real estate crisis because of the analyst's inability to "predict large-scale unpredictable and irregular events" (Taleb, 2012, p. 6) – known as black swans. Taleb offered his black swan theory to describe such events which, when they occur, surprise the analyst and those influenced to agree with the faulty prediction. The event may have a substantial negative effect on society. The fundamental problem concerning forecasting these events is that the probability of events that occur rarely cannot be computed. Taleb refers to those who believe they can use their econometric models to predict accurately as being a "fragilista" – analysts who fervently believe in their ability to identify the reasons behind economic outcomes. Unfortunately, a fragilista "defaults to thinking that what he [or she] doesn't see is not there, or what he does not understand does not exist. At the core, he tends to mistake the unknown for the nonexistent" (Taleb, 2012, p. 8).

The threat to societies from such a perspective is that it underlies policies based upon the arrogant, misguided belief that the "scientific knowledge" possessed by fragilistas enables them to both create effective policies and forecast their outcomes. An egregious example of this occurred prior to the financial and real estate crises in 2008. Fragilistas that included Nobel Prize winner Joseph Stiglitz and Peter Orzag, the first Director of the Office of Management and Budget in the Obama administration, predicted prior to 2008 that there was no risk of default for either Fannie Mae or Freddie Mac. Their forecasts contributed to an absence of policy response to the growing fragility of the financial and real estate industries as the housing bubble grew – making them "dangerous" as their views were made public and gave credibility, especially among other fragilistas and their followers who attend the World Economic Forum in Davos, to their belief in the absence of default risk. Among the problems with their perspective was that they had "no clue about the fragility of [economic] systems" since they possessed a "harmful misunderstanding of small probabilities by the economics establishment. It is a severe disease, one that explains why economists will blow us up again" (Taleb, 2012, pp. 386–7).

Orthodox economists combine their belief in the reliability of econometric forecasts with blind faith in unregulated markets. Examples of influential fragilistas who held this belief are three of the principal economic policy makers who contributed significantly to the 2008 financial and real estate crises: Alan Greenspan, Lawrence Summers, and Ben Bernanke. All three believed strongly "that big, private, lightly regulated financial institutions are good for America" (Johnson and Kwak, 2011, p. 162). Some observers believe that "there came to be no truer believer in the ideology of free markets, financial innovation, and deregulation" than Greenspan. His "faith-based regulation" of financial markets instead of prudent government regulations was perhaps more influential than anyone else, with the possible exception of Milton Friedman, in that "failed experiment" (Goodman, 2009, p. 217). When faced proposals from leaders of Congress or federal regulators to regulate derivatives, which ultimately became highly toxic, he "fiercely objected" while arguing that the "good will of Wall Street" required only "self regulation" (Goodman,

2008). Summers, who is on record as having claimed that "[t]he laws of economics are like the laws of engineering. ... One set of laws works everywhere" (Klein, 2007, p. 275), argued fervently that Wall Street investment firms' top management would behave responsibly so that the financial system would function smoothly as a result. He also should be credited with being one of the prime proponents of financial industry deregulation as well as an aggressive, foghorn-like voice against subsequent attempts to regulate financial derivatives. Meanwhile Bernanke consistently exhibited considerable faith that the mortgage crisis would not spill over into the macro economy. Even after the 2008 financial crisis he continued to "sing the praises of financial innovation" (Johnson and Kwak, 2011, p. 107) which indicates a quintessential case of blind faith in unregulated markets.

Other fragilistas who possessed a strong faith-based conviction in the desirability of deregulated financial markets made their own faulty forecasts that further contributed to the financial crisis. During 2007, soon-to-be-appointed Treasury Secretary (in 2009) Timothy Geithner believed that the US economy was not in any danger of recession. A few months earlier in a Federal Open Market Committee of the Federal Reserve Board meeting, Geithner, the vice chairman, argued that despite some problems with the housing market the US economy looked reasonably well, while the reigning Treasury Secretary, Henry Paulson, dismissed the subprime mortgage issue as not being a serious problem.

These fragilistas, and nearly all other orthodox economic policy makers, rarely question the end results of failed policies because they agree with the orthodox means used to implement these policies. They consistently have endorsed top-down policies created like a chef prepares a recipe, namely add specific ingredients in a specific order, process them, and a predetermined outcome will occur – just like making chocolate chip cookies. An egregious example has been globalization. Freer trade and investment worldwide has enabled Americans to purchase a plethora of low-priced electronic goods and video games, among other products, and to almost effortlessly disseminate information such as what they had for lunch to their entire social network. Unfortunately what free trade advocates failed to recognize is that in nearly all economies throughout the world since the 1950s where globalization policies based upon the free market fundamentalism championed by the orthodox economists like themselves have been introduced the outcomes ultimately have been negative for all but a small percentage of wealthy individuals or families.

It is noteworthy, however, to examine the reaction of the three aforementioned fragilistas representing Wall Street, as well as nearly all World Bank and IMF economists, to the US 2008 financial crisis. Rather than advocate the same type of free market policies that are the bedrock of globalization policies they forcefully argued that the US government must permit the irresponsibly managed large US investment banks not to fail by providing them with billions of bailout subsidies. As one expert analyst pointed out, these three "chose the blank check option, over and over again" (Johnson and Kwak, 2011, p. 173). This corporate welfare came at unprecedented public expense, as "[n]ever before had so much taxpayer money [which ultimately could exceed $100 billion] been dedicated to save an industry from the consequences of its own mistakes" (Johnson and Kwak, 2011, p. 165).

One final characteristic of orthodox economists that helps to explain why there is little in orthodox economists' research about corporate welfare is their group-think culture which almost exclusively focuses on individual behavior as the basis for all economic activity. This focus is supported by wealthy private interests, particularly through consulting contracts provided to prominent orthodox economists. These wealthy private sector interests are, in turn, part of what one researcher describes as a "group culture" that "discourages economists from recognizing this group culture or the powerful organizations that support it" (Van den Berg, 2014). The outcome is that much of the orthodox economists' research focuses on a "mythical market system that actually has little resemblance" (Van den Berg, 2014) to the type of corporate welfare economy the United States has become.

Notes

1   Orthodox thinkers adopt such a perspective because of the narrow, ideological graduate economic education and the economic perspective instilled in them, leading to their fervent single-minded championing of a pro-democratic, free market ideology. Having been imbued with a systematized body of orthodox economic theory that validates a particular institutional structure (a "free market economy"), and the corresponding values inherent in this structure, they go on to use their economic theory as a weapon in what is essentially an ideological crusade. Due to such education "economics remains caught in a set of assumptions which not only serve enormously important ideological purposes, but also offers little help in understanding the modern world" (Manicas, 2007). No alternative to their abstract notion of a free market economy is considered.

2   After the 2008 financial crisis had occurred Greenspan, confronted with his free market values and perspective, eventually "admitted that his faith had been excessive" (Goodman, 2009, p. 17).

Bibliography

Aiken, K. 1994. Not Long Ago a Smoking Chimney Was a Sign of Prosperity: Corporate and Community Response to Pollution at the Bunker Hill Smelter in Kellogg, Idaho. *Environmental History Review*. Vol. 18, Number 2, Summer, pp. 67–86.

Allen, B. 2007. Exxon-Mobil-Funded Think Tank Solicits Criticism of Report on Global Warming, EthicsDaily.com, February 7. www.ethicsdaily.com/exxon-mobil-funded-think-tank-solicits-criticism-of-report-on-global-warming-cms-8502

Alperovitz, G. 2011. Worker-Owners of America, Unite! *New York Times*, December 14. www.nytimes.com/2011/12/15/opinion/worker-owners-of-america-unite.html?_r=0

Anderson, A. F. 1998. Book Review: *Field of Schemes: How the Great Stadium Swindle Turns Public Money into Private Profit*, *Marquette Sports Law Review* 8(2), Spring. http://scholarship.law.marquette.edu/cgi/viewcontent.cgi?article=1260&context=sportslaw

Anderson, R. 2014. Pharmaceutical Industry Gets High on Fat Profits, BBC News, November 6. www.bbc.com/news/business-28212223

Angresano, J. 2010. The Financial, Real Estate, and Macroeconomic Crises: Precursors to the Decline of the USA Empire, Conference papers, Varna University of Economics, "Science and Economy" Publishing, Vol. 1: 276–96.

Angresano, J. 2007. *French Welfare State Reform*, London: Anthem Press.

Angresano, J. 2005. China's Development Strategy: A Game of Chess that Countered Orthodox Development Advice, *Journal of Socio-Economics*, 34: 471–98.

Applebaum, B. 2012. Family Net Worth Drops to Level of Early '90s, Fed Say, *New York Times*, June 11. www.nytimes.com/2012/06/12/business/economy/family-net-worth-drops-to-level-of-early-90s-fed-says.html

Applebaum, B. 2011. A Recovery That Repeats Its Painful Precedents, *New York Times*, July 28. www.nytimes.com/2011/07/29/business/economy/as-growth-slows-us-recovery-seems-to-repeat-a-pattern.html?pagewanted=all

Armour, S. 2012. Snack Attack: Moms Take On Nutella, Fruit Roll-Ups, *Bloomberg Business*, June 21. www.bloomberg.com/bw/articles/2012-06-21/snack-attack-moms-take-on-nutella-fruit-roll-ups

Aswell, T. 2014. Legislative Members of ALEC Check their Principles at Door When It Comes to Accepting Farm Subsidy (Welfare) Payments, *Louisiana Voice*, April 23. http://theind.com/LaLaLand/alec-toadies-have-no-problemwith-corporate-welfare-3216/

Babiak, P. and Hare, R. 2006. *Snakes in Suits: When Psychopaths Go to Work*, New York: Harper.

Badal, S. 2010. *Entrepreneurship and Job Creation: Leveraging the Relationship*, Washington, DC: Gallup, World Headquarters. www.nifa.org/downloads/entrepreneurshipandjobcreation10711.pdf

Bacon, J. 2013. Fracking-Harmed Residents Confront EPA and Demand Reopened Investigation, *Environmental Action*, August 13. http://environmental-action.org/blog/fracking-harmed-residents-confront-epa-and-demand-reopened-investigation/

Baker, D. 2014. Fund Managers Tax Break: Because Wall Streeters Want Your Money, *Huffington Post*, April 14. www.huffingtonpost.com/dean-baker/the-hedge-fund-managers-t_b_5148468.html

Baker, D. 2008. Trade and Inequality: The Role of Economists, *Post-Autistic Economics Review*, Issue 45. www.paecon.net/PAEReview/issue45/Baker45.pdf

Bakhtiari, E. 2008. Palinomics in Alaska – Taxing and Spending, *The Moderate Voice*, September 9. http://themoderatevoice.com/22557/palinomics-in-alaska-taxing-and-spending/

Bandow, D. 2012. Where to Cut the Federal Budget? Start by Killing Corporate Welfare, August 20. www.forbes.com/sites/dougbandow/2012/08/20/where-to-cut-the-federal-budget-start-by-killing-corporate-welfare/

Barr, N. 2004. *Economics of the Welfare State*, 4th edn, Oxford: Oxford University Press.

Barshay, J. 2014. Measuring the Cost of Federal Student Loans to Taxpayers, *Washington Monthly*, June 16. www.washingtonmonthly.com/college_guide/blog/measuring_the_cost_of_federal.php

Bass, F. 2012. Rich–Poor Gap Widest in Republican-Leaning States, Census Shows, *Yahoo!Finance*, March 9. www.justiceunited.net/2012_03_01_archive.htm

Bello, M. 2012. More than 1.4 Million Families Live on $2 a Day Per Person, *USA Today*, February 24. www.sanders.senate.gov/newsroom/news/?id=6FAA189F-C06A-47B5-B8CE-E70EB8DAF713

Berg, S. and Southorn, D. 2014. For New Boise Hawks Owners, An Old Pitch, *Idaho Statesman*, September 24. www.idahostatesman.com/2014/09/24/3391332_for-new-hawks-owners-old-pitch.html?rh=1

Bittman, M. 2013A. The F.D.A.'s Not-Really-Such-Good-News, *New York Times*, December 17. www.nytimes.com/2013/12/18/opinion/bittman-the-fdas-not-really-such-good-news.html?pagewanted=all

Bittman, M. 2013B. Welfare for the Wealthy, *New York Times*, June 4. http://opinionator.blogs.nytimes.com/2013/06/04/welfare-for-the-wealthy/

Bjerga, A. and Bykowicz, J. 2014. A Farm Bill Only a Lobbyist Could Love, *Bloomberg Business*, January 30. www.bloomberg.com/bw/articles/2014-01-30/farm-bill-draws-lobbyist-horde

Blodget, H. 2012A. American Incomes Are Falling and Near-Retirees Are Getting Crushed: Study, *Yahoo!Finance*, August 24. http://finance.yahoo.com/blogs/daily-ticker/american-incomes-falling-near-retirees-getting-crushed-study-150139666.html

Blodget, H. 2012B. The Middle Class Is Broke: Pew Study Reveals Real Problem with Economy, *Yahoo!Finace*, August 23. http://finance.yahoo.com/blogs/daily-ticker/middle-class-broke-pew-study-reveals-real-problem-155018682.html

Blodget, H. 2011. Matt Taibbi: Goldman Sachs Executives Lied to Their Customers and Congress, *Yahoo!Finance,* May 17. http://finance.yahoo.com/blogs/daily-ticker/matt-taibbi-goldman-sachs-executives-lied-customers-congress-175044553.html

Blood Horse. 2014. Tax Break on Racehorses Passes Congress, December 16. www.bloodhorse.com/horse-racing/articles/89213/tax-break-on-racehorses-passes-congress

Bloomberg Businessweek. 2015. Is a $15 Minimum Wage Too High? August 10–23. www.bloomberg.com/news/articles/2015-08-06/is-a-15-minimum-wage-too-high-

Bloomberg Businessweek. 2014. Big Enough to Drive a Government Contract Through, July 14–20. http://resourcecenter.businessweek.com/reviews/big-enough-to-drive-a-government-contract-through

Bloomberg Businessweek. 2013. The Great Gatsby Curve: How Inequality Became a Household Word, December 12. www.bloomberg.com/bw/articles/2013-12-05/obama-talks-inequality-and-mobility-going-full-gatsby

Bloomberg Politics. 2015. Big Corn Butters Up the 2016 Hopefuls, March 9–15. www.bloomberg.com/politics/articles/2015-03-05/big-corn-butters-up-the-2016-hopefuls

Blow, C. M. 2013. Billionaires' Row and Welfare Lines, *New York Times,* October 25. www.nytimes.com/2013/10/26/opinion/blow-billionaires-row-and-welfare-lines.html

Blow, C. M. 2011. Empire at the End of Decadence, *New York Times,* February 18. www.nytimes.com/2011/02/19/opinion/19blow.html

Boesler, M. and Kearns, J. 2015. Fed's "Revolving Door" Spins Faster as Banks Set to Boost Hiring, *Washington Post,* January 30. http://washpost.bloomberg.com/Story?docId=1376-NGDQC46VDKHY01-6CBN77V3L9H8I4QLBI0N9MTT71

Bollier, D. 2014. *Think Like a Commoner,* Gabriola Island, BC, Canada: New Society Publishers.

Bovard, J. 1995. Archer Daniels Midland: A Case Study in Corporate Welfare, Policy Analysis No. 241, Cato Institute, September 26. www.cato.org/pubs/pas/pa-241.html

Brandon, E. 2012. Poverty Increasing among Retirees, *Yahoo!Finance,* May 21. http://finance.yahoo.com/news/poverty-increasing-among-retirees-164453772.html

Brodwin, D. 2015. Fast Track to a Bad Deal: Congress Shouldn't Give the President Authority to Fast Track a Lousy Trade Deal, *US News and World Report,* February 17. www.usnews.com/opinion/economic-intelligence/2015/02/17/fast-track-for-the-trans-pacific-partnership-is-a-bad-deal

Brooks, D. 2013. What Data Can't Do, *New York Times,* February 18. www.nytimes.com/2013/02/19/opinion/brooks-what-data-cant-do.html?_r=0

Brooks, D. 2012A. The Two Economies, *New York Times,* April 9. www.nytimes.com/2012/04/10/opinion/brooks-the-two-economies.html

Brooks, D. 2012B. America Is Europe, *New York Times,* February 23. www.nytimes.com/2012/02/24/opinion/brooks-america-is-europe.html?hp

Brooks, D. 2010. The Broken Society, *New York Times,* March 19. www.nytimes.com/2010/03/19/opinion/19brooks.html

Bureau of Labor Statistics. 2012. The Employment Situation – June 2012. www.bls.gov/news.release/pdf/empsit.pdf

Business Insider. 2010. 22 Statistics that Prove the Middle Class Is Being Systematically Wiped Out of Existence in America, July 15. www.businessinsider.com/22-statistics-that-prove-the-middle-class-is-being-systematically-wiped-out-of-existence-in-america-2010-7

Business Pundit. 2011. 10 Charts that Illustrate What's Wrong with the America, March 16. www.businesspundit.com/10-charts-that-illustrate-whats-wrong-with-the-america/lisay/

Cagan, J. and deMause, N. 1998. *Field of Schemes: How the Great Stadium Swindle Turns Public Money into Private Profit*, Monroe, ME: Common Courage Press.

Callenbach, E. 2008. The Hollowing Out of the American Empire, *Cascadia Commons*, June 16. www.cascadiacommons.org/index.php.callenbach

Campbell, B. M. 2015. Chris Christie's Exxon Settlement Is Bad for New Jersey, *New York Times*, March 4. www.nytimes.com/2015/03/05/opinion/chris-christies-exxon-settlement-is-bad-for-new-jersey.html

Campione, J. 2014. Wall Street Wins in $1.1 Trillion Spending Bill, But Who Loses? *Yahoo!Finance*, December 12. http://finance.yahoo.com/news/wall-street-wins-in--1-1-trillion-spending-bill--but-who-loses-162059497.html

Cannadine, D. 2006. *Mellon*, New York: Alfred A. Knopf.

Carney, J. 2013. Insider Trading in Our Nation's Capital Just Got Easier, *Yahoo!Finance*, April 17. http://finance.yahoo.com/news/insider-trading-nations-capital-just-123453723.html

Carville, J. 2012. Middle Class "Hit by Truck," *Yahoo!Finance*, 2013. http://finance.yahoo.com/news/james-carville-middle-class-hit-003512805.html

Cato Institute, 1999. Corporate Subsidies in the Federal Budget, Congressional Testimony of Stephen Moore, Director of Fiscal Policy Studies, Washington, DC, June 30. www.cato.org/testimony/ct-sm063099.html

Catts, T., Robison, P. and Kolet, I. 2013. No Renaissance for U.S. Factory Workers as Pay Stagnates, *Bloomberg.com news*, November 21. www.bloomberg.com/news/articles/2013-11-21/no-renaissance-for-u-s-factory-workers-as-pay-stagnates

Censky, A. 2012. The 86 Million Invisible Unemployed, *CNN Money*, May 4. http://money.cnn.com/2012/05/03/news/economy/unemployment-rate/index.htm

Censky, A. 2011A. A Rough 10 Years for the Middle Class, *CNN Money*, October 14. http://money.cnn.com/2011/09/21/news/economy/middle_class_income/index.htm

Censky, A. 2011B. Middle-class Income Fell in the Last Decade, *CNNMoney.com*, September 23. http://money.cnn.com/2011/09/21/news/economy/middle_class_income/index.htm

Censky, A. 2011C. How the Middle Class Became the Underclass, *Yahoo!Finance*, February 16. www.sodahead.com/living/how-the-middle-class-became-the-underclass-does-this-make-you-angry-disillusionedor-motivated/question-1517643/

Center for Responsive Politics. 2015A. Sen. Christopher Dodd, Center for Responsive Politics, March 9. www.opensecrets.org/politicians/industries.php?cycle=Career&cid=N00000581

Center for Responsive Politics. 2015B. Oil and Gas, Center for Responsive Politics, February 2. https://www.opensecrets.org/industries/indus.php?ind=E01++ and DirtyEnergyMoney.com "Exxon Mobil"

Center for Responsive Politics. 2014. Top Industries, Center for Responsive Politics. https://www.opensecrets.org/lobby/top.php?indexType=i&showYear=2014

Center for Responsive Politics. 2010. Oil and Gas: Top Contributors to Federal Candidates, Parties, and Outside Groups, Center for Responsive Politics. www.opensecrets.org/industries/contrib.php?cycle=2010&ind=e01

Chatterjee, P. 2009. *Halliburton's Army*, New York: Nation Books.

Christie, L. 2010. Census Bureau Reports New Spike in Poverty, *CNNMoney.com*, September 16. http://money.cnn.com/2010/09/16/news/economy/Census_poverty_rate/index.htm

Christie, L. and Stewart, R. 2012. Countrywide Issued Hundreds of VIP Loans to Buy Influence, Report Says, *CNN Money*, July 5. http://money.cnn.com/2012/07/05/real_estate/countrywide-mortgage/

Citizens for Responsibility and Ethics in Washington. 2015. Natural Cash – Fracking Industry Contributions to Congress, Citizens for Responsibility and Ethics in Washington, May. www.citizensforethics.org/pages/natural-cash-fracking-industry-contributions-to-congress

Citizens for Responsibility and Ethics in Washington. 2009. Crew Releases Fifth Annual Most Corrupt Members of Congress Report, Citizens for Responsibility and Ethics in Washington, July 9. www.citizensforethics.org/press/entry/crew-releases-fifth-annual-most-corrupt-members-of-congress-report

CNN. 2009. New American Embassy Opens in Baghdad, January 5. www.cnn.com/2009/WORLD/meast/01/05/iraq.main/index.html?_s=PM:WORLDde

CNN Money. 2015. NFL Gets Billions in Subsidies from U.S. Taxpayers, January 30. http://money.cnn.com/2015/01/30/news/companies/nfl-taxpayers/

Coates, D. and Humphreys, B. R. 2004. Caught Stealing: Debunking the Economic Case for D.C. Baseball, Briefing Paper No. 89, Cato Institute, October 27. www.cato.org/publications/briefing-paper/caught-stealing-debunking-economic-case-dc-baseball

Coburn, T. A. 2011. Subsidies of the Rich and Famous, November. www.coburn.senate.gov/public/index.cfm?a=Files.Serve&File_id=bb1c90bc-660c-477e-91e6-91c970fbee1f

Cohan, W. D. 2012. Rethinking Robert Rubin, *Bloomberg Businessweek*, September 20. www.bloomberg.com/bw/articles/2012-09-19/rethinking-robert-rubin

Cohan, W. D. 2011. The Reform that Wasn't, *New York Times*, March 30. http://opinionator.blogs.nytimes.com/2011/03/30/the-reform-that-wasnt/

Cohen, S. 2012. Faces beyond the Numbers of Long-term Unemployed, *Yahoo!Finance*, February 11. http://finance.yahoo.com/news/faces-beyond-numbers-long-term-152829723.html

Collins, G. 2013. The House Just Wants to Snack, *New York Times*, July 12. www.nytimes.com/2013/07/13/opinion/collins-the-house-just-wants-to-snack.html

Commons Magazine. 2011. In Wisconsin, Governor Walker's Secret Privatization Agenda: Selling Off State Assets with No Bids Hidden in the Fine Print of Budget Repair Bill, February 25. www.onthecommons.org/wisconsin-governor-walkers-secret-privatization-agenda

Conference Board Consumer Confidence Index. 2010. Consumer Confidence Index: Down Slightly but Well Below Historical Trend, December 28. http://seekingalpha.com/article/239308-consumer-confidence-index-up-slightly-but-well-below-historical-trend

Confessore, N. 2015. Koch Brothers' Budget of $889 Million for 2016 Is on Par with Both Parties' Spending, *New York Times*, January 26. www.nytimes.com/2015/01/27/us/politics/kochs-plan-to-spend-900-million-on-2016-campaign.html

Confessore, N. and Chozick, A. 2015. Emerging Hillary Clinton Team Shows Signs of Disquiet, *New York Times*, February 10. www.nytimes.com/2015/02/11/us/politics/emerging-clinton-team-shows-signs-of-disquiet.html?_r=0

Confessore, N., Cohen, S. and Yourshaug, K. 2015. Small Pool of Rich Donors Dominates Election Giving, *New York Times*, August 1.

CorpWatch, 2009. Book Release: Halliburton's Army: How a Well-Connected Texas Oil Company Revolutionized the Way America Makes War. www.corpwatch.org/article.php?id=15287

Coy, P. 2012. The Gap between Rich and Poor Widens, *Bloomberg Businessweek*, October11.www.businessweek.com/articles/2012-10-11/the-gap-between-rich-and-poor-widens

Crutsinger, M. 2011. Americans Cut Spending for First Time in 20 Months, *Yahoo!News*, August 2. http://news.yahoo.com/americans-cut-spending-first-time-20-months-123819626.html

Curtin, S. 2012. The American Dream Shrinks: Avg. Net Worth Falls 40% from 2007–2010, *Yahoo!Finance*, June 12. http://finance.yahoo.com/blogs/daily-ticker/american-dream-shrinks-avg-net-worth-falls-40-160150749.html

Curtin, S. 2011. The Top 5 Facts about America's Richest 1%, *Yahoo! Finance*, October 11. http://finance.yahoo.com/blogs/daily-ticker/top-5-facts-america-richest-1-183022655.html

Daily Kos, 2014. Someone Finally Polled the 1% – And It's Not Pretty, *Daily Kos*, May 29. https://www.dailykos.com/story/2014/05/29/1302820/-Someone-finally-polled-the-1-And-it-s-not-pretty

Daly, H. and Farley, J. 2011. *Ecological Economics*, Washington, DC: Island Press.

Davidson, P. 2012. Is Economics a Science? Should Economics Be Rigorous? *Real-World Economics Review*, No. 59. http://rwer.wordpress.com/2012/03/12/rwer-issue-59/

Dayen, D. 2014. The Farm Bill Still Gives Wads of Cash to Agribusiness. It's Just Sneakier about It, *New Republic*, February 4. www.newrepublic.com/article/116470/farm-bill-2014-its-even-worse-old-farm-bill

Dayen, D. 2010. Brooksley Born Excoriates Alan Greenspan: "You Failed," *Firedoglake*, April 7. http://news.firedoglake.com/2010/04/07/brooksley-born-excoriates-alan-greenspan-you-failed/

DeHaven, T. and Edwards, C. 2012. Will the House Block the Farm Bill Pig-Out? *The Hill*, June 18. www.downsizinggovernment.org/will-house-block-farm-bill-pig-out

Delaney, A. 2010. Lawmakers Ignore Call to Promise Not to Become Lobbyists, *Huffington Post*, April 22. www.unz.org/Pub/HuffingtonPost-2010apr-07847

Dennis, S. T. 2011. Democrats Target McConnell's Horse-Racing Tax Break, June 30. www.rollcall.com/issues/56_148/mitch-mcconnell-horse-racing-tax-break-206938-1.html

DeParle, J. 2011. Top Earners Not So Lofty in the Days of Recession, *New York Times*, December 12. www.nytimes.com/2011/12/13/business/economy/recession-crimped-incomes-of-the-richest-americans.html

DeParle, J., Gebeloff, R. and Tavernise, S. 2011. Older, Suburban and Struggling, "Near Poor" Startle the Census, *New York Times*, November 26. www.nytimes.com/2011/11/19/us/census-measures-those-not-quite-in-poverty-but-struggling.html?pagewanted=all

de Rothschild, F. L. 2013. A Costly and Unjust Perk for Financiers, *New York Times*, February 24. www.nytimes.com/2013/02/25/opinion/carried-interest-an-unjust-privilege-for-financiers.html

Diamond, J. 2005. *Collapse*, New York: Penguin Books.

Dickler, J. 2011. CBO Study Shows Growing Income Disparity, *CNNMoney.com*, October 26. http://money.cnn.com/2011/10/26/news/economy/cbo_income/index.htm

Dodd, R. 2007. Tax Breaks for Billionaires: Loophole for Hedge Fund Managers Costs Billions in Tax Revenue, Economic Policy Institute, Policy Memo No. 120, July 24. www.epi.org/publication/pm120/

Domhoff, G. W. 2015. Who Rules America? Wealth, Income, and Power. http://whorulesamerica.net/power/wealth.html

Dorning, M. 2012. Romney's "Very Poor" at Highest in 35 Years as Safety Gaps Grow, *Bloomberg Business*, February 3. http://mobile.bloomberg.com/news/2012-02-03/romney-s-very-poor-at-highest-percentage-in-35-years-as-safety-gaps-grow

Dorning, M. 2011. The Slow Disappearance of the American Working Man, *Bloomberg Businessweek*, August 25. www.businessweek.com/magazine/the-slow-disappearance-of-the-american-working-man-08242011.html

Drinkard, J. 2005. Drugmakers Go Furthest to Sway Congress, *USA TODAY Money*, April 25. http://usatoday30.usatoday.com/money/industries/health/drugs/2005-04-25-drug-lobby-cover_x.htm

Drucker, J. and Dudley, R. 2015. Wal-Mart Has $76 Billion in Undisclosed Overseas Tax Havens, *Bloomberg Business*, June 16. www.bloomberg.com/news/articles/2015-06-17/wal-mart-has-76-billion-in-overseas-tax-havens-report-says

Drutman, L. 2014. How Big Pharma (and Others) Began Lobbying on the Trans-Pacific Partnership Before You Ever Heard of It, *Sunlight Foundation*, March 13. http://sunlightfoundation.com/blog/2014/03/13/tpp-lobby/

Dwyer, J. 2007. Vantage Point: Arrogance Takes Down Madison Square Garden, *New York Times*, October 3. www.nytimes.com/2007/10/03/sports/03iht-vantage.1.7730107.html

Easley, J. 2013. MSNBC's Chuck Todd Says It's Not His Job to Challenge Republican Lies, *PoliticusUSA*, September 18. www.politicususa.com/2013/09/18/msnbcs-chuck-todd-job-challenge-republican-lies.html

Easterly, W. 2006. *The White Man's Burden*, New York: Penguin.

Edsall, T. B. 2015. The Lobbying Bonanza, *New York Times*, June 10. www.nytimes.com/2015/06/10/opinion/the-lobbying-bonanza.html

Edsall, T. B. 2013A. The Political–Monetary Complex, *New York Times*, October 15. http://mobile.nytimes.com/2013/10/16/opinion/edsall-the-political-monetary-complex.html

Edsall, T. B. 2013B. Can the Government Actually Do Anything about Inequality? *New York Times*, September 10. http://opinionator.blogs.nytimes.com/2013/09/10/can-the-government-actually-do-anything-about-inequality/

Edwards, C. 2009. Downsizing the Federal Government, Cato Institute, March. www.downsizinggovernment.org/government-cost-overruns

Egan, T. 2011. Conservative Cash Crop, *New York Times*, July 1. http://opinionator.blogs.nytimes.com/2011/07/01/conservative-cash-crop/

Eggen, D. and Helderman, R. S. 2012. Santorum Reports Millions in Income as Washington Consultant, *Washington Post.com*, February 16. www.washingtonpost.com/politics/santorum-reports-millions-in-income-as-washington-consultant/2012/02/16/gIQAVGknIR_story.html

Eirenreich, B. 2001. *Nickel and Dimed*, New York: Henry Holt.

Ejiochi, I. 2014. How the NFL Makes More Money than Any Pro Sport, *CNBC*, September 4. www.cnbc.com/2014/09/04/

Elderd, C. 2014. Walt Disney Got Better Deal than a Florida Tax Credit, *Watchdog.com*, April 21. http://watchdog.org/139875/walt-disney/

Environmental Working Group. 2013. Farm Subsidy Data base. http://farm.ewg.org/index.php

ESPN. 2013. Ultimate Scoundrel, September 24. http://espn.go.com/sportsnation/story/_/id/9677383/most-dishonest-owner-sports-miami-marlins-jeffrey-loria-espn-magazine

ESPN. 2007. Stern Criticizes City, State Governments in Sonics Dealings, November 8. http://sports.espn.go.com/nba/news/story?id=3100691

Etzioni, A. 2010. Warning: Profit-Making Colleges Are After You, *Huffington Post*, June 29. www.huffingtonpost.com/amitai-etzioni/warning-profit-making-col_b_629213.html

Farrell, H. 2014. Five Questions on Regulating For-Profit Colleges, *Washington Post*, May 29. www.washingtonpost.com/blogs/monkey-cage/wp/2014/05/29/five-questions-on-regulating-for-profit-colleges/

Field, K. 2010. Government Vastly Undercounts Defaults, *The Chronicle*, July 11. http://chronicle.com/article/Many-More-Students-Are/66223/

Finkle, V. 2014. Tough Choices Ahead for Jeb Hensarling, *American Banker*, April 10. www.americanbanker.com/issues/179_70/tough-choices-ahead-for-jeb-hensarling-1066810-1.html

Frank, R. 2012. The Rich, Very Rich, and, Now, the "Volatile Rich," *Yahoo!Finance*, July 13. http://finance.yahoo.com/news/rich-very-rich-now-volatile-173653430.html

Froomkin, D. 2011. How the Oil Lobby Greases Washington's Wheels, *HuffPost Politics*, April 6. www.huffingtonpost.com/2011/04/06/how-the-oil-lobby-greases_n_845720.html

Fulbrook, E. 2012. The Political Economy of Bubbles, *Real-World Economics Review*, No. 59. www.paecon.net/PAEReview/issue59/Fullbrook59.pdf

Fulbrook, E. 2009. The Meltdown and Economics Textbooks, in *The Handbook of Pluralist Economics Education*, ed. Jack Reardon. London: Routledge.

Fulton, D. 2015. Dark Cloud of ALEC Converges at Annual Corporate-Political Lovefest, *Common Dreams*, July 23. www.commondreams.org/news/2015/07/23/dark-cloud-alec-converges-annual-corporate-political-lovefest

Fusfeld, D. R. 2002. *The Age of the Economist*, 9th edn, Boston, MA: Addison Wesley.

Gabriel, Trip. 2013. Clouds Spread to Democratic Side of Virginia Governor's Race, *New York Times*, August 2. www.nytimes.com/2013/08/03/us/clouds-spread-to-democratic-side-of-virginia-governors-race.html

Galbraith, J. K. and Hale, J. T. 2014. The Evolution of Economic Inequality in the United States, 1969–2012: Evidence from Data on Inter-industrial Earnings and Inter-regional Incomes, *World Economic Review*, Vol. 3: 1–19. http://wer.worldeconomicsassociation.org/papers/the-evolution-of-economic-inequality-in-the-united-states-1969-2012/

Gallucci, M. 2015. Oil Trains: Crude Oil Involved in North Dakota Train Derailment and Fire Was Less Flammable than State Limits, *International Business Times*, May 8. www.ibtimes.com/oil-trains-crude-oil-involved-north-dakota-train-derailment-fire-was-less-flammable-1914570

Garrett, R. 2010. Fraudulent Tactics Lure Students to For-Profit Colleges, *Education change.org*. www.refusethesilence.com/2010/08/question-the-college-con/

Garrick, D. 2015. Past Failures Key to Chargers' L.A., *San Diego Union Tribune*, June 27. www.sandiegouniontribune.com/news/2015/jun/27/chargers-stadium-nfl-pitch-unsuccessful-attempts/?st

Genuine Progress. 2015. Genuine Progress Indicator. http://genuineprogress.net/genuine-progress-indicator/

Gillespie, P. 2014. 3 Black Eyes in the U.S. Job Market, *CNNMoney*, October 17. http://finance.yahoo.com/news/3-black-eyes-u-job-131600037.html

Glantz, A. 2014. Taxpayer Funds Are Lifeline for More than 100 For-Profit Schools, The Center for Investigative Reporting, October 9. https://www.revealnews.org/article-legacy/taxpayer-funds-are-lifeline-for-more-than-100-for-profit-schools/

Glaser, J. 2012. Romney's Military Advisors Work for Corporate-Welfare Defense Contractors, *AntiWar.Blog*, October 22. http://antiwar.com/blog/2012/10/22/romneys-military-advisors-work-for-corporate-welfare-defense-contractors/

Glassman, G. 2014. Correlations: Taxes and Growth, *Bloomberg Businessweek*, January 2. www.bloomberg.com/bw/articles/2014-01-02/correlations-high-corporate-taxes-economic-growth-can-coexist

Gold, H. 2011. New Recession Begins Next Year, Shilling Says, *MarketWatch.com*, June 24. www.marketwatch.com/story/new-recession-begins-next-year-shilling-says-2011-06-24

Goldstein, J. 2012. How the 1 Percent and the 99 Percent Are Doing, in 1 Table, *NPR.org*, March 5. www.npr.org/blogs/money/2012/03/05/147974102/how-the-1-percent-and-the-99-percent-are-doing-in-1-table

Goleman, D. 2013. Rich People Just Care Less, *New York Times*, October 5. http://opinionator.blogs.nytimes.com/2013/10/05/rich-people-just-care-less/

Goleman, D. 2009. *Ecological Intelligence*, New York: Crown Publishing.

Gongloff, M. 2012. New York Fed's Libor Documents Reveal Cozy Relationship between Regulators, Banks, *Huffington Post*, July 13. www.huffingtonpost.com/2012/07/13/new-york-fed-libor-documents_n_1671524.html

Goodman, P. S. 2009. *Past Due*, New York: Henry Holt.

Goodman, P. S. 2008. Taking a Hard Look at the Greenspan Legacy, *New York Times*, October 9. www.nytimes.com/2008/10/09/business/economy/09greenspan.html?pagewanted=all

Goodwin, L. 2011. More than $6 Billion in Iraq Reconstruction Funds Lost, *Yahoo!News*, June 13. http://news.yahoo.com/blogs/lookout/more-6-billion-iraq-reconstruction-funds-lost-174047033.html

Gorenstein, P. 2011A. The Rich Are Back! Luxury Spending Jumps as Income Disparity Widens, *Yahoo!Finance*, April 15. http://finance.yahoo.com/blogs/daily-ticker/rich-back-luxury-spending-jumps-income-disparity-widens-20110415-094912-274.html

Gorenstein, P. 2011B. It's Good to Be the King: CEO Pay Up Big 2010, Not So Much for the Average Worker, *Yahoo!Finance*, April 11. http://finance.yahoo.com/blogs/author/peter-gorenstein/archive/10.html

Grant, J. 2011. Price and Punishment, Book Review: *The Illusion of Free Markets*, *Wall Street Journal*, December 13. http://online.wsj.com/article/SB10001424052748704034804576026012320513404.html

Greeley, B. 2012. The Fed Takes a Crash Course in Finance, *Bloomberg Business*, August 3. www.bloomberg.com/bw/articles/2012-08-30/the-fed-takes-a-crash-course-in-finance

Greenblatt, M. 2012. Man Blows Whistle on For-Profit College, *ABC News*, November 26. http://news.yahoo.com/man-blows-whistle-profit-college-152357622--abc-news-topstories.html

Greenpeace. 2015. Koch Industries: Secretly Funding the Climate Denial Machine, Greenpeace. www.greenpeace.org/usa/en/campaigns/global-warming-and-energy/polluterwatch/koch-industries/

Greenwald, G. 2009. Larry Summers, Tim Geithner and Wall Street's Ownership of Government, *Salon,* April 4. www.salon.com/2009/04/04/summers/singleton/

Greenwald, R. and Sloan, M. 2012. The Real Scandal Involving Generals, *HuffPost Politics*, November 19. www.huffingtonpost.com/robert-greenwald/once-a-soldier-always-a-s_b_2161490.html

Griffin, D. and Johnston, K. 2012. Army to Congress: Thanks, but No Tanks, October 12. http://security.blogs.cnn.com/2012/10/09/army-to-congress-thanks-but-no-tanks/

Griffiths, D. 2014. Americans Give Up Passports as Asset Disclosure Rules Start, *Bloomberg Businessweek*, April 7. www.bloomberg.com/news/2014-08-06/americans-give-up-passports-as-asset-disclosure-rules-start.html

Gross, D. 2012A. America Is Headed Toward an Age of Descent, *Yahoo!Finance*, April 13. http://finance.yahoo.com/blogs/daniel-gross/america-headed-toward-age-descent-edward-luce-140827727.html9

Gross, D. 2012B. Unemployment May Be Down, But So Are Wages and Benefits, *Yahoo!Finance*, April 2. http://finance.yahoo.com/blogs/daily-ticker/reich-superficial-labor-market-improvements-masks-erosion-wages-133111886.html

Gross, D. 2011. Here's the Real Adult Conversation on Deficits: The U.S. Has a Taxing Problem, *Yahoo!Finance*, April 12. http://finance.yahoo.com/blogs/daniel-gross/real-adult-conversation-deficits-u-taxing-problem-152801137.html

Gross, D. 2007. Income Inequality, Writ Larger, *New York Times*, June 10. www.nytimes.com/2007/06/10/business/yourmoney/10view.html?pagewanted=print

Gruley, B. 2012. The Man Who Bought North Dakota, *Bloomberg Business*, January 19. www.bloomberg.com/bw/magazine/the-man-who-bought-north-dakota-01192012.html

Gumbel, A. 2007. Poverty Gap in US Has Widened under Bush, *CommonDreams. org*, February 27. www.commondreams.org/cgi-bin/print.cgi?file=/headlines 07/0227-02.htm

Hacker, J. S. and Pierson, P. 2010. *Winner Takes All Politics*, New York: Simon & Schuster.

Halberstam, D. 1992. *The Best and the Brightest*, 20th edn, New York: Ballantine Books.

Hamburger, T. and Wallsten, P. 2013. The U.S. Sugar Industry: Names to Know, *Washington Post*, December 7. www.washingtonpost.com/politics/the-us-sugar-industry-names-to-know/2013/12/07/840811fe-5ecf-11e3-be07-006c776266ed_story.html

Handley, M. 2012. Americans Are the Wealthiest but Not the Happiest, *Yahoo!Finance*, May 22. http://finance.yahoo.com/news/americans-wealthiest-not-happiest-163028373.html

Hanford, E. 2012. The Case Against For-Profit Colleges and Universities, American Public Media, September. http://americanradioworks.publicradio. org/features/tomorrows-college/phoenix/case-against-for-profit-schools. html

Harjani, A. 2014. Hedge Fund Manager Pay Rises to $2.4 Million, *CNBC*, November 6. www.cnbc.com/2014/11/06/

Harkins, D. 2000. Dominant Media Insiders Fired over Monsanto/BGH Expose, *Idaho Observer*, December. www.proliberty.com/observer/20001204.htm

Harshaw, T. 2010. Will the Jobless Cost Democrats Their Jobs? *The Smart Money WordPress.com*, July 3. http://thesmartmoney.wordpress.com/2010/07/03/will-the-jobless-cost-democrats-their-jobs-by-tobin-harshaw-in-the-n-y-times/

Harwell , D. and Hobson, W. 2015. The NFL Is Dropping Its Tax-Exempt Status. Why that Ends Up Helping Them Out, *Washington Post*, April 28. www. washingtonpost.com/news/business/wp/2015/04/28/the-nfl-is-dropping-its-tax-exempt-status-why-that-ends-up-helping-them-out/

Hechinger, J. 2010. Stripper Regrets Art Degree Profitable for Goldman, *Bloomberg*, August 6. www.bloomberg.com/news/articles/2010-08-05/stripper-s-college-degree-profitable-for-goldman-finds-70-000-was-wasted

Helmen, C. 2013. World's Happiest Countries, *Forbes* in *Yahoo! Travel*, January 15. http://travel.yahoo.com/ideas/world-s-happiest-countries-233204795.html

Herbert, B. 2011A. Losing Our Way, *New York Times*, March 26. www.nytimes. com/2011/03/26/opinion/26herbert.html

Herbert, B. 2011B. When Democracy Weakens, *New York Times*, February 11. www. nytimes.com/2011/02/12/opinion/12herbert.html

Herbert, B. 2011C. Misery with Plenty of Company, *New York Times*, printed in *The HutchNews.com*, January 13. www.hutchnews.com/Wirecolumns/herbert 011011--1

Herbert, B. 2011D. The Data and the Reality, *New York Times*, January 5. www. nytimes.com/2010/12/28/opinion/28herbert.html

Herbert, B. 2010A. Winning the Class War, *New York Times*, November 27. www. nytimes.com/2010/11/27/opinion/27herbert.html

Herbert, B. 2010B. The Horror Show, *New York Times*, August 10. www.nytimes. com/2010/08/10/opinion/10herbert.html

Herbert, B. 2010C. A Sin and a Shame, *New York Times*, July 30. www.nytimes. com/2010/07/31/opinion/31herbert.html

Herbert, B. 2010D. Long-Term Economic Pain, *New York Times*, July 26. www.nytimes.com/2010/07/27/opinion/27herbert.html

Herszenhorn, D. M. 2007. Farm Subsidies Seem Immune to an Overhaul, *New York Times*, July 26. www.nytimes.com/2007/07/26/washington/26farm.html?_r=0

Hertsgaard, M. 2014. The Petro States of America, *Bloomberg Businessweek*, February 7. www.bloomberg.com/bw/articles/2014-02-27/oil-industrys-power-in-u-dot-s-dot-petro-state-shapes-keystone-xl-debate

Hicken, M. 2014. Elizabeth Warren: Obama's Economic Team Chose Wall Street over Families, *CNN Money*, October 13. www.cuinsight.com/elizabeth-warren-obamas-economic-team-chose-wall-street-over-families.html#sthash.6bXS9gPJ.dpuf

Hopkins, C. and Schmidt, R. 2013. Ex-Senator Gregg Said to Be Top Candidate to Lead Bank Lobby, *Bloomberg News*, May 9. www.bloomberg.com/news/articles/2013-05-09/ex-senator-gregg-said-to-be-top-candidate-to-lead-bank-lobby

Horn, S. 2013. Censored EPA PA Fracking Water Contamination Presentation Published for First Time, *DeSmog*, August 5. www.desmogblog.com/2013/08/05/censored-epa-pennsylvania-fracking-water-contamination-presentation-published-first-time

Hudson, M. 2011. How Economic Theory Came to Ignore the Role of Debt, *Real-World Economics Review*, No. 57. http://rwer.wordpress.com/2011/09/06/rwer-issue-57-michael-huds

International Herald Tribune. 2006. A Marie Antoinette Moment, January 3. www.nytimes.com/2006/01/02/opinion/02iht-edcorp.html

International Monetary Fund. 2015. U.S. Needs to Finish Financial Reforms, *IMF Survey Magazine*, July 7. www.imf.org/external/pubs/ft/survey/so/2015/POL070715A.htm

Israel, J. 2013. Secret Koch Fund Decries "Corporate Welfare" and Stimulus but Funds Their Top Defender, *Nation of Change*, September 15. www.nationofchange.org/secret-koch-fund-decries-corporate-welfare-and-stimulus-funds-their-top-defender-1379254052

Jamrisko, M. 2014. Yellon's Philosophy: The More Data, the Better, *Bloomberg Businessweek*, July 17. www.businessweek.com/articles/2014-07-17/feds-yellen-goes-beyond-unemployment-rate-to-craft-policy

Jensen, H. 1981. An Opportunistic Interpretation of Adam Smith's Inquiry, pp. 2, 3, 13–14, and 18. Taken from Smith, *An Inquiry into the Nature and Causes of the Wealth of Nations*, 2 volumes, Glasgow Edition, eds. R. H. Campbell and A. S. Skinner, Indianapolis: Liberty Press/Liberty Classics, 1981 (originally published in 1776). Paper presented at the History of Economics Society, Charleston, SC, June 20–23, 1997.

Jensen, H. 1976. Sources and Contours of Adam Smith's Conceptualized Reality in the Wealth of Nations, *Review of Social Economy*, 34(3): 259–74.

Jilani, Z. 2012. Goldman Sachs Is Paying Dick Gephardt's Lobbying Firm to Weaken Financial Regulations, *Republic Report*, May 19. www.republicreport.org/2012/gephardt-lobbying-doddfrank/

Johnson, S. 2015, The Republican Strategy to Repeal Dodd-Frank, *Baseline Scenario*, January 7. http://baselinescenario.com/2015/01/07/the-republican-strategy-to-repeal-dodd-frank/

Johnson, S. 2009. The Quiet Coup, *The Atlantic,* May. www.theatlantic.com/magazine/archive/2009/05/the-quiet-coup/307364/

Johnson, S. and Kwak, J. 2011. *13 Bankers: The Wall Street Takeover and the Next Financial Meltdown,* New York: Vintage Books.

Juhasz, J. 2013. Why the Iraq War Was Fought, *CNN.com,* April 15. www.cnn.com/2013/03/19/opinion/iraq-war-oil-juhasz/

Kahn, S. 2013. We Are Not All in This Together, *New York Times,* December 14. http://opinionator.blogs.nytimes.com/2013/12/14/we-are-not-all-in-this-together/?_r=0

Kahneman, D. 2011. *Thinking, Fast and Slow,* New York: Farrar, Strauss and Giroux.

kaiserEDU.org. 2012. U.S. Health Care Costs. www.kaiseredu.org/issue-modules/us-health-care-costs/background-brief.aspx

Khimm, S. 2012. Tim Pawlenty: The New Face of the GOP–Wall Street Alliance, *Washington Post,* September 20. www.washingtonpost.com/blogs/ezra-klein/wp/2012/09/20/tim-pawlenty-the-new-face-of-the-gop-wall-street-alliance/

Kiersh, A. 2009. Lockheed Opposes Defense Cuts, but Donates to Friends and Foes Alike, *Opensecrets.org.* www.opensecrets.org/news/2009/07/lockheed-opposes-defense-cuts/

Kim, C. 2013. Should You Renounce Your Citizenship? *Yahoo!News,* February 13. http://finance.yahoo.com/news/should-you-renounce-your-citizenship-144048875.html

Kingkade, T. 2012. For-Profit Colleges Collect $32 Billion, 3 Lose Federal Aid Eligibility for Failing 90/10 Rule, *Huffington Post,* September 28. www.huffingtonpost.com/2012/09/27/for-profit-colleges-lose-federal-aid-90-10_n_1920190.html

Kingsolver, B. 2007. *Animal, Vegetable, Miracle,* New York: Harper.

Kinzer, S. 2006. *Overthrow,* New York: Times Books.

Klein, N. 2014. *This Changes Everything: Capitalism Versus the Climate,* New York: Simon & Schuster.

Klein, N. 2007. *The Shock Doctrine,* New York: Picador.

Konczal, M. 2014. The Financial Regulation Congress Is Quietly Trying to Destroy in the Budget, Roosevelt Institute, December 10. www.nextnewdeal.net/rortybomb/financial-regulation-congress-quietly-trying-destroy-budget

Korn, M. 2012A. Nearly 50% of Americans Believe Wealthy Lifestyle Is Unattainable: The Hill, *Yahoo!Finance,* July 17. http://finance.yahoo.com/blogs/daily-ticker/nearly-50-americans-believe-wealthy-lifestyle-unattainable-hil-125001839.html

Korn, M. 2012B. NYC's Luxury Housing Market Booms, While American Dream Fades for Most, *Yahoo!Finance,* March 22. http://finance.yahoo.com/blogs/daily-ticker/nyc-luxury-housing-market-booms-while-american-dream-170316774.html

Korn, P. 2013. Max Baucus, the Senator from K Street – A Poster Boy for Campaign Finance Reform, *Huffington Post,* May 8. www.huffingtonpost.com/pearl-korn/max-baucus-the-senator-fr_b_3229915.html

Kravitz, D. and Rugaber, C. S. 2011. Americans' Equity in Their Homes Near a Record Low, *Grand Junction Free Press,* June 9. www.gjfreepress.com/article/20110609/APF/1106090845

Kretzmann, S. 2015. Bribery Is a Bargain for Big Oil, *HuffPost Green,* January 22. www.huffingtonpost.com/stephen-kretzmann/bribery-is-a-bargain-for-_b_6516236.html

Kristof, N. D. 2015. Peerless Republicans for President: Trump, Carson and Fiorina, *New York Times*, October 8. www.nytimes.com/2015/10/08/opinion/nicholas-kristof-3-peerless-republicans-for-president-trump-carson-and-fiorina.html?_r=0

Kristof, N. D. 2012. The White Underclass, *New York Times*, February 8. www.nytimes.com/2012/02/09/opinion/kristof-the-decline-of-white-workers.html

Kristof, N. D. 2011. Our Banana Republic, *New York Times*, February 15. http://www.nytimes.com/2011/2/15/opinion/07kristof.html

Kristof, N. D. 2010. A Hedge Fund Republic? *New York Times*, November 18. www.nytimes.com/2010/11/18/opinion/18kristof.html

Krugman, P. 2015A. Wall Street Vampires, *New York Times*, May 11. www.nytimes.com/2015/05/11/opinion/paul-krugman-wall-street-vampires.html?_r=0

Krugman, P. 2015B. Cranking Up for 2016, *New York Times*, February 20. www.nytimes.com/2015/02/20/opinion/paul-krugman-cranking-up-for-2016.html

Krugman, P. 2014A. Our Invisible Rich, *New York Times*, September 28. www.nytimes.com/2014/09/29/opinion/paul-krugman-our-invisible-rich.html?_r=0

Krugman, P. 2014B. Those Lazy Jobless, *New York Times*, September 21. www.nytimes.com/2014/09/22/opinion/paul-krugman-those-lazy-jobless.html?emc=eta1

Krugman, P. 2014C. Charlatans, Cranks and Kansas, *New York Times*, June 29. www.nytimes.com/2014/06/30/opinion/paul-krugman-charlatans-cranks-and-kansas.html?_r=0

Krugman, P. 2014D. Now That's Rich, *New York Times*, May 8. www.nytimes.com/2014/05/09/opinion/krugman-now-thats-rich.html?rref=opinion&_r=2

Krugman, P. 2014E. Wall Street's Revenge: Dodd-Frank Damaged in the Budget Bill, *New York Times*, December 14. www.nytimes.com/2014/12/15/opinion/paul-krugman-dodd-frank-damaged-by-the-budget-bill.html

Krugman, P. 2013A. Hunger Games, U.S.A., *New York Times*, July 14. www.nytimes.com/2013/07/15/opinion/krugman-hunger-games-usa.html

Krugman, P. 2013B. Makers, Takers, Fakers, *New York Times*, January 27. www.nytimes.com/2013/01/28/opinion/krugman-makers-takers-fakers-.html?_r=0

Krugman, P. 2012A. The Conscience of a Liberal, *New York Times*, July 8. http://krugman.blogs.nytimes.com/2012/07/08/taxes-at-the-top/?emc=eta1

Krugman, P. 2012B. Lobbyists, Guns and Money, *New York Times*, March 27. www.nytimes.com/2012/03/26/opinion/krugman-lobbyists-guns-and-money.html

Krugman, P. 2012C. States of Depression, *New York Times*, March 5. www.nytimes.com/2012/03/05/opinion/krugman-states-of-depression.html

Krugman, P. 2012D. Moochers against Welfare, *New York Times*, February 16. http://topics.nytimes.com/top/opinion/editorialsandoped/oped/columnists/paulkrugman/index.html

Krugman, P. 2012E. Things Are Not O.K., *New York Times*, February 6. www.nytimes.com/2012/02/06/opinion/krugman-things-are-not-ok.html

Krugman, P. 2012F. Who's Very Important, *New York Times*, July 12. www.nytimes.com/2012/07/13/opinion/krugman-whos-very-important.html

Krugman, P. 2011A. The Social Contract, *New York Times*, September 22. www.nytimes.com/2011/09/23/opinion/krugman-the-social-contract.html

Krugman, P. 2011B. The Wrong Worries, *New York Times*, August 5. www.nytimes.com/2011/08/05/opinion/the-wrong-worries.html

Krugman, P. 2011C. Shock Doctrine, U.S.A., *New York Times*, February 24. www.nytimes.com/2011/02/25/opinion/25krugman.html

Krugman, P. 2010A. Wall Street Whitewash, *New York Times*, December 16. www.nytimes.com/2010/12/17/opinion/17krugman.html

Krugman, P. 2010B. Fear and Favor, *New York Times*, October 4. www.nytimes.com/2010/10/04/opinion/04krugman.html?_r=0

Krugman, P. 2010C. Defining Prosperity Down, *New York Times*, August 1. www.nytimes.com/2010/08/02/opinion/02krugman.html

Krugman, P. 2006. Graduates Versus Oligarchs, *New York Times*, February 27, p. A19.

Kuriloff, A. and Preston, D. 2012. In Stadium Building Spree, U.S. Taxpayers Lose $4 Billion, *Bloomberg Business*, September 4. www.bloomberg.com/news/articles/2012-09-05/in-stadium-building-spree-u-s-taxpayers-lose-4-billion

Lancaster, J. 2001. For Big Hog Farms, Big Subsidies, *Washington Post*, August 17. www.washingtonpost.com/archive/politics/2001/08/17/for-big-hog-farms-big-subsidies/909f27dd-3631-41de-9904-9c7ab44f60e8/

Lange, J. 2012. Data Points to Weaker Economic Momentum, *Yahoo!Finance*, April 30. http://finance.yahoo.com/news/u-march-personal-incomes-rise-123210987.html

Lauerman, J. 2013. For-Profit Colleges Aim to Relax Draft Student Debt Rules, *Bloomberg Business*, September 8. www.bloomberg.com/news/articles/2013-09-09/for-profit-colleges-aim-to-relax-draft-student-debt-rules

Lawson, T. 2012. Mathematical Modelling and Ideology in the Economics Academy: Competing Explanations of the Failings of the Modern Discipline? *Economic Thought*, Vol. 1: 3–22. http://etdiscussion.worldeconomicsassociation.org/?post=mathematical-modelling-and-ideology-in-the-economics-academy-competing-explanations-of-the-failings-of-the-modern-discipline

Learsey, R. J. 2007. $20 Billion Later Halliburton Moves Headquarters to Dubai, *Huffington Post*, March 12. www.huffingtonpost.com/raymond-j-learsy/20-billion-later-hallibur_b_43196.html

Lehmann, C. 2011. Nightly News Stays Mum on GEs $0 Tax Bill, *Yahoo!News*, March 30. http://news.yahoo.com/blogs/cutline/nightly-news-stays-mum-ge-0-tax-bill-20110330-055057-274.html

Leonhardt, D. 2014A. The Great Wage Slowdown, Looming Over Politics, *New York Times*, November 11. www.nytimes.com/2014/11/11/upshot/the-great-wage-slowdown-looming-over-politics.html?abt=0002&abg=0

Leonhardt, D. 2014B. Inequality Has Actually Not Risen Since the Financial Crisis, *New York Times*, February 15. www.nytimes.com/2015/02/17/upshot/inequality-has-actually-not-risen-since-the-financial-crisis.html

Leonhardt, D. 2012A. Standard of Living Is in the Shadows as Election Issue, *New York Times*, October 23. www.nytimes.com/2012/10/24/us/politics/race-for-president-leaves-income-slump-in-shadows.html?pagewanted=all&_r=0

Leonhardt, D. 2012B. A Closer Look at Middle-Class Decline, *New York Times*, July 23. http://finance.yahoo.com/news/closer-look-middle-class-decline-192705261.html

Levisohn, B., Silver-Greenberg, T. F. and Francis, T. 2009. Old Banks, New Lending Tricks, *Bloomberg Business*, August 5. www.bloomberg.com/bw/magazine/content/09_33/b4143020536818.htm

Lewin, T. 2015. Government to Forgive Student Loans at Corinthian Colleges, *New York Times*, June 8. www.nytimes.com/2015/06/09/education/us-to-forgive-federal-loans-of-corinthian-college-students.html

Lichtblau, E. 2010. Ex-Regulators Get Set to Lobby on New Financial Rules, *New York Times*, July 27. www.nytimes.com/2010/07/28/business/28lobby.html?pagewanted=all

Lipton, E. 2014A. Energy Firms in Secretive Alliance with Attorneys General, *New York Times*, December 6. www.nytimes.com/2014/12/07/us/politics/energy-firms-in-secretive-alliance-with-attorneys-general.html?_r=0

Lipton, E. 2014B. Missouri Attorney General Puts Limit on Contributions, *New York Times*, November 19. www.nytimes.com/2014/11/20/us/missouri-attorney-general-chris-koster-puts-limit-on-contributions.html?_r=0

Lipton, E. 2013. Tax Lobby Builds Ties to Chairman of Finance Panel, *New York Times*, April 7. www.nytimes.com/2013/04/07/us/politics/tax-lobby-builds-ties-to-max-baucus.html?pagewanted=all

Lipton, E. and Protess, B. 2013. Banks' Lobbyists Help in Drafting Financial Bills, *New York Times*, May 23. http://dealbook.nytimes.com/2013/05/23/banks-lobbyists-help-in-drafting-financial-bills/

LiveLeak. 2011. Insider Trading on Capitol Hill? *Yahoo!News*, May 30. www.liveleak.com/view?i=0c1_1306879639

Livesay, H. C. 1975. *Andrew Carnegie and the Rise of Big Business*, New York: Harper Collins.

Los Angeles Times. 2010. Pentagon Can't Account for $8.7 Billion in Iraqi Funds, July 26. http://articles.latimes.com/2010/jul/26/world/la-fg-iraq-funds-20100727

Lubin, G. 2011A. 23 Mind-Blowing Facts about Income Inequality in America, *BusinessInsider.com*, November 7. www.businessinsider.com/new-charts-about-inequality-2011-11?op=1#ixzz246ZAUB8C

Lubin, G. 2011B. Falling out of the Middle Class: A Statistical Look at the People Who Have Lost the Most, *Yahoo!Finance*, September 6. http://finance.yahoo.com/blogs/daily-ticker/falling-middle-class-statistical-look-people-lost-most-023139283.html

Luhby, T. 2011A. Economic Insecurity Hits More than 1 in 5 Americans, *CNNMoney*, November 28. http://money.cnn.com/2011/11/28/news/economy/americans_insecurity/index.htm

Luhby, T. 2011B. Poverty Grows in Rick Perry's Texas, *CNNMoney.com*, September 20. http://money.cnn.com/2011/09/18/news/economy/poverty_perry_texas/index.htm

Lycklama, M. 2015. Boise Hawks' New Owners Hope to Build Multi-Use Development, *Idaho Statesman*, July 3. www.idahostatesman.com/2015/07/03/3881149/boise-hawks-new-owners-hope-to.html

Lynch, D. J. 2013. Safety Net for Crops Means $14 Billion Tab for Taxpayers, *Bloomberg News*, September 10. www.bloomberg.com/news/articles/2013-09-10/crop-insurers-14-billion-some-see-as-money-laundering

Lynch, D. J. and Bjerga, A. 2013. Taxpayers Turn U.S. Farmers into Fat Cats with Subsidies, *Bloomberg Business*, September 8. www.bloomberg.com/news/articles/2013-09-09/farmers-boost-revenue-sowing-subsidies-for-crop-insurance

Lyster, L. 2013. "Want to Cut Government Waste? Find the $8.5 Trillion the Pentagon Can't Account For," *Yahoo!Finance*, November 25. http://finance.yahoo.com/blogs/daily-ticker/want-cut-government-waste-8-5-trillion pentagon-142321339.html

Manicas, P. T. 2007. Endogenous Growth Theory: The Most Recent "Revolution" in Economics? *post-autistic economics review*, No. 41, March 5: 39–53. www.paecon.net/PAEReview/issue41/Manicas41.pdf

Mantell, R. 2010. Labor Force Polarized as Middle-Skill Jobs Disappear: Report, *Yahoo!Finance*, April 30. http://finance.yahoo.com/career-work/article/109424/labor-force-polarized-as-middle-skill-jobs-disappear-report?mod=career-worklife_balance&sec=topStories&pos=5&asset=&ccode=

Marisol, B. 2012. More than 1.4 Million Families Live on $2 a Day Per Person. *USA Today*, February 24. http://usatoday30.usatoday.com/news/nation/story/2012-02-23/extreme-poverty-increase/53227386/1

Mattera, P. and Purinton, A. 2004. Shopping for Subsidies: How Wal-Mart Uses Taxpayer Money to Finance Its Never-Ending Growth, May. www.goodjobsfirst.org/sites/default/files/docs/pdf/wmtstudy.pdf

Matus, M. 2013. Monsanto Hires Former Senator Blanche Lincoln as Washington Lobbyist, October 17. http://inhabitat.com/monsanto-hires-former-senator-as-washington-lobbyist/

Mazzucato, M. 2013. *The Entrepreneurial State: Debunking Public vs. Private Sector Myths*, London: Anthem Press.

McIntyre, D. A. 2010. The 10 American Industries that May Never Recover, *24/7Wall ST*, September 15. http://finance.yahoo.com/banking-budgeting/article/110592/the-10-american-industries-that-will-never-recover

McMaken, L. 2011. 5 Outrageous CEO Spending Abuses and Perks, *Yahoo!News*, August 3. http://news.yahoo.com/5-outrageous-ceo-spending-abuses-perks-135334463.html

Mehta, A. and Mulvany, L. 2012. The Army Tank that Could Not Be Stopped, *PublicIntegrity.org*, July 30. www.publicintegrity.org/2012/07/30/10325/army-tank-could-not-be-stopped

Melone, M. J. 2012. When Profit-Raking Disney and the Daytona Speedway Beg Florida for Corporate Welfare, *FlaglerLive.com*, January 19. http://flaglerlive.com/33260/disney-daytona-speedway-welfare/

Meyer, J. and Cooper, P. 2014. Sugar Subsidies Are a Bitter Deal for American Consumers, e21 Economic Policies for the 21st Century at the Manhattan Institute, June 23.

Mider, Z. 2015. Koch Calls for End to "Corporate Welfare" for Wall Street, *Bloomberg Politics*, August 1. www.bloomberg.com/politics/articles/2015-08-02/koch-calls-for-end-to-corporate-welfare-for-wall-street

Mider, Z. R. 2013. Wal-Mart's Waltons Maintain Their Billionaire Fortune, *Bloomberg Business*, September 12. www.bloomberg.com/news/articles/2013-09-12/how-wal-mart-s-waltons-maintain-their-billionaire-fortune-taxes

Milliman. 2009. Healthcare. http://us.milliman.com/solutions/healthcare/

Monbiot, G. 2011. The Self-Attribution Fallacy, November 7. www.monbiot. com/2011/11/07/the-self-attribution-fallacy/

Moore, M. 2011. Video – America is NOT Broke, *MichaelMoore.com*, March 5. www. michaelmoore.com/words/mike-friends-blog/america-is-not-broke

Moore S. 1999. Corporate Subsidies in the Federal Budget, Cato Congressional Testimony, June 30. www.cato.org/testimony/ct-sm063099.html

Morgan, D. 2012. One in Four Americans without Health Coverage: Study, *Reuters*, April 19. www.reuters.com/article/2012/04/19/us-usa-healthcare-insurance-idUSBRE83I17420120419

Morgan, D. 2007. Corn Farms Prosper, but Subsidies Still Flow, *Washington Post*, September 28. www.washingtonpost.com/wp-dyn/content/article/2007/09/27/AR2007092702054.html

Morgan, D., Cohen, S. and Gau, G. M. 2006. Powerful Interests Ally to Restructure Agriculture Subsidies, *Washingtonpost.com*, December 22. www.washingtonpost.com/wp-dyn/content/article/2006/12/21/AR2006122101634_...#sthash.PkPrAvuM.dpuf

Mosk, M. and Ross, B. 2012. Rick Santorum, "Stealth Lobbyist," *abcnews.go.com*, January 5. http://abcnews.go.com/Blotter/rick-santorum-stealth-lobbyist/story?id=15298204

Murphy, R. 2011. Tax Havens, Secrecy Jurisdictions and the Breakdown of Corporation Tax, *Real-World Economics Review*, No. 57. http://rwer.wordpress.com/2011/09/06/rwer-issue-57-richard-murphy/

Nader, R. 2003. *Cutting Corporate Welfare*, New York: Seven Stories Press. www.ontheissues.org/Archive/Corporate_Welfare_Government_Reform.htm

Napach, B. 2012. Corporate Tax Loopholes = Corporate Socialism, *Yahoo!Finance*, September 21. http://finance.yahoo.com/blogs/daily-ticker/corporate-tax-loopholes-corporate-socialism-pulitzer-prize-winner-121242544.html

Nash, J. and Deprez, E. E. 2014. Las Vegas Balks at Stadium Debt Amid Taxpayers Backlash, October 7. www.bloomberg.com/news/2014-10-08/las-vegas-balks-at-stadium-debt-amid-taxpayers-backlash.html

National Center for Children in Poverty. 2015. Child Poverty. www.nccp.org/topics/childpoverty.html

Negrin, M. 2012. Newt Gingrich: The Lobbyist Who Wasn't, *abcnews*, January 24. http://abcnews.go.com/Politics/OTUS/newt-gingrich-lobbyist/story?id=15430694

Nesto, M. 2012. Lobbying Works! Big Spenders Reap Big Stock Gains Says Trennert, *Yahoo!Finance*, July 23. http://finance.yahoo.com/blogs/breakout/lobbying-works-big-spenders-reap-big-stock-gains-143308537.html

New York Times. 2015A. Predatory Colleges Find Friends in Congress, June 25. www.nytimes.com/2015/06/25/opinion/predatory-colleges-find-friends-in-congress.html

New York Times. 2015B. Banks as Felons, or Criminality Lite, May 22. www.nytimes.com/2015/05/23/opinion/readers-of-the-daily-news.html

New York Times. 2015C. Coke Tries to Sugarcoat the Truth on Calories, August 14. www.nytimes.com/2015/08/14/opinion/coke-tries-to-sugarcoat-the-truth-on-calories.html

New York Times. 2014A. Call to Congress. End Loophole for Tax on Elite, November 14. www.nytimes.com/2014/11/15/business/idea-for-new-congress-end-a-tax-break-for-the-elite.html

New York Times. 2014B. Job Growth but No Raises, November 7. www.nytimes. com/2014/11/08/opinion/job-growth-but-no-raises.html

New York Times. 2014C. Lobbying to Influence Attorney Generals, October 29. www.nytimes.com/2014/10/29/us/lobbyists-bearing-gifts-pursue-attorneys-general.html

New York Times. 2014D. Secretly Buying Access to a Governor, October 7. www. nytimes.com/2014/10/08/opinion/secretly-buying-access-to-a-governor.htm l?emc=eta1&gwh=A66797D255F8DF559227DE9E1617CA4C&gwt=pay&asset Type=opinion

New York Times. 2014E. Kansas' Ruinous Tax Cuts, July 13. www.nytimes. com/2014/07/14/opinion/kansas-ruinous-tax-cuts.html

New York Times. 2014F. The Capitol's Spinning Door Accelerates, February 2. www.nytimes.com/2014/02/03/opinion/the-capitols-spinning-door-accelerates.html

New York Times. 2013A. The Money Behind the Shutdown Crisis, September 17. www.nytimes.com/2013/09/18/opinion/the-money-behind-the-shutdown-crisis.html

New York Times. 2013B. Insider Influence in the Commonwealth, August 15. www. nytimes.com/2013/08/16/opinion/insider-influence-in-the-commonwealth. html

New York Times. 2013C. "A" Is for Avoidance, May 25. www.nytimes.com/ 2013/05/26/opinion/sunday/a-is-for-avoidance.html

New York Times. 2013D. Quietly Killing a Consumer Watchdog, February 10. www. nytimes.com/2013/02/11/opinion/quietly-killing-a-consumer-watchdog. html

New York Times. 2012. False Promises, July 12. www.nytimes.com/2012/07/31/ opinion/false-promises-at-for-profit-colleges.html

New York Times. 2011A. Illegal, Just Not on Capitol Hill, December 14. www. nytimes.com/2011/12/15/opinion/insider-trading-is-illegal-just-not-on-capitol-hill.html?_r=0

New York Times. 2011B. Runaway Spending on War Contractors, September 17. www.nytimes.com/2011/09/18/opinion/sunday/runaway-spending-on-war-contractors.html

New York Times. 2010A. The Unemployed Held Hostage, Again, November 27. www.nytimes.com/2010/11/28/opinion/28sun1.html

New York Times. 2010B. The Recession's Awful Impact, September 16. www. nytimes.com/2010/09/17/opinion/17fri2.html

New York Times. 2008. Senator Dodd's Notion of Courtesy, October 21. www. nytimes.com/2008/10/21/opinion/21tue3.htmlputs-limit-on-contributions. html?_r=0

New York Times. 2006. A Marie Antoinette Moment, *International Herald Tribune*, January 3. www.highbeam.com/doc/1P1-116929416.html

Nixon, R. 2014. Review of Naomi Klein, *This Changes Everything*, *New York Times*, November 6. www.nytimes.com/2014/11/09/books/review/naomi-klein-this-changes-everything-review.html

Nixon, R. 2013. Farm Subsidies for Nonfarmers May Continue as Lawmakers Deadlock Again, *New York Times*, September 10. www.nytimes. com/2013/09/10/us/politics/farm-subsidies-for-nonfarmers-may-continue-as-lawmakers-deadlock-again.html

Nocera, J. 2015. Corporate Welfare for the Kochs, *New York Times*, October 10. www.nytimes.com/2015/10/11/opinion/sunday/corporate-welfare-for-the-kochs.html

Nocera, J. 2011. The Big Lie, *New York Times*, December 23. www.nytimes.com/2011/12/24/opinion/nocera-the-big-lie.html

Nussbaum, A. 2015. What Should We Tell the Kids about Climate Change? *Bloomberg Politics*, February 15. www.bloomberg.com/politics/articles/2015-02-06/what-should-we-tell-the-kids-about-climate-change-

OECD Health Statistics. 2014. How Does the United States Compare? www.oecd.org/unitedstates/Briefing-Note-UNITED-STATES-2014.pdf

Ohlemacher, S. 2011. Super-Rich See Federal Taxes Drop Dramatically, *Yahoo!Finance*, April 17. http://finance.yahoo.com/news/Super-rich-see-federal-taxes-apf-3022452208.html?x=0

OpenSecrets.Org. 2015. Ranked Sectors. April. https://www.opensecrets.org/lobby/indus.php?id=H&year=a

Organic Consumers Association. 2014. Biggest Fool in Congress? Stop Pompeo from Supporting the Food Industry's Bill to Preempt GMO Labeling Laws! Organic Consumers Association, April 11. http://salsa3.salsalabs.com/o/50865/p/dia/action3/common/public/?action_KEY=13596

Ozanian, M. 2014. The NFL's Most Valuable Teams, *Forbes*, August 20. www.forbes.com/sites/mikeozanian/2014/08/20/the-nfls-most-valuable-teams/

Parker, A. and Weisman, J. 2014. Spending Bill Hits Snags, but Congress Thinks It Can Avoid Shutdown, *New York Times*, December 10. www.nytimes.com/2014/12/11/us/trillion-dollar-spending-pact-angers-campaign-finance-watchdogs.html

Passell, P. 1998. Economic Scene; Rich Nation, Poor Nation. Is Anyone Even Looking for a Cure? *New York Times*, August 13. www.nytimes.com/1998/08/13/business/economic-scene-rich-nation-poor-nation-is-anyone-even-looking-for-a-cure.html

Patterson, O. and Cowles, J. 2015. Overreliance on the Pseudo-Science of Economics, *New York Times*, February 9. www.nytimes.com/roomfordebate/2015/02/09/are-economists-overrated/overreliance-on-the-pseudo-science-of-economics

Pear, R. 2011A. Top Earners Doubled Share of Nation's Income, Study Finds, *New York Times*, October 25. www.nytimes.com/2011/10/26/us/politics/top-earners-doubled-share-of-nations-income-cbo-says.html

Pear, R. 2011B. Recession Officially Over, U.S. Incomes Kept Falling, *New York Times*, October 9. www.nytimes.com/2011/10/10/us/recession-officially-over-us-incomes-kept-falling.html

Pelofsky, J. 2009. Senator Harkin Defends Earmark to Research Pig Odor, *Reuters*, March 4. http://blogs.reuters.com/talesfromthetrail/2009/03/04/senator-harkin-defends-earmark-to-research-pig-odor/

Piketty, T. 2014. *Capital in the Twenty-First Century,* Cambridge, MA: Harvard University Press.

Piketty, T. and Saez, E. 2007. How Progressive Is the U.S. Federal Tax System? A Historical and International Perspective, *Journal of Economic Perspectives*, 21(1): 3–24.

Porter, E. 2012. A Nation with Too Many Tax Breaks, *New York Times*, March 13. www.nytimes.com/2012/03/14/business/a-nation-with-too-many-tax-breaks-economic-scene.html

Potter, W. 2013. Big Pharma's Stranglehold on Washington, The Center for Public Integrity, February 11. www.publicintegrity.org/2013/02/11/12175/opinion-big-pharmas-stranglehold-washington

Powell, M. 2015A. Sports Owners Dip into the Public's Purse, Despite Their Billions in the Bank, *New York Times*, July 21. www.nytimes.com/2015/07/22/sports/sports-owners-dip-into-the-publics-purse-despite-their-billions-in-the-bank.html?ref=sports

Powell, M. 2015B. James L. Dolan, A Consummate 1 Percenter, *New York Times*, February 14. www.nytimes.com/2015/02/15/sports/jim-dolan-consummate-1-percenter.html?ref=sports

Powell, M. 2015C. Bucks' New Owners Get House-Warming Gift of Public Money, *New York Times*, August 14. www.nytimes.com/2015/08/15/sports/bucks-new-owners-get-house-warming-gift-of-public-money.html?ref=sports

Powell, M. 2014. Sniffing for Dollars at Home of the Vikings, *New York Times*, November 2. www.nytimes.com/2014/10/03/sports/football/sniffing-for-dollars-at-home-of-the-vikings.html

Powell, M. 2010. Though Leery of Washington, Alaska Feasts on Its Dollars, *New York Times*, August 18. www.nytimes.com/2010/08/19/business/19stimulus.html?_r=0

Prante, G. 2008. Attention Iowa: Your Ethanol Subsidies Have Little Economic or Environmental Justification, Tax Foundation, February 7. http://taxfoundation.org/blog/attention-iowa-your-ethanol-subsidies-have-little-economic-or-environmental-justification

Prins, N. 2015. Wall Street + Washington Revolving Door Is More Dangerous than Ever, *Yahoo!Finance*, April 1. http://finance.yahoo.com/news/nomi-prins-on-the-revolving-door-between-washington-and-wall-street-191158164.html

Protess, B. 2015. A Heated Path Toward S.&P.'s Legal Settlement with Prosecutor, *New York Times*, February 2. http://dealbook.nytimes.com/2015/02/02/a-heated-path-toward-standard-poors-legal-settlement-with-regulators/

Protess, B. 2014. S.&P. Nears Settlement with Justice Dept. over Inflated Ratings, *New York Times*, January 12. http://dealbook.nytimes.com/2015/01/12/s-p-nears-settlement-with-justice-over-inflated-ratings/

Protess, B. 2013. Big Banks Get Break in Rules to Limit Risks, *New York Times*, May 15. http://dealbook.nytimes.com/2013/05/15/compromise-seen-on-derivatives-rule/

Protess, B. and Scott, M. 2012. Bank Scandal Turns Spotlight to Regulators, *New York Times*, July 9. http://dealbook.nytimes.com/2012/07/09/libor-scandal-intensifies-spotlight-on-bank-regulators/?_r=0

Protess, B. and Silver-Greenberg, J. 2014. Prosecutors Suspect Repeat Offenses on Wall Street, October 29. http://dealbook.nytimes.com/2014/10/29/prosecutors-wrestling-with-wall-streets-repeat-offenders/?emc=eta1

Puzzanghera, J. 2015. As Export–Import Bank Charter Expires, Backers Warn of Economic Damage, *Los Angeles Times*, June 30. www.latimes.com/business/la-fi-export-import-bank20150630-story.html

Pyle, T. 2015. The Iowa Caucuses Have a Winner – Ethanol, *Wall Street Journal*, March 25. www.wsj.com/articles/thomas-pyle-the-iowa-caucuses-have-a-winner-ethanol-1427324726

Quigley, B. 2014. Ten Examples of Welfare for the Rich and Corporations, *Huffington Post*, January 14. www.huffingtonpost.com/bill-quigley/ten-examples-of-welfare-for-the-rich-and-corporations_b_4589188.html

Rattner, S. 2014. Inequality Is Getting Worse, *New York Times*, November 16. www.nytimes.com/2014/11/17/opinion/inequality-unbelievably-gets-worse.html?emc=eta1

Real-World Economics Review. 2010. Greenspan, Friedman and Summers Win Dynamite Prize in Economics, *Real-World Economics Review* blog. https://rwer.wordpress.com/2010/02/22/greenspan-friedman-and-summers-win-dynamite-prize-in-economics/

Reichl, R. 2014. The FDA's Blatant Failure on Food, *New York Times*, July 30. www.nytimes.com/2014/07/31/opinion/the-fda-blatant-failure-on-food.html

Reinberg, S. 2012. Many U.S. Families Struggle to Pay Medical Bills, *Yahoo!Finance*, March 7. http://news.yahoo.com/many-u-families-struggle-pay-medical-bills-140204312.html

Rich, M. 2010. For the Unemployed over 50, Fears of Never Working Again, *New York Times*, September 21. www.nytimes.com/2010/09/20/business/economy/20older.html?pagewanted=all

Riley, Charles. 2012. Long-term Unemployment Crisis Rolls On, *CNNMoney*, June 11. http://money.cnn.com/2012/06/11/news/economy/long-term-unemployment/index.htm

Ritholz, B. 2013. How McDonald's and Wal-Mart Became Welfare Queens, *Bloombergview*, November 13. www.bloombergview.com/articles/2013-11-13/how-mcdonald-s-and-wal-mart-became-welfare-queens

Rmuse. 2015. Scott Walker Intends to Rob Taxpayers to Enrich Billionaires, *PoliticusUSA*, June 11. www.politicususa.com/2015/06/11/scott-walker-intends-rob-taxpayers-enrich-billionaires.html

Robertson, L. 2013. False Assumptions on the Health Care Law, *FactCheck.org*, July 11. www.factcheck.org/2013/07/false-assumptions-on-the-health-care-law/

Rodrik, D. 2002. Feasible Globalizations, NBER Working Paper 9129, September. www.nber.org/papers/w9129.pdf

Rogers, D. 2015. Bigger Subsidies under New Farm Bill Program, *Politico*, March 9. www.politico.com/story/2015/03/farm-bill-subsidies-115907.html

Rosenberg, D. 2012. We Are Living in a Modern Day Depression, *Yahoo!Finance*, June 25. http://finance.yahoo.com/blogs/daily-ticker/living-modern-day-depression-david-rosenberg-121332909.html

Rosenberg, T. 2011. To Beat Back Poverty, Pay the Poor, *New York Times*, January 3. http://opinionator.blogs.nytimes.com/2011/01/03/to-beat-back-poverty-pay-the-poor/

Rosenthal, E. 2011. TransCanada Pipeline Foes See Bias in U.S. E-Mails, *New York Times*, October 3. www.nytimes.com/2011/10/04/science/earth/04pipeline.html

Roth, B. 2011. For-Profit Colleges Field Team of Top Lobbyists, *Roll Call*, May. www.rollcall.com/issues/56_114/-205206-1.html

Roth, Z. 2011A. Greenspan: Too Much Regulation Slowing Growth, *Yahoo!News,* March 15. http://news.yahoo.com/blogs/lookout/greenspan-too-much-regulation-slowing-growth-20110315-083033-963.html

Roth, Z. 2011B. Separate but Unequal: Charts Show Growing Rich–Poor Gap, *Yahoo!News,* February 23. http://news.yahoo.com/blogs/lookout/separate-unequal-charts-show-growing-rich-poor-gap-20110223-141311-132.html

Roth, Z. 2011C. Workers' Share of National Income Plummets to Record Low, *Yahoo!News,* June 14. http://news.yahoo.com/blogs/lookout/workers-share-national-income-plummets-record-low-163749508.html

Roy, A. 2012. Capitalism: A Ghost Story, *Outlook India.com,* March 26. www.outlookindia.com/article.aspx?280234

RT Question More. 2014. Congress Considers Blocking GMO Food Labeling, *Rt.com,* April 9. http://rt.com/usa/congress-considers-blocking-gmo-labeling-480/

Rubin, R. 2015. U.S. Companies Are Stashing $2.1 Trillion Overseas to Avoid Taxes, *Bloomberg Business,* March 4. www.bloomberg.com/news/articles/2015-03-04/u-s-companies-are-stashing-2-1-trillion-overseas-to-avoid-taxes

Rufermarch, C. 2015. End This Corporate Welfare, *New York Times,* March 23. www.nytimes.com/2015/03/23/opinion/end-this-corporate-welfare.html

Rugaber, C. S. 2015. Incomes Rise for Bottom 99 pct.; US Inequality Still Worsens, *Yahoo!Finance,* June 30. http://finance.yahoo.com/news/incomes-rise-bottom-99-pct-193440203.html

Rugy, V. 2015. The Export–Import Bank Subsidizes the Already Wealthy, *New York Times,* March 16. www.nytimes.com/roomfordebate/2015/03/16/should-congress-save-the-export-import-bank/the-export-import-bank-subsidizes-the-already-wealthy

Salant, J. D. 2014. Congress Makes NASA Finish Useless $350 Million Structure, *Bloomberg Business,* January 8. www.bloomberg.com/news/articles/2014-01-08/congress-makes-nasa-finish-useless-350-million-structure

Salant, J. D. 2013A. Lobbying from Capitol to K Street in a Hot Second, *Bloomberg Businessweek,* May 27. http://magsreview.com/bloomberg-businessweek-may-27-2013/5458-lobbying-from-capitol-to-k-street-in-a-hot-second.html

Salant, J. D. 2013B. Congress Members Spring for Money to Lobby After Election, *Bloomberg Business,* May 12. www.bloomberg.com/news/articles/2013-05-08/congress-members-sprint-for-money-to-lobby-after-election

Salant, J. D. and Capaccio, T. 2014. The Pentagon Loves to Pay Top Dollar, *Bloomberg Business,* July 17. www.bloomberg.com/bw/articles/2014-07-17/defense-department-overpays-for-bell-helicopter-parts

Salmon, F. 2009. Recipe for Disaster: The Formula That Killed Wall Street, *Wired Magazine,* February 24. http://archive.wired.com/techbiz/it/magazine/17-03/wp_quant?currentPage=all

Samuelsohn, D. and Palmer, A. 2013. Defense Industry Finds Few Old Friends on Hill, *PoliticoPro,* February 24. www.politico.com/story/2013/02/defense-industry-finds-few-old-friends-on-hill-87991.html

Sanati, C. 2014. Collateralized Loan Obligations: Our Next Financial Nightmare, *Fortune,* April 10. http://fortune.com/2014/04/10/collateralized-loan-obligations-our-next-financial-nightmare/

Scherzer, L. 2012. Where Have All the "Good" Jobs Gone? *Yahoo!Finance*, August 1. http://finance.yahoo.com/blogs/the-exchange/where-good-jobs-gone-195409412.html

Schultz, D. 2014. The Vikings Stadium Deal Is a Study in Diminishing Returns, *MinnPost*, March 19. www.minnpost.com/community-voices/2014/03/vikings-stadium-deal-study-diminishing-returns

Schumpeter, J. 1962. *Capitalism, Socialism and Democracy*, 3rd edn, New York: Harper & Row.

Segall, L. and Censky, A. 2011. Job Growth Stalls, Layoffs Surge, *CNNMoney*, August 3. http://money.cnn.com/2011/08/03/news/economy/jobs_challenger_adp/index.htm

Shah, A. 1999. Monsanto's Influence, *Global Issues*, January 2. www.globalissues.org/article/162/some-examples#MonsantosInfluence

Sheppard, K. 2014. Federal Government Still Spending Billions to Subsidize Fossil Fuels, *HuffPost Politics*, July 9. www.huffingtonpost.com/2014/07/09/fossil-fuel-subsidies_n_5572346.html

Shilling, G. 2010. Middle Class in Crisis: America Needs a Reality Check, *Yahoo!Finance*, November 15. http://finance.yahoo.com/tech-ticker/middle-class-in-crisis-america-needs-a-reality-check-gary-shilling-says-535609.html

Silver-Greenberg, J., Protess, B. and Eavis, P. 2014. New Scrutiny of Goldman's Ties to the New York Fed after a Leak, *New York Times*, November 19. http://dealbook.nytimes.com/2014/11/19/rising-scrutiny-as-banks-hire-from-the-fed

Silverman, E. 2015. Senators Re-Introduce Bill to Allow Imported Medicines from Canada, *Wall Street Journal Pharmalot*, January 9. http://blogs.wsj.com/pharmalot/2015/01/09/senators-re-introduce-bill-to-allow-imported-medicines-from-canada/

Sirota, D., Harvey, C. and Legum, J. 2004. Wal-Mart Welfare, *Alternet*, May 27. www3.alternet.org/story/18816/wal-mart_welfare

Slivinski, S. 2007. The Corporate Welfare State, Policy Analysis No. 592, Cato Institute, May 14. www.cato.org/pubs/pas/pa592.pdf

Slome, W. W. 2012. Experts vs. Dart-Throwing Chimps, *Investing Caffeine*, July 8. http://investingcaffeine.com/2012/07/08/experts-vs-dart-throwing-chimps/

Smialek, J. 2014. Top 1 Percent Is Richer than Data Shows, ECB Paper Finds, *Bloomberg Business*, July 14. www.bloomberg.com/news/articles/2014-07-14/top-1-percent-is-richer-than-data-shows-ecb-paper-finds

Smith, A. 2012. The Middle Class Falls Further Behind, *CNNMoney*, August 22. http://money.cnn.com/2012/08/22/news/economy/middle-class-pew/index.html

Snyder, J. S. 2009. Clinton Says Don't Blame Him, *Time*, February 16.

Snyder, M. 2010. 22 Statistics That Prove the Middle Class Is Being Systematically Wiped Out of Existence in America, *Business Insider*, July 15. www.businessinsider.com/22-statistics-that-prove-the-middle-class-is-being-systematically-wiped-out-of-existence-in-america-2010-7?op=1

Social Security Advisory Board. 2009. The Unsustainable Cost of Health Care, September. www.ssab.gov/documents/TheUnsustainableCostofHealthCare_508.pdf

Soederberg, S. 2015. The Student Loan Crisis and the Debtfare State, *truthout.org*, May 31. www.truth-out.org/news/item/31074-the-student-loan-crisis-and-the-debtfare-state

Sontag, D. 2014. Where Oil and Politics Mix, *New York Times*, November 23. www.nytimes.com/interactive/2014/11/24/us/north-dakota-oil-boom-politics.html

Sorkin, A. R. 2008. Behind the Deal, the Hand of the Fed, *New York Times*, March 25. www.nytimes.com/2008/03/25/business/25sorkin.html

Spear, S. 2014. Samso: World's First 100% Renewable Energy-Powered Island Is a Beacon for Sustainable Communities, *EcoWatch*, May 1. http://ecowatch.com/2014/05/01/samso-renewable-energy-island-sustainable-communities/

Spencer, J., Hughlett, M. and Herb, J. 2014. In Congress, No One Beats the Influential Beet Lobby, *Star Tribune*, November 10. www.startribune.com/politics/statelocal/138264909.html

Standard and Poor's/Case–Shiller National U.S. Home Price Index. 2015. www.standardandpoors.com/indices/sp-case-shiller-home-price-indices/en/us/?indexId=spusa-cashpidff--p-us----

Standard and Poor's/Case–Shiller National U.S. Home Price Index. 2009. Falling House Prices Spread beyond the Sun Belt, April 2. www.project.org/info.php?recordID=445

Stein, J., Marley, P. and Spicuzza, M. 2015. State Jobs Agency Gave Loans, Credits to Firms without Financial Review, *Milwaukee Journal Sentinel*, June 19. www.jsonline.com/news/statepolitics/state-jobs-agency-gave-loans-credits-to-firms-without-financial-review-b99523031z1-308521291.html

Steorts, J. L. 2005. The Sugar Industry and Corporate Welfare, *National Review*, July 18. http://reclaimdemocracy.org/sugar_industry_subsidies/

Steverman, B. 2014. What the Economy Has Done to the Family, *Bloomberg Business*, November 10. www.bloomberg.com/news/articles/2014-11-10/how-the-bad-economy-breaks-up-families

Stiglitz, G. E. 2013. A Tax System Stacked against the 99 Percent, *New York Times*, April 14.

Stiglitz, J. 2012. Student Debt and the Crushing of the American Dream, *New York Times*, May 12.

Stiglitz, J. 2009A. Wall Street's Toxic Message, *Vanity Fair*, July, pp. 84–5.

Stiglitz, J. 2009B. Obama's Ersatz Capitalism, *New York Times*, March 31. www.nytimes.com/2009/04/01/opinion/01stiglitz.html

Stolberg, S. G. 2013. Reaping Profit after Assisting on Health Law, *New York Times*, September 17. www.nytimes.com/2013/09/18/us/politics/reaping-profit-after-assisting-on-health-law.html?pagewanted=all

Stone, G. and Campbell, T. C. 2011. *Forks over Knives: The Plant-Based Way to Health*, New York: The Experiment.

Story, L. 2012. As Companies Seek Tax Deals, Governments Pay High Price, *New York Times*, December 1. www.nytimes.com/2012/12/02/us/how-local-taxpayers-bankroll-corporations.html?pagewanted=all

Story, L. and Lowrey, A. 2013. The Fed, Lawrence Summers, and Money, *New York Times*, August 10. http://mobile.nytimes.com/2013/08/11/business/economy/the-fed-lawrence-summers-and-money.html

Strauss, D. 2012. Senate Defeats McCain Amendment on Canadian Pharmacies, *The Hill*, May 24. http://thehill.com/blogs/floor-action/senate/229405-senate-defeats-mccain-amendment-on-canadian-pharmacies

Strom, S. 2013. Food Politics Creates Rift in Panel on Labeling, *New York Times*, April 10. www.nytimes.com/2013/04/11/business/a-dismissal-raises-questions-about-objectivity-on-food-policy.html

Strom, S. 2012. Has "Organic" Been Oversized, *New York Times*, July 7. www.nytimes.com/2012/07/08/business/organic-food-purists-worry-about-big-companies-influence.html

Super, D. A. 2014. A Costly and Outrageous Tax Break, *New York Times*, December 2. www.nytimes.com/2014/12/03/opinion/a-costly-and-outrageous-tax-break.html?emc=eta1&_r=0

Taleb, N. 2012. *Antifragile: Things That Gain from Disorder*, London: Allen Lane.

Taleb, N. 2007. *The Black Swan: The Impact of the Highly Improbable*, New York: Random House.

Task, A. 2012. Marion Nestle on The (Big) Business of Food Stamps: "Here's Where the Profits Come in," *Yahoo!Finance*, June 15. http://finance.yahoo.com/blogs/daily-ticker/marion-nestle-big-business-food-stamps-where-profits-164228337.html

Tavernise, S. 2012. Life Expectancy Drops for Least-Educated Whites, *International Herald Tribune*, September 21. http://graphics8.nytimes.com/images/ihtfrontpage/europefrontpage.pdf

Tavernise, S. 2011. Study Finds Big Spike in Poorest in the U.S., *New York Times*, November 3. www.nytimes.com/2011/11/04/us/extreme-poverty-is-up-brookings-report-finds.html?_r=1

Taxpayers for Common Sense. 2013. Corn Ethanol Subsidies Are Alive and Well, October 16. www.taxpayer.net/library/article/corn-ethanol-subsidies-are-alive-and-well

Taxpayers for Common Sense. 2011. Big Oil, Big Corn: An In-depth Look at the Volumetric Ethanol Excise Tax Credit, June 23. www.taxpayer.net/library/article/big-oil-big-corn-an-in-depth-look-at-the-volumetric-ethanol-excise-tax-cred

Taylor, O. 1960. *A History of Economic Thought*, Cambridge, MA: Harvard University Press.

Teachout, Z. 2014. *Corruption in America*, Cambridge, MA: Harvard University Press.

Tergesen, A. 2015. In Retirement Ranking, 18 Countries Beat the U.S., *Yahoo!Finance*, February 10. http://finance.yahoo.com/news/retirement-ranking-18-countries-beat-175150981.html

The Economist. 2014. Milking Taxpayers, February 14. www.economist.com/news/united-states/21643191-crop-prices-fall-farmers-grow-subsidies-instead-milking-taxpayers

The Economist online. 2011. Market Troubles, April 6. www.economist.com/blogs/dailychart/2011/04/public_opinion_capitalism

The Progress Report. 2006. World's Biggest Corporation Is a Welfare Queen, April 7. www.progress.org/tpr/worlds-biggest-corporation-is-a-welfare-queen/

Todaro, M. P. and Smith, S. C. 2014. *Economic Development*, 12th edn, Chapter 5. New York: Pearson.

Tone, H. 2015. *WSJ* Defends Shuttered For-Profit College Despite Evidence of Fraud, *Media Matters for America*, April 28. http://mediamatters.org/blog/2015/04/28/wsj-defends-shuttered-for-profit-college-despit/203452

Transparency International. 2014. *Corruption Perceptions Index 2014: Results*. www.transparency.org/cpi2014/results

Tritch, T. 2014. So, Where's My Pay Raise? *New York Times*, December 24. http://takingnote.blogs.nytimes.com/2014/12/24/so-wheres-my-pay-raise/?emc=eta1

Trull, J. 2015. For-Profit Colleges: What You Need to Know Before Taking on Student Loan Debt, March 16. https://studentloanhero.com/featured/for-profit-colleges-what-you-need-to-know-before-taking-on-student-loan-debt/

Turkewitz, J. 2015. Environmental Agency Uncorks Its Own Toxic Water Spill at Colorado Mine, *New York Times*, August 10. www.nytimes.com/2015/08/11/us/durango-colorado-mine-spill-environmental-protection-agency.html

TV. Natural News.com. 2011. Bill Maher Interviews Dr. T. Colin Campbell – Forks Over Knives, July 16. http://tv.naturalnews.com/v.asp?v=35EAFE39BAC6762A7113FB0AA7802655

Tyson, L. D. 2011. Tackling Income Inequality, *Yahoo!Finance*, November 18. www.gainesville.com/article/20111118/ZNYT01/111183003

Uchitelle, L. 2000. Middle-Class Pinch: The Joneses Can't Keep Up, *International Herald Tribune*, September 11, p. 6.

Udland, M. 2014. Steve Ballmer Paid $2 Billion for the Clippers, but He Might Get Half that Back in Tax Breaks, *Business Insider*, October 27. www.businessinsider.com/steve-ballmer-la-clippers-tax-break-report-2014-10

Union of Concerned Scientists, 2007. Smoke, Mirrors and Hot Air: How ExxonMobil Uses Big Tobacco's Tactics to Manufacture Uncertainty on Climate Science, January. www.ucsusa.org/sites/default/files/legacy/assets/documents/global_warming/exxon_report.pdf

US Department of Education. 2014. Obama Administration Takes Action to Protect Americans, March 14. www.ed.gov/news/press-releases/obama-administration-takes-action-protect-americans-predatory-poor-performing-career-colleges

US Government Accountability Office. 2008. Superfund: Funding and Reported Costs of Enforcement and Administration Activities, July 18. www.gao.gov/new.items/d08841r.pdf

US Senate Committee on Health, Education, Labor and Pensions. 2012. Harkin: Report Reveals Troubling Realities of For-Profit Schools, July 30. www.help.senate.gov/ranking/newsroom/press/harkin-report-reveals-troubling-realities-of-for-profit-schools

Van Buren, P. 2011. *We Meant Well: How I Helped Lose the Battle for the Hearts and Minds of the Iraqi People*, New York: Henry Holt.

Van den Berg, H. 2014. How the Culture of Economics Stops Economists from Studying Group Behavior and the Development of Social Cultures, *World Economic Review*, Vol. 3: 53–68.

Viswanatha, A. 2015. Banks to Pay $5.6 Billion in Probes, *Wall Street Journal*, May 20. www.wsj.com/articles/global-banks-to-pay-5-6-billion-in-penalties-in-fx-libor-probe-1432130400

Walker, D. 2014. In San Francisco an Arena Emerges with No Public Subsidy, *Milwaukee Journal Sentinel*, February 8. www.jsonline.com/news/milwaukee/

in-san-francisco-an-arena-emerges-with-no-public-subsidy-b99440
899z1-291176061.html

Walker, D. 2013. Publicly Funded Sports Arenas Add Little to Local Economy, Report Says, *Milwaukee Wisconsin Journal Sentinel*, April 5. www.jsonline.com/ news/milwaukee/publicly-funded-sports-arenas-add-little-to-local-economy-report-says-cc9ehcj-201706591.html

Walsh, M. W. and Story, L. 2013. A Stealth Tax Subsidy for Business Faces New Scrutiny, *New York Times*, March 4. www.nytimes.com/2013/03/05/business/ qualified-private-activity-bonds-come-under-new-scrutiny.html

Walsh, S. 2015. Conservative ALEC Conference Opens in San Diego amid Protests, July 22. www.kpbs.org/news/2015/jul/22/conservative-alec-conference-opens-amid-protests/

Walshe, S. 2013. End Corporate Welfare for McDonald's. Better Yet, Raise the Minimum Wage, *The Guardian*, October 30. www.theguardian.com/ commentisfree/2013/oct/30/mcdonalds-helpline-food-stamps-minimum-wage

Ward, D. 2009. The Money Taboo in Health Reform Coverage: Industry Donations to Powerful Players Often Go Unmentioned, *Fairness and Accuracy in Reporting*, November 1. http://fair.org/extra-online-articles/the-money-taboo-in-health-reform-coverage/

Ward, K. 2014. Sallie Mae: How Feds Fuel Student-Loan Fiasco, *Watchdog.org*, February 10. http://watchdog.org/127888/student-loan-debt/

Weise, K. 2014. The For-Profit College that's Too Big to Fail, *Bloomberg Business*, September 25. www.bloomberg.com/bw/articles/2014-09-25/corinthian-colleges-for-profit-and-too-big-to-fail

Weisman, J. and Lipton, R. 2015. In New Congress, Wall St. Pushes to Undermine Dodd-Frank Reform, *New York Times*, January 13. www.nytimes. com/2015/01/14/business/economy/in-new-congress-wall-st-pushes-to-undermine-dodd-frank-reform.html

Wessel, D. 2011. What's Wrong with America's Job Engine? *Wall Street Journal*, July 27. http://online.wsj.com/article/SB100014240531119047723045764688205826 15858.html

Wexler, A. 2013. Big Sugar Is Set for a Sweet Bailout, *Wall Street Journal*, March 13. www.wsj.com/articles/SB10001424127887324096404578356740206766164

Williams, E. D. 2015. Chargers: No Bending to Pressure, *ESPN.com*, February 17. http://espn.go.com/nfl/story/_/id/12335606/san-diego-chargers-issue-stern-threat-city-hall-panel

Wines, M. 2014. Behind Toledo's Water Crisis, a Long-Troubled Lake Erie, *New York Times*, August 4. www.nytimes.com/2014/08/05/us/lifting-ban-toledo-says-its-water-is-safe-to-drink-again.html?emc=eta1&_r=1

Wiseman, P. 2011A. Pain of Job Crisis Goes Well Beyond the Unemployed, *Yahoo!Finance*, October 9. http://finance.yahoo.com/news/Pain-of-job-crisis-goes-well-apf-1617669023.html

Wiseman, P. 2011B. A Boom in Corporate Profits, a Bust in Jobs, Wages, *MSNBC*, July 22. www.msnbc.msn.com/id/43860044/ns/business-stocks_ and_economy/t/boom-corporate-profits-bust-jobs-wages/

Wiseman, P. and Leonard, C. 2011. Unemployed Face Tough Competition: Underemployed, *Yahoo!Finance*, September 4. http://finance.yahoo.com/ news/Unemployed-face-tough-apf-2863640197.html

Wolff, E. N. 2009. *Poverty and Income Distribution*, 2nd edn, Malden, MA: Wiley-Blackwell.

Wolin, S. 2010. *Democracy Incorporated: Managed Democracy and the Specter of Inverted Totalitarianism*, Princeton, NJ: Princeton University Press.

World Economic Forum. 2015. Competitiveness Rankings 2014/2015. http://reports.weforum.org/global-competitiveness-report-2014-2015/rankings/

Wright, G. and Gallegos, S. 2014. Despite Lower Rates, More than 650,000 Defaulted on Federal Student Loans: For-Profits Account for Nearly Half of All Defaults, The Institute for College Access & Success, September 24. http://ticas.org/sites/default/files/legacy/pub_files/CDR_2014_NR.pdf

Yen, H. 2012. 1 in 2 New Graduates Are Jobless or Unemployed, *Yahoo!Finance*, April 22. http://finance.yahoo.com/news/1-2-graduates-jobless-under employed-140300522.html

Yen, H. 2011A. Census Shows 1 in 2 People Are Poor or Low-Income, *Yahoo!Finance*, December 15. http://finance.yahoo.com/news/census-shows-1-2-people-103940568.html

Yen, H. 2011B. US Wealth Gap between Young and Old Is Widest Ever, *Yahoo!News*, November 7. http://news.yahoo.com/us-wealth-gap-between-young-old-widest-ever-050259922.html

Yen, H. 2011C. US Poverty at New High: 16 Percent, or 49.1 M, *Memphis Daily News*, November 8. www.memphisdailynews.com/news/2011/nov/8/us-poverty-at-new-high-16-percent-or-491m//print

Yen, H. 2010D. Census: Number of Poor May Be Millions Higher, MSNBC, September 16. www.msnbc.msn.com/id/40930573/ns/us_news-life/t/census-number-poor-may-be-millions-higher/

Yen, H. and Sidoti, L. 2010. US Poverty on Track to Post Record Gain in 2009, *CherokeeTribune.com*, September 12. http://cherokeetribune.com/view/full_story/9496742/article-U-S--poverty-on-track-to-post-record-gain-in-2009

Ying, L. 2010. Estimating Entrepreneurial Jobs: Business Creation is Job Creation, U.S. Small Business Administration. Paper presented at American Economic Association Annual Meeting, Denver, January 8, 2011.

Young, A. 2013. Cheney's Halliburton Made $39.5 Billion on Iraq War, *International Business Times*, March 20. http://readersupportednews.org/news-section2/308-12/16561-focus-cheneys-halliburton-made-395-billion-on-iraq-war

Zall, M. 2001. The Pricing Puzzle, *Modern Drug Discovery*, 4(3): 36–8, 41, 42. http://pubs.acs.org/subscribe/archive/mdd/v04/i03/html/03zall.html

Zepezauer, M. and Naiman, A. 1996. *Take the Rich Off Welfare*, Tucson, AZ: Odonian Press. www.thirdworldtraveler.com/Corporate_Welfare/Military_Fraud.html

Zimbalist, A. and Noll, R. G. 1997. Sports, Jobs, & Taxes: Are New Stadiums Worth the Cost? *Brookings*, summer. www.brookings.edu/research/articles/1997/06/summer-taxes-noll

Index

Taylor & Francis eBooks

Helping you to choose the right eBooks for your Library

Add Routledge titles to your library's digital collection today. Taylor and Francis ebooks contains over 50,000 titles in the Humanities, Social Sciences, Behavioural Sciences, Built Environment and Law.

Choose from a range of subject packages or create your own!

Benefits for you

» Free MARC records
» COUNTER-compliant usage statistics
» Flexible purchase and pricing options
» All titles DRM-free.

Benefits for your user

» Off-site, anytime access via Athens or referring URL
» Print or copy pages or chapters
» Full content search
» Bookmark, highlight and annotate text
» Access to thousands of pages of quality research at the click of a button.

REQUEST YOUR **FREE** INSTITUTIONAL TRIAL TODAY	**Free Trials Available** We offer free trials to qualifying academic, corporate and government customers.

eCollections – Choose from over 30 subject eCollections, including:

Archaeology	Language Learning
Architecture	Law
Asian Studies	Literature
Business & Management	Media & Communication
Classical Studies	Middle East Studies
Construction	Music
Creative & Media Arts	Philosophy
Criminology & Criminal Justice	Planning
Economics	Politics
Education	Psychology & Mental Health
Energy	Religion
Engineering	Security
English Language & Linguistics	Social Work
Environment & Sustainability	Sociology
Geography	Sport
Health Studies	Theatre & Performance
History	Tourism, Hospitality & Events

For more information, pricing enquiries or to order a free trial, please contact your local sales team:
www.tandfebooks.com/page/sales

Routledge Taylor & Francis Group	The home of Routledge books	**www.tandfebooks.com**